THE ARMIES AND WARS OF THE SUN KING 1643–1715

Volume 1: The Guard of Louis XIV

René Chartrand

'This is the Century of the Soldier', Fulvio Testi, Poet, 1641

Helion & Company

Helion & Company Limited
Unit 8 Amherst Business Centre
Budbrooke Road
Warwick
CV34 5WE
England
Tel. 01926 499 619
Email: info@helion.co.uk
Website: www.helion.co.uk
Twitter: @helionbooks
Visit our blog at http://blog.helion.co.uk/

Published by Helion & Company 2019
Designed and typeset by Serena Jones
Cover designed by Paul Hewitt, Battlefield Design (www.battlefield-design.co.uk)
Printed by Henry Ling Limited, Dorchester, Dorset

Text © René Chartrand 2019
Illustrations © as individually credited
Colour plates 1–5 by Ed Dovey © Helion & Company 2019
Cover: Fusiliers of the Gardes Françaises charging, early 1690s. The plug bayonets' narrow grips are inserted in the musket barrels. Print after JOB. Private collection. Author's photo.

Every reasonable effort has been made to trace copyright holders and to obtain their permission for the use of copyright material. The author and publisher apologise for any errors or omissions in this work, and would be grateful if notified of any corrections that should be incorporated in future reprints or editions of this book.

ISBN 978-1-911628-60-6

British Library Cataloguing-in-Publication Data.
A catalogue record for this book is available from the British Library.

All rights reserved. No part of this publication may be reproduced, stored in a retrieval system, or transmitted, in any form, or by any means, electronic, mechanical, photocopying, recording or otherwise, without the express written consent of Helion & Company Limited.

For details of other military history titles published by Helion & Company
Limited, contact the above address, or visit our website: http://www.helion.co.uk

We always welcome receiving book proposals from prospective authors.

Contents

Preface & Acknowledgements	5
1. Young Louis XIV	8
2. Into Personal Rule	27
3. Foreign Intrigues and Adventures	39
4. The Sun King's *Blitzkrieg*	57
5. The Army's Command	70
6. Senior Officials and Officers	78
7. The World of Senior Officers	110
8. Orders of Chivalry	123
9. The Royal Guard: Units *Au Dedans du Louvre*	135
10. The Royal Guard: Units *Au Dehors du Louvre*	161
11. The Royal Guard: Infantry	181
12. Other Guard Units	197
Appendix I: Royal Guard Cavalry Uniforms in Army Lists	202
Appendix II: Order of Battle at the Compiègne Review, September 1698	203
Appendix III: Opponent Armies: the Spanish Army of the 17th Century	204
Colour Plate Commentaries	208
Bibliography	213

Preface and Acknowledgements

Peace is the dream of wise men;
War is the history of mankind
Louis-Philippe, Comte de Ségur (1753–1830)

To delve into the era of the Sun King is to look into our own present world. Has anything changed 350 years later? Yes, but all the fundamentals that humans had to face then are with us today: wars, religious strife, ruthless competition between nations by force of arms and knavery, love of pomp and pageantry, adulation or hatred of strong leaders, the search for truth, fascination with discovery and technical progress such as development of better weapons; the list goes on and on.

Indeed, many elements that shape our world today came forth in Louis XIV's France. Modest-sized professional armies became very numerous, an early form of conscription appeared, firepower became dominant on battlefields, transforming tactics, the organisation of armies was much improved and the impact of large armies on national economies became a prime concern since it had repercussions on manufacturing, employment and banking; indeed, wars could be profitable. There was an increased pan-European and overseas view in Louis XIV's France with geo-strategic and geo-political outlooks thus favouring elaborate protocols in diplomacy. French culture, including a large chunk of its military culture, came to be seen as the world's finest. Indeed, armies always export their national culture as values of the dominant power.

These and many more topics are presented in this series of four volumes, of which this is the first. We recount Louis XIV's rather turbulent reign since it was mostly a succession of wars, with the main details of battle tactics and, more fundamentally, of the personalities and the armies that were largely on campaign nearly constantly from the mid 17th century to the early 18th century. An important part of each volume is devoted to the many units in the French army outlining their histories and material culture – arms, uniforms and colours; here it must be pointed out that the author was a curator specialising in military topics. We add that for showing those aspects, each volume will have a couple of hundred images, many of which are by forgotten military artists whose works were often the source for later renderings by younger artists. Each volume has also five especially commissioned plates that will concentrate mainly on showing, often for the first time, lesser-seen topics.

THE ARMIES AND WARS OF THE SUN KING 1643–1715: VOLUME 1

The Sun King, Louis XIV of France, 1665. Copy of a bust by Gian Lorenzo Bernini. City of Quebec collection. Author's photo.

This first volume starts in 1638 when Louis was born and ends in 1671. The intervening years were filled with conflicts against Spain, the Fronde civil war, foreign adventures and the Sun King's *blitzkrieg*. There follow short biographies of the men who shaped and led Europe's finest and largest army, their knighthoods and lifestyles. The last substantial part is devoted to the royal guard – it was far more than a personal bodyguard, it was the showpiece portion of the army leading by example amongst its many ramifications.

The second volume will cover the Dutch War (1672–1678) and other events ending in the later 1680s. The evolution of the line infantry, both the regiments raised in France and the many mercenary units, will be described in all its main aspects.

The third volume will cover the War of the League of Augsburg (1689–1697). The Gendarmerie, line cavalry, dragoons and light cavalry will be its other main topic.

The fourth volume will start at the outset of the War of the Spanish Succession (1702–1714) ending with the Sun King's passing in 1715. Artillery, engineering, light troops, constabulary troops, health care, chaplains and the huge and varied militia structure that mustered hundreds of thousands of men, often armed and uniformed, everywhere in the kingdom, will be amongst the topics presented followed by a bibliography.

Each volume will have a few appendices including glances at the opposing armies. Details on certain subjects such as arms, colours and standards will also be found in future volumes.

PREFACE AND ACKNOWLEDGEMENTS

We wish to acknowledge most humbly and with considerable gratitude the assistance from many individuals and institutions over the last half century. We cite here Francis Back (Montréal), Giancarlo Boeri (Rome), Jean and Raoul Brunon (Salon-de-Provence), William Y. Carman (Sutton, UK), Robert Delort (Paris), Kevin Gélinas (Saint-Sévère, Québec), Eugène Lelièpvre (Paris), Michel Pétard (Saint-Sébastien-sur-Loire, France), the kind staff of the Archives Nationales (Paris), the Anne S.K. Brown Military Collection at the Brown University Library (Providence, USA), the Canadian War Museum (Ottawa), Library and Archives Canada (Ottawa), the Library of Congress (Washington), the Louvre (Paris), the Musée de l'Armée (Paris and Salon-de-Provence), The National Archives (Kew), the Rijksmuseum (Amsterdam), the Service Historique de la Défense (Vincennes) are amongst the many persons and institutions that have kindly greeted us over the years.

We further wish to thank Charles Singleton and Serena Jones, whose mastery of editorial as well as historical aspects has tuned a pile of digital files into the attractive present publication with their colleagues at Helion as well as Edward Dovey for his fine plates. And last but not least, Dr. Luce Vermette, historian of lifestyles and of art who happens to be my beloved and very encouraging and patient spouse.

Finally the inevitable errors or misinterpretations rest solely with the author – *Errare humanum est*.

René Chartrand
Gatineau (Québec)

1

Young Louis XIV

Louis XIV was born in tumultuous times into a turmoiled family. His father, Louis XIII, had been married to Anne of Austria in 1615. Both were 14 years old. It was of course a diplomatically arranged marriage to warm relations between the French royal family of Bourbon with the Hispano-Germanic royal and Imperial Hapsburg family. She was a princess from the Spanish branch of her family, had blond hair and might have been prettier but for the long "Hapsburg nose" that Louis also had since his family tree had Hapsburg ancestors. They immediately did not take to each other and soon led separate private lives while usually smiling together at public ceremonies.

Years passed and no royal heirs appeared. The estrangement appears to have been even more acute after the 10 November 1630 Day of Dupes when Louis XIII foiled a plot to oust prime minister Cardinal Richelieu from power. This was masterminded by the Queen Mother, Marie de Médicis, and a group of nobles. She was exiled for life and some nobles were executed as Louis XIII trusted more the outstanding statesman that Cardinal Richelieu was rather than any other person. His queen was in the untrustworthy category. So the advent of a Dauphin – the heir to the throne of France – seemed even more remote.

By late 1637, France was now involved in the Thirty Years' War, the management of which the King left to his marshals while he often went hunting at his small lodge at Versailles. In December, he was on the way to Versailles, but there was such a bad storm with rain and thunder that it was considered more prudent to stop at the Louvre in Paris, the palace where the Queen resided. According to an account by Father Griffet, Louis XIII accepted the suggestion since he would find supper and lodging there. Queen Anne greeted him and, for once, they seem to have been at ease with each other's company. "They supped together" Griffet related. It must have been a pleasant evening for he added that: "The king spent the night with the queen, and nine months later Anne of Austria had a son, whose unexpected birth brought universal joy to the entire kingdom." Frenchmen now had a Dauphin, as the prince to be king was called, and rejoiced since his advent most likely would

YOUNG LOUIS XIV

LVDOVICVS XIV FRANCIÆ
ET NAVARRÆ REX
Christianissimus. P. de Iode ex   P. Rucholle f.

1-1 Louis XIV, as king of France at five years old in 1643. This print shows the infant monarch wearing the royal robes trimmed with ermine fur, over which is seen the grand collar of the Order of the Holy Spirit. He holds the marshal's baton of command indicating that the king is the supreme authority over the armed forces and the government. Courtesy Rijksmuseum, Amsterdam. RP-P-1910-2319.

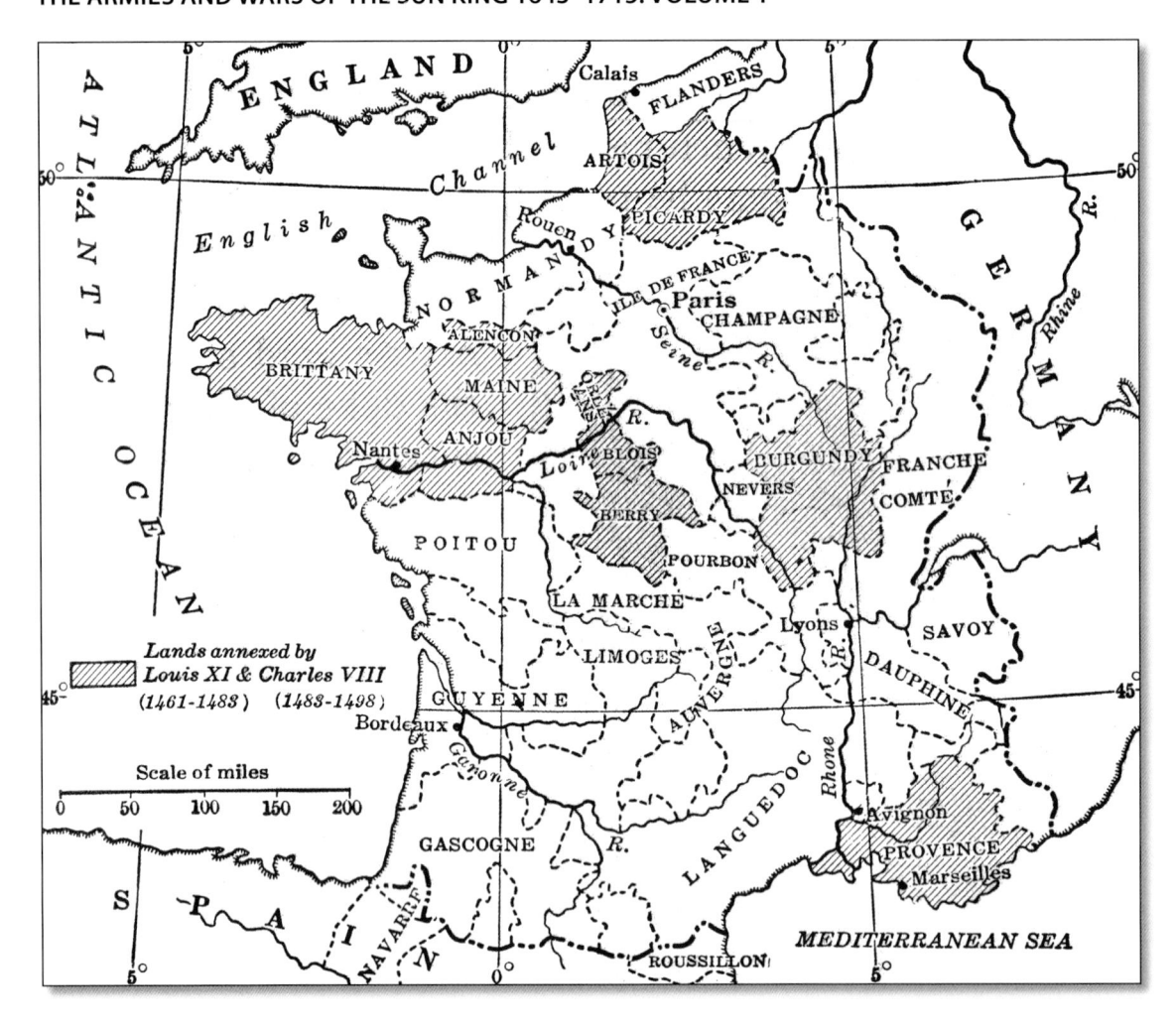

THE ARMIES AND WARS OF THE SUN KING 1643–1715: VOLUME 1

1-2 Map of France showing its unification, 1461–1498. The shaded areas are those provinces that were incorporated into the kingdom between 1461 and 1498. The eastern frontiers had rather fluctuating borders thereafter. Private collection. Author's photo.

avert a future civil war between self-appointed candidates to the throne on the death of a king having no son.[1]

The birth occurred on 5 September 1638. Louis XIII died on 14 May 1643 and thus, the young Dauphin became Louis XIV, King of France. He was not yet five years old so his mother was declared regent. Cardinal Richelieu had died on 4 December 1642 so the affairs of state passed on to the man he had recommended as prime minister, Cardinal Jules Mazarin. He was shrewd, patient, would promise much to keep friend and foe in hopes of rewards and, most of all, was tenacious in his aims. While politics were rife in Paris following the death of Louis XIII, a very important event occurred in north-eastern France.[2]

---

1 Griffet quoted in: Joseph Barry, 'Sex and the King of France', *Horizon* (Summer 1968), Vol. X, No. 3, p. 119. There was another pleasant meeting between Louis XIII and his queen that led to the birth in 1640 of Philippe, Louis XIV's younger brother. Gossip was rife that Louis XIII's paternity was dubious…

2 It should be mentioned that cardinals – regarded as princes of the church – at that time were not necessarily priests like today. They were very senior administrators with substantial political

Rocroi

On 19 May 1643, a Spanish army of 27,000 men under the command of Francisco de Melo was crushed by a French army of about 25,000 men led by Louis de Bourbon, Duc d'Enghien (known from 1646 as the Prince de Condé) who was the 21-year-old cousin of Louis XIV. Although he had a somewhat nominal command of his army who was under the administrative supervision of experienced Marshal François de L'Hôpital, Condé already showed remarkable tactical and command abilities. He had studied the cavalry tactics employed by Swedish King Gustavus Adolphus, notably thanks to one of his army's cavalry commanders, Major-General Jean de Gassion who had served in the Swedish army. Condé's army had up to 8,000 cavalrymen and his opponent had some 9,000. On 16 May, Condé learned of Louis XIII's death, but kept the news secret so as to not disrupt the good morale of his troops. Three days later, both armies clashed. Melo's troops advanced on the French centre and took some of its artillery while Marshal L'Hôpital, who commanded that sector, was hard pressed. Condé with Gassion's cavalry were on the right attempting to outflank, with some success, the Spanish. At that point, the chances of either side winning were about even. Normally, Condé would have drawn back and reinforced his centre. Instead, in what has been called a stroke of genius, he pressed on the cavalry charge at full gallop – Swedish style – and this destabilised some of the famed Spanish *tercio* units. They eventually broke ranks and ran, and a rout ensued spreading panic to the rest of the Spanish army. Melo lost some 12,000 men while Condé lost 4,000. The French army captured 200 colours, 60 standards, 24 guns and the baggage, including money meant to pay the Spanish army. Condé then brought his army to Thionville which, after a two-month siege, capitulated on 10 August followed by the surrender of Sierk on 3 September.[3]

Rocroi was an outstanding victory that turned the fate of the war in favour of France. But it was much more than that. The feared Spanish *tercios* who almost reigned on the battlefield since the 16th century were definitely proven as outclassed thanks to the French army's tactics. After a rather unremarkable period, the French army was proving to be a very lethal force led by talented commanders with innovative notions. Besides Condé, young General Henri de Turenne was also drawing attention. So, following Rocroi, the balance of military power and influence gradually shifted to France that, in turn, gave it more weight in European affairs.

In the short term, there was more fighting against both the Spanish and some of their German allies. In the fall, French troops in Germany had suffered defeats, Marshal de Guébrillant being killed there on 24 November 1643. Without much opposition, Bavarian Marshal Franz Baron von Mercy

---

powers who usually originated from the high nobility. Both Richelieu and Mazarin were outstanding statesmen and might even be with an army during a campaign.

3 Charles Sevin, Marquis de Quincy, *Histoire militaire du règne de Louis le Grand, roi de France* (Paris, 1726), vol. 1, pp. 2–6; Paul Lacroix, *L'Armée depuis le Moyen-Age jusqu'à la Révolution* (Paris: Firmin-Didot, c,1880), pp. 260–265; André Corvisier, *Dictionnaire d'art et d'histoire militaires (Paris: PUF, 1988)*, pp. 737–738.

THE ARMIES AND WARS OF THE SUN KING 1643–1715: VOLUME 1

1-3 The battle of Rocroi, 19 May 1643. Fought only five days after five year old Louis XIV became king, it was an outstanding victory by the Prince de Condé that crushed much of Spain's power and influence in Europe.
Print after Maurice Leloir. Private collection. Author's photo.

moved in 1644 to besiege Fribourg with an army of 15,000 men and this weakly defended city capitulated. Meanwhile, the French court ordered Condé with his 10,000 men to join Marshal Turenne and march against Mercy at Fribourg. While Turenne spread his troops on the outskirts, Condé took the initiative to attack Mercy. There was robust fighting for the next two days, Condé being narrowly missed by a cannonball that took off his saddle's pommel while Marshal de Gramont's horse was killed, but, by 5 August, the Bavarians withdrew exhausted leaving behind six cannons and two mortars as well as their baggage.[4]

In 1645, Turenne was in Germany leading a French army of about 9,000 men. On 2 May, he encountered Mercy's 9,600 Bavarians at Marienthal (also called Herbsthausen and Mergentheim). General Rosen had not carried out Turenne's instructions, Mercy saw Rosen's fault in the French's dispositions and successfully attacked. A general rout followed and Turenne tried to save what he could of his army after losing 59 colours and some 2,600 men. In early August, the French army, which now included troops from Saxe-Weimar, had recuperated and Condé had been sent to reinforce Turenne. The French force was met at Nördlingen by Mercy and General Johann von Werth with some 12,000 Bavarians and 4,000 troops of the Holy Roman Empire. The Franco-Saxon troops attacked in the afternoon of 3 August, the Bavarians counter-attacked and broke the French right wing led by Condé who managed to contain the opponents. Meanwhile Turenne's left wing now charged into the Imperial troop, which scattered and turned into a rout. Marshal Mercy was killed and the French took 70 colours and 4,000 prisoners. It was a resounding French success. There followed more battles of less consequence, the last major engagement being at Lens on 20 August 1648. There, Condé's 16,000 men faced 18,000 men of the Spanish army of Flanders under Archduke Leopold Wilhelm. While the French centre managed to contain the Spanish, Condé's cavalry successfully overran the Spanish flanks which crushed Wilhelm's army, half being lost. This last major victory sealed Condé's reputation as one of the best generals of his time.[5]

On 24 October 1648, Peace of Westphalia was signed by most participants, Spain continuing a not very effective war against France until 1659. The human and economic legacy of the Thirty Years' War was generally awful for most countries. Some 180,000 soldiers had been killed or mortally wounded in battle. Others who had perished from disease were likely much more numerous and vast numbers of civilians had succumbed due to the war's miseries. Northern Germany and central Europe had decreases of over half their population in some areas and their economies collapsed. Even Spain, in spite of the silver and gold it drew from its American domains, was nearly ruined. Politically, the cohesion of the Hapsburg's Holy Roman Empire exploded into a multitude of small German states while certain of its parts gained strength such as Bavaria,

---

4   Marquis de La Houssaye and Isaac de La Peyrère, 'Rocroi, Fribourg et Lens', *Bibliothèque de souvenirs & récits militaires*, P. Gaulot, ed (Paris: Henri Gautier, c.1900), No. 83, pp. 135–149.
5   Turenne, 'Marienthal et Norlingen', *Bibliothèque de souvenirs & récits militaires*, P. Gaulot, ed. (Paris: Henri Gautier, c.1900), No. 80, pp. 34–64; A. Ledieu, *Esquisses militaires de la Guerre de Trente Ans* (Lille and Paris: J. Lefort, 1888), pp. 169–177.

1-4 (above): Marshal Louis de Bourbon, Prince de Condé, c.1648. Commonly called Le Grand Condé, Louis de Bourbon (1621–1686) was an elder cousin of Louis XIV and one of the best generals of his times. Portrait by Juste van Egmont. Musée Condé, Chantilly. Author's photo.

1-5 (left): Anne of Austria, 1625–1626. Anne of Austria (1601–1666) was queen of France as the wife of King Louis XIII and mother of Louis XIV. She was a woman of will and purpose. From 1643, she assumed the role of Regent of France during a period of great political instability, some of it caused by her actions. Painting from the studio of Peter Paul Rubens. Courtesy Rijksmuseum, Amsterdam. SK-C-296.

Brandenburg and Austria. Sweden also gained territories and power in northeastern Europe. As for France, it was the biggest winner. It had suffered little from the depredations of war, had Europe's largest population at about 20 million souls and its economy was not greatly affected. It thus could hope for hegemony over European affairs. However, internal conflicts were about to upset these ambitions.[6]

The *Frondes*

Within France, many were unsatisfied for a variety of political reasons. One faction was the Paris Parliament which wished to have more independence from the regency of Queen Mother Anne of Austria and especially from Prime Minister Mazarin, whose style of government made him scorned by many. Nevertheless, he had enormous influence over the Queen and had also gained actual control of the royal government. On 16 August 1648, the day of the celebrations for the French army's victory at Lens, the Queen had leading members of Parliament, notably the popular councillor Pierre Broussel, arrested for disrespect to royal authority. Many believed it was a trumped-up charge and it sparked the start of the first Fronde. Many in Paris were outraged, the city militia mustered and, in true Parisian style, barricades went up on many streets in protest. After three days of effervescence, things calmed down enough for a delegation of members of Parliament to advise the Queen to soften her grip and release the members of Parliament. She would not hear of it, nor would Mazarin.

Coming back from the fruitless meeting, Parliament President Matthieu Molé was mocked and set upon by militiamen asking where was Broussel and also the hated Mazarin. The intellectual Paul de Conti and the coadjutor of Paris (later Cardinal) de Retz sided with Parliament and also demanded the dismissal of the scorned Mazarin, seen as the evil influence on the Queen. De Retz was especially skilled as a politician and was remembered by Bussy-Rabutin as "hardy, turbulent, popular, the soul of the intrigues of the Fronde" further mentioning that his private life "was even more amazing". He had an "air of greatness, a genial impetuosity" that were "the image of his conduct".[7]

Sensing the situation was worsening, the Queen and Mazarin had the members of Parliament released, but secretly plotted their next action. This came during the night of 5 to 6 January 1649 when the Queen and Mazarin moved out of the royal palace with young Louis XIV to the chateau of Saint-Germain-en-Laye. The next day, there was stupor in the city, but also joy at being rid of Mazarin. But civil war was now a reality as royal troops under

---

6 Lucien Bély, Jean Bérenger and André Corvisier, *Guerre et paix dans l'Europe du XVIIe siècle* (Paris: SEDES, 1991), chapter 1.
7 The remarks on Cardinal de Retz are inscribed below in a portrait in Bussy-Rabutin's chateau: 'Hardi, turbulent, populaire, l'âme des intrigues de la Fronde, sa vie privée fut encore plus étonnante. Il a laissé des mémoires écrits avec un aire de grandeur, une impétuosité de génie, une inégalité, qui sont l'image de sa conduite.'

1-6 Cardinal Jules Mazarin, 1660. He was prime minister from 1643 to 1661 and, although unpopular, managed to keep France united and preserve the powers of the royal government through the Fronde rebellions. Portrait by Pierre Mignard. Chateau d'Ancy-le-Franc, Burgundy. Author's photo

Prince Condé arrived, beat back the militia and entered Paris on 8 February. A truce was agreed and, eventually, Louis XIV came back to Paris on 8 August.

Matters might have ended there had it not been for Princes Condé, Conti and Longueville whose arrogance and hatred of Mazarin knew no bounds. This led to renewed fighting between different factions with parts of the army in one camp and parts in another faction. Central command all but collapsed and even Turenne was serving Longueville for a short time. Mazarin fled to Cologne, but his influence was great and he continued to mastermind schemes to restore royal authority under his control. Thus, in a spectacular move, the Queen now had Princes Condé, Conti and Longueville arrested on 18 January 1650. This sparked the "Fronde of the Nobles" or "of the Princes" as many noblemen now sided with them. The princes were released, but the civil strife went on.

In all this, many saw their salvation in the young king who was immensely popular with the common people. Fearing he would be taken away again, the royal palace was besieged by a huge crowd headed by thousands of city militiamen at two in the morning of 9 February 1651. They wanted to see the king now! Escape was impossible so young Louis was led to his bed and feigned sleep while hundreds of Parisian militiamen quietly passed by his bed with his mother nearby. Thinking their beloved young king was asleep and safe, the rioting crowd dispersed.

But the young monarch was not asleep. This event, which was a traumatic experience, had a very profound effect on him. He knew he lived in an era when his own life was at stake in times of turmoil; Henri IV, his grandfather had been assassinated and, in England, King Charles I had been executed by order of his own parliament. This shaped his belief that autocratic rule was the only solution in governance. It also instilled a lifelong aversion to Paris and its turbulent and revolutionary populace. He could do nothing immediately but his time would come.

The Fronde, whose many twists and turns are difficult to understand and worse to explain, went on after a respite. Some were for Mazarin and royal power, the nobles headed by Condé wanted to rule in place of Mazarin's royal government and Cardinal de Retz was more or less for expanded powers for Paris and its Parliament. No less than the late King's brother, Gaston d'Orléans, an eternal political schemer, was also a dissident of his own nephew! All were looking to nullify whatever power the young king might eventually have, get rid of Mazarin and govern the country. So all were engaged in a three-way power struggle. Again, part of the army and militias were in each camp and occasionally battled each other. Nevertheless, the Queen's regency retained enough military and political support to hold on. On 7 September 1651, Louis XIV officially attained his majority, but he was only 13 years old and a de facto regency remained, controlled by Mazarin and the Queen Mother.

1-7 (right, top): The arrest of Pierre Broussel, a leading member of the Paris Parliament, 16 August 1648. This event sparked the Fronde civil war. Print after F. Lix. Private collection. Author's photo.

1-8 (right) Outbreak of the Fronde in Paris, August 1648. One of the many incidents was the mocking crowd of armed militiamen setting upon a delegation of members of the Paris Parliament which had failed to obtain the release of two of its members. A militiaman even pulled the beard of Parliament's President Molé. Print after Maurice Leloir. Private collection. Author's photo.

1-9 (above): Jean-François Paul de Gondi, Cardinal de Retz, c.1652. One of the most prominent leaders of the Fronde in Paris. He actually became a cardinal in February 1652 and is shown wearing his cardinal's robes. Unsigned portrait. Chateau de Bussy-Rabutin, Burgundy. Author's photo.

1-10 (right): Arrest of princes de Condé, de Conti and the Duc de Longueville, 18 January 1650. Although later released, these arrests encouraged a new uprising, this time by some noble families and became nicknamed *la Fronde des nobles* (the Fronde of the nobles). Print after Lix. Private collection. Author's photo.

1-11 (left): Coat of arms of Henri d'Orléans, Duc de Longueville. A diplomat, he led the French delegation at the negotiations that culminated in the 1648 Treaty of Westphalia that ended the Thirty Years' War. He then became a leader of the Fronde with his brothers-in-law Condé and Conti. Banished from court, he passed away in 1668. Blue shield with gold lilies, silver label and baton. From a mural painting. Musée Condé, Chantilly. Author's photo.

YOUNG LOUIS XIV

1-12 (left): Cassock for a mid 17th century soldier. This one was most likely for a Spanish soldier, being red with a white Burgundy cross. Spanish colours also bore this insignia noted by *La Grande Mademoiselle* who saw them in Paris during the Fronde in June 1652. Some of Condé's Spanish soldiers probably had such cassocks. The Hermitage, St. Petersburg, Russia. Author's photo.

1-13 (below): Fighting between Marshal Turenne's and the Prince de Condé's troops at the gate of Saint-Antoine, 2 July 1652. Note the smoke rising from the guns in the old castle of the Bastille (at upper right) firing on the royal army. Contemporary print. Private collection. Author's photo..

1-4 The *Grande Mademoiselle* ordering the guns of the Bastille to fire on royal troops, 2 July 1652. Print after Maurice Leloir. Private collection. Author's photo.

Seeing this, Condé quit Paris for Bordeaux and there accepted an alliance with the Spanish to which Conti, Longueville and many nobles also adhered to. But not all – the witty Duc d'Orléans nicknamed Condé *le lion* (the lion), Conti *le singe* (the monkey) and Longueville *le renard* (the fox) that summed up well their characters in the public's mind.[8]

It was outright treason and it made many others rally to the Queen Mother and Mazarin if the Kingdom of France was to remain French. De Retz was put aside while Marshal Turenne, like most of the army, definitely chose the royal party. It was reinforced by Mazarin who led 8,000 royal troops and approached Paris. He joined the royal army led by Turenne who took overall military command. The capital had been recently occupied by Condé's troops. Mademoiselle de Montpensier – nicknamed *La Grande Mademoiselle* – had

---

8   Gustave Toudouze, *Le Roy Soleil* (Paris: Boivin, 1908), p. 8.

somewhat taken over command of the Fronde's troops in Paris and later recalled her "great satisfaction and at the same time great amazement to think that [she] made Spanish cannons of the King of Spain roll through Paris and [see passing troops bearing] red colours with [white] St. Andrew's [actually Burgundy] crosses." There was some heavy fighting between Turenne's royal army and Condé's partly Spanish troops outside the Saint-Antoine gate and leading into the centre of Paris. On 2 July 1652, Condé's soldiers were being beaten back and he might have been captured had it not been for *La Grande Mademoiselle* who ordered the guns of the old, but still redoubtable Bastille castle to open fire on Turenne's royal army. In spite of that, Turenne's troops prevailed although they were slowed down in their progress to secure the city. This allowed Condé to get away to Spanish Flanders, but *La Grande Mademoiselle's* action was the last straw for many Frenchmen. Still, she was later forgiven and even re-admitted to Louis XIV's court. Why? She was the daughter of Louis XIII's brother, Gaston d'Orléans, and thus of the "royal blood" being cousin of the King as well as an outstandingly flamboyant personality. She was also possibly the most wealthy woman in Europe. In any event, on 4 July, the young king made a triumphant entry into Paris.[9]

To most Frenchmen, the only way out of France's civil strife lay with the royal government and its army. There were other battles in the next couple of months, but the Fronde of the Nobles was doomed and it collapsed. Given a choice between treasonous nobles supported by Spain and their young king, even with the Queen and Mazarin who at least were loyal to him and to France, the overwhelming feeling in the population and of the army was to rally to royal authority. On 21 October 1652, Louis XIV with his court, which had been safely outside the capital, usually at Saint-Germain-en-Laye, was back in Paris and so was Cardinal Mazarin as prime minister. The Frondes of the Parliament and of the Nobles were finished. In their stead, the roots of absolute autocratic power by the head of state were firmly planted.[10]

"I am the state"

While Cardinal Mazarin was still, in reality, governing France, Louis had been crowned on 7 June 1654 and thereafter asserted increasingly strongly a small part of his powers. At that time, the Paris Parliament was also the kingdom's legislative body tasked with registering the royal edicts. This was

---

9 *Mémoires de Mademoiselle de Montpensier* (Amsterdam: Jean-Frédéric Bernard, 1729), Vol. 2, pp. 85–86. Anne-Marie-Louise d'Orléans, Duchesse de Montpensier (1627–1693) inherited her great wealth from her mother Marie de Bourbon who died five days after her birth. Her flamboyant behaviour at the battle of Saint-Antoine was generally much disapproved of, even by her scheming father. She went into exile at her Saint-Fargeau estate for five years until forgiven and allowed to appear again at the royal court. She eventually again drew controversy by her torrid love affair with the Duke de Lauzun. See her biography by Michel Le Moël, *La Grande Mademoiselle* (Paris: Fallois, 1994).

10 Quincy, *Histoire militaire*, Vol. 1. pp. 113–140 has details on the many engagements during the Fronde for 1649 to 1652. See also R. Quarré de Verneuil, *L'armée en France depuis Charles VII jusqu'à la Révolution 1439–1789* (Paris: J. Dumaine, 1880), Vol. 2, pp. 229–233.

1-15 King Louis XIV at 14 years old. Private collection. Author's photo.

a routine task and, as usual, various edicts had been duly proclaimed on 20 March 1655, but the Parliament decided to debate on their content. Louis was infuriated. He had witnessed dissent to royal authority during the Fronde years and could not stand any disrespect. This included the actions, past and present, of Parliament. Learning while hunting at nearby Vincennes that the Paris Parliament was still discussing the edicts he had signed, he considered its action to be *lèse-majesté* (disrespect to His Majesty), galloped to the legislative assembly, marched into the meeting hall with his suite, took his seat in the king's chair and summoned the assembled members telling them, in effect, that *l'état c'est moi* (I am the state). They would no longer tamper with his edicts because he dissolved Parliament on the spot.

This was not an elected chamber like the one in England. As Voltaire put it, to think of French Parliaments as representing the people was ridiculous. Nevertheless, their legal role as courts of law continued. But henceforth, political debates and decisions were in the realm of the royal court and nowhere else. Louis XIV may not have said the famous "I am the state" often quoted in histories, but his assertive action was generally applauded. Amongst the people as well as the nobility, parliamentarians had a dubious reputation, especially as many became remarkably wealthy when in office.

Young Louis had deeper motivations. He later wrote that the parliaments in the kingdom had dangerously "elevated themselves too much" during his minority. They had to be brought under control. Their authority, when opposed to the King's, was often "very bad" no matter how "good their intentions" were and they had to be brought down. Cardinal Mazarin, assessing the maturing Louis XIV, concluded that "he had enough stuff to make four kings and one honest man."[11]

The Advent of the Sun King

Now secure if not yet in power, the young Louis and his court were treated to many concerts and plays to forget the horrors of the past civil wars and herald times of optimism for the kingdom. For all its troubles, it was still the largest and most powerful country in Europe. And, by the time he was 15, Louis had a growing awareness that his destiny would be exceptional; he would open the vast potential of his nation and raise it to its zenith – to the sun itself.

---

11 Voltaire (François-Marie Arouet), *Le Siècle de Louis XIV*, (Berlin, 1751) from the (Paris: Gallimard, 2015) edition pp. 911–912; *Mémoires de Louis* XIV, Jean Longnon, ed. (Paris: Tallandier, 1928), p. 41; Toudouze, *Le Roy Soleil*, pp. 16–18.

YOUNG LOUIS XIV

1-16 The rise of the Sun King, 1655. The 15-year-old king's fascination with the sun was proclaimed when he assumed the role of the rising sun in an operatic ballet given at the royal theatre in 1655, dressed in a magnificent golden costume. His courtiers later convinced him to adopt the sun as his badge. Print after Maurice Leloir. Private collection. Author's photo.

He was growing to be handsome and loved the arts to the point of even dancing ballet at the court's theatre during 1655. In a combination ballet and theatrical production titled *La Nuit* (the night), he played the part of the rising sun dressed in a magnificent gold costume and reciting almost prophetic verses such as: "a divine hand has given me the reins; a great goddess has sustained my rights; … I [the sun] am the star of the kings".

This infatuation with the sun as a symbol of power was also mentioned in his own memoirs. He related that his courtiers had "agreeably flattered the ambition of a young king" and they convinced him to adopt both the "terrestrial globe of the earth" with the motto *nec pluribus impar* as well as that of the sun because he would "surely govern other empires" just as "the sun lights other worlds, if they are equally exposed to his rays". Convinced that the sun was his best badge, it eventually appeared on his buildings and on "an infinity of other things". When this occurred is not clear, but could be as early as 1656 or as late as 1662.[12]

The Latin motto he chose, *nec pluribus impar*, literally translated comes out as "Not unequal to many", which was and remains quite obscure and somewhat confusing. Another version is "above all others", notably given by

---

12 *Mémoires de Louis XIV*, pp. 125–126; Voltaire, *Le Siècle de Louis XIV* p. 416 attributes one Douvrier, an antiquarian, to have come up with this badge; Toudouze, *Le Roy Soleil*, pp. 15–16.

1-17 The sun badge of the Sun King and his motto, mid 17th century. Print after JOB. Private collection. Author's photo.

Voltaire in his history, which was certainly in tune with the young Sun King's vision of himself. Coming from the ambitious young Louis XIV, the sense of its meaning certainly had a strong "second to none" feeling, especially as, from the 1660s, it was cast on the French army's pieces of ordnance and embroidered on a multitude of military standards and flags, always with the sun's badge with its long rays. "Opponents beware, the Sun is rising" and its burning rays can reach you, was its implicit message.

Progress of the War with Spain

Meanwhile, Spain had never signed the 1648 peace treaties and kept up a somewhat latent military pressure on France. After the Fronde, the French army regained much of its cohesion thanks to a more stable government. Turenne and other generals were able to repulse any Spanish attempt to violate its borders. The French army nevertheless went on campaign every spring after having raised some levies and temporary regiments to its modest-sized regular force. Accurate figures on the strength of the French army are elusive, but it seems to have hovered at about 100,000 men, more or less. However, like the Spanish, it was deployed in several areas so that there appears to have been no overwhelming advantage facing opponents. The area of operation was mainly in Flanders as usual, part of it being French and part being a Spanish domain although its inhabitants were mainly Walloon and Flemish. French contingents were also seen in northern Italy against the Spanish in the Milanese and in Catalonia. By 1654, the internal struggles due to the Frondes had ended. "Sovereign [royal] power was restored and the people's disobedience repressed" as Quincy put it.

The King was crowned on 7 June 1654 and the fortress of Stenay fell to Marshal Turenne's French army on 2 August. The young king arrived at the front to encourage the troops and, after a long siege by the Marquis de Faber, the city of Sédan capitulated. The French army being absorbed by that siege, Spanish troops led by the Prince of Condé laid siege to Arras whose small French garrison was first reinforced and finally relieved by a strong army led by Marshal Turenne and several other marshals. The King then came to Arras for a triumphant entry congratulating Governor de Montjeu and his garrison for a brilliant defence. This was followed by the siege and capture of Le Quesnoy and the relief of Rozes in Catalonia.[13]

The French army had now reassumed its redoubtable force and went from a defensive stance during the Fronde to more offensive operations. The war then went on with more sieges in Flanders, the French slowly gaining the advantage over the Spanish. All this was fought between relatively small armies in a fairly limited territory, much as it had been for decades if not centuries previously. To be sure, the inhabitants of the areas where combat occurred were devastated, but this was a small portion on the borders of the opposing nations. The young Sun King, who went on the occasional moral-boosting visits to the troops in the field, must have learned and appreciated the tactical aspects explained by such masters as Marshals Turenne and Faber. Yet, one wonders if he did not perceive a lack of military strategy in spite of his young age. We feel he did perceive it because, once in effective autocratic power, he had strategic vision in a grand scale and took the necessary measures to build up the largest army in Europe to carry it out.

1-18 Marshal Henri de la Tour d'Auvergne, Vicomte de Turenne, c.1660. Arguably the most outstanding general of his times. Print after P. de Champeigne. Private collection. Author's photo.

Dunkirk and the Peace of the Pyrenees

By 1657, the wily Cardinal Mazarin, who was certainly not a military strategist, was looking for a way to end the somewhat deadlocked, "tit for tat" war with Spain. He had negotiated an almost unholy alliance with England, then governed by the Puritan dictator of England, Oliver Cromwell, who had executed King Charles I. Cromwell had already attacked Spanish possessions in the West Indies taking Jamaica. Spain also possessed Dunkirk at the time. An English expeditionary corps of 6,000 men joined Turenne's army creating much interest amongst the French because they wore red uniforms – a novelty as the French army was not uniformed at the time. It was not until May 1658, when

---

13 Quincy, *Histoire militaire*, Vol. 1. pp. 181–196.

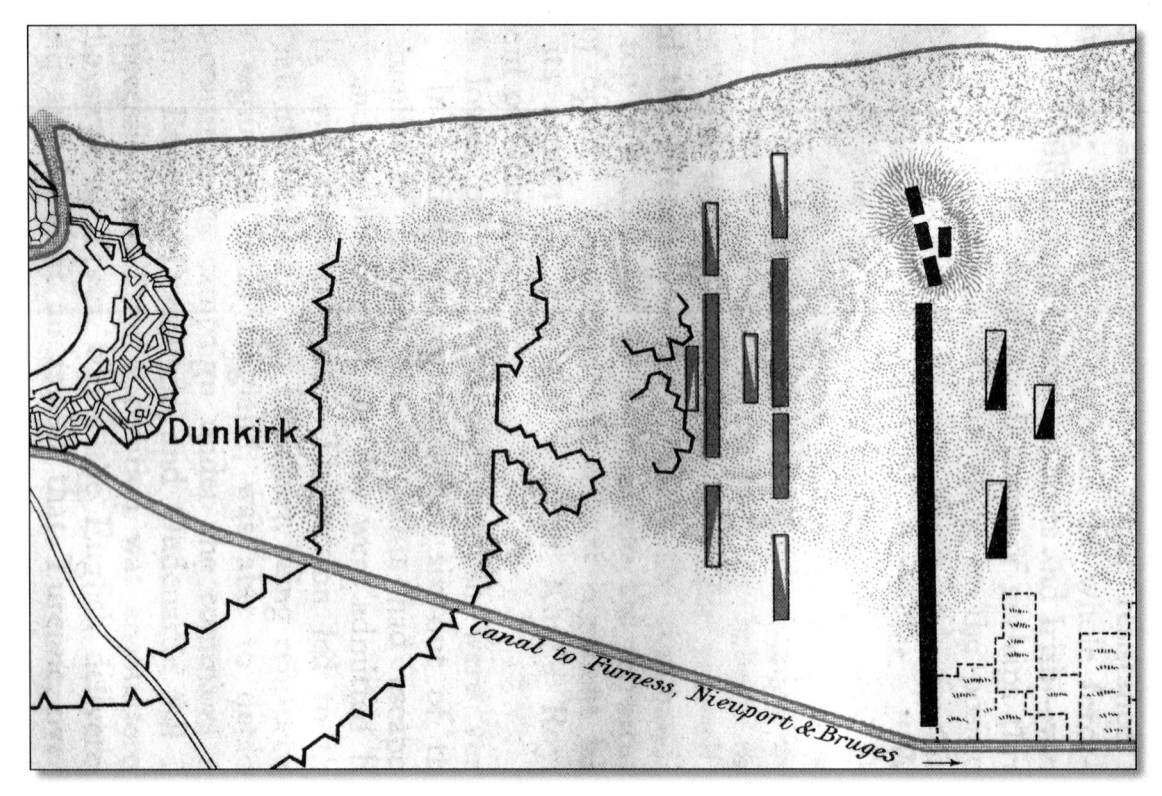

1-19 Plan of the Battle of the Dunkirk Dunes, 14 June 1658. At left, the Franco-English troops, at right the Spanish troops. The decisive action was the allied assault and capture of the high Dunes held by Spanish, which turned their army's flank and led to a costly defeat. From Fortescue's *History of the British Army*, Vol. 1. Author's photo.

Dunkirk was invested by the Franco-English force, that a decisive campaign got under way. In June, Turenne's army of 15,000 men with the English corps of 6,000 men faced Don Juan of Austria's 15,000 men that had come to raise the siege. Some Spanish troops took position in sand dune heights east of the city. On 14 June, Turenne's troops attacked, the English being in the heart of the action, ran up the dunes ultimately driving their defenders and the whole Spanish force into retreat. Some 3,000 were killed and wounded and another 4,000 were taken prisoner. The Battle of the Dunes sealed Dunkirk's fate and it capitulated 10 days later. Louis XIV entered the city triumphant.[14]

Imperial Spain that had made other nations tremble in past times was vanquished, never to rise again to its former, eminent 16th-century glory. Rocroi, and now Dunkirk, had shattered its military reputation. But it still was a power to be reckoned with. In the negotiations that led to the 1659 Peace Treaty of the Pyrenees, it was agreed that Prince Condé would be pardoned and allowed back into France. The province of Artois, the city of Arras, some Spanish Flanders towns, Luxembourg, Roussillon and Pignerol in the Alps were ceded to France. Furthermore, the daughter of King Felipe IV of Spain "and the Indies" would marry Louis XIV of France. On 7 June 1660, the Spanish *infanta*, Marie-Thérèse of Austria, met Louis at the Island of Pheasants and, two days later, they were married at Saint-Jean-de-Luz. Both were the same age. They went on a triumphal promenade, being hailed in every town, all the way to Paris.

---

14   John W. Fortescue, *A History of the British Army* (London: Macmillan, 1899), Vol. 1, pp. 270–274; Quincy, *Histoire militaire*, Vol. 1, pp. 234–238.

2

Into Personal Rule

On 9 March 1661, Cardinal Mazarin passed away. Louis immediately took steps to make sure that no one would ever again be above him. Since the Fronde, he had a clear idea of what to do. He would reduce the kingdom's parliaments to simply legal courts that mutely registered royal edicts and he would slash the powers of the nobility by transferring much of the government's non-military activities to the middle-class bourgeoisie. He also had great military ambitions.

Up to Mazarin's death, there were varying levels of control that depended largely on the first minister of the government. For instance, the government headed by Cardinal Richelieu, who was Louis XIII's head of government, favoured a centralised administrative structure to have a more efficient royal administration. However, royal power itself, although theoretically absolute, was in fact exercised by high-ranking officials such as Cardinals Richelieu and Mazarin. Their royal appointment had more to do with a tradition of privilege granted to individuals who seemed the best to manage the kingdom's government. Because of the structure behind the collection of revenue, such posts as tax collecting could ensure substantial wealth to those responsible while the kingdom's top financial officer could rise to being one of the richest individuals in the country.

Louis immediately called a meeting of the ministers of the kingdom: Hughes de Lionne at foreign affairs, Michel Le Tellier for internal affairs and in particular the army, Nicolas Fouquet at finance and Archbishop Harlay for religious matters; they were told by the 22-year-old king that henceforth, he assumed the function of prime minister, that all state matters would first be submitted to him and to no one else. It was a remarkable transformation for a young king who was renowned for his love of parties and gallant ladies to suddenly assume as well the dreary duties of a real reigning monarch with its paperwork and endless meetings. The ministers gave their full support to the King's autocratic vision of government. They discovered a hard-working Louis, who was revealed to be much smarter than they anticipated at "the

2-1 Minister of finance Fouquet receives the Sun King at his palace of Vaux-le-Vicomte, 17 August 1661. The king is shown with a numerous suite that includes a few Cent-Suisses guards with their halberds. Fouquet's outlandish show of wealth was his undoing. Print after Maurice Leloir. Private collection. Author's photo.

job of being king" as he merrily put it, and were simply inspired when he outlined his strategic objectives to make France much grander in the world.[1]

Le désorde régnait partout (Disorder reigned everywhere)

As he assumed power during 1661, that is how the Sun King in his 1660s *Mémoires* summed up the state of affairs he found. The atmosphere at the royal court was one perpetual intrigues with individuals "having imaginary rights" on whatever was their fancy permanently currying ministers for favours such as official posts and once they had the post, say of provincial

---

[1] *Mémoires de Louis XIV*, pp. 24–30; Camille Rousset, *Histoire de Louvois et de son administration politique et militaire jusquà la paix de Nimègue* (Paris: Didier, 1864), Vol. 1, pp. 15–16

governor, they were hard to control. There was "no demand" for favours from courtiers that was not accompanied by veiled threats of worse to come; gratifications were demanded as a right rather than expected as a bonus. Finances were "totally exhausted" to the point that the royal household and even the King had to resort to credit, yet abundance and great luxury was also evident amongst the privileged. The church "besides its usual problems" was a nest of theocratic arguments bordering on schisms. The "smallest fault" of the nobility was to have "an infinite number of usurpers" that were not actually noble or had "bought with money" their titles without being of any use to the King. Much more serious was "the tyranny" that some nobles imposed "on some of my provinces" while some few, real nobles that they were, might indulge in duels in spite of royal regulations formally forbidding such behaviour. The administration of justice was also almost hopeless to reform, having been corrupted by appointments of officials through "hazard and by money".

As for the army, it was equally out of direct control. Its management was actually under the authority of colonel generals, the most powerful by far being the colonel general of French infantry. His power, wrote the young king, "was infinite: the appointment of lower ranking officers was attached to it" so that officers royal commissions were actually controlled by the colonel general. This gave him the possibility to "appoint everywhere his own creatures" making the colonel general "more the master of the main [armed] forces of the realm than the king". Furthermore, the colonel general collected a brokerage fee on every commission since these were the days when prospective officers had to purchase their rank. The ranks had no actual fixed price so it was like a stock market operation insofar as fluctuations, the guards and the few other permanent units commanding high prices. Colonel generals of foreign infantry and mounted troops had generally similar powers, but were less important since they involved much smaller corps.

Also out of direct control were the governors and their garrison troops of the *places de guerre* such as fortresses. As a result, governors "who abused so often their powers" were rampant and their garrison's soldiers depended more on the governors than on the King. These places cost "immense" sums of money to the royal treasury that were supposed to be spent on the upkeep the fortifications, but were in fact often diverted to the pockets of governors and their friends thus "making them too powerful and too absolute". Even the modest royal guard was not beyond reproach when it came to discipline.

In conclusion, thought Louis XIV, if a king becomes lax his authority is weakened and, ultimately, "everything falls" upon the common people who is then ruled "by thousands and thousands of small tyrants instead of the legitimate king whose indulgence has created all this disorder". The solution was clear: greater rigour.[2]

---

2 *Mémoires de Louis XIV*, pp. 15–17, 43–45.

Taking Control of the Treasury

To achieve his many ambitions, a lot of money was needed. Especially for the army that Louis wished to reform and expand. A strong navy would also have to be built and subsidies encouraging commerce and industry be invested. In his last days, Cardinal Mazarin had obviously seen the man Louis really was and the great king that he could be. Ever wily, Mazarin recommended that a secret minister be appointed who would only report to the King the actual financial state of France. For that post, Jean-Baptiste Colbert, son of a textile merchant, was recommended and accepted by the King. Colbert had a genial ability in financial matters combined with an extraordinary devotion to his work. His first task was to audit the practices of the kingdom's superintendent of finance, Nicolas Fouquet, who was the more reluctant minister in spite of proclaiming his full support to the Sun King. His personal revenues appeared high as he had even built a luxurious chateau for himself and his own courtiers; his personal motto *Quo non ascendet* (to what height will he rise?) revealed a suspiciously ambitious attitude. On 17 August 1661, Fouquet even invited the King to a grand reception at his Vaux-le-Vicomte chateau where luxury not even seen at the royal court was displayed. The evening's entertainment even featured a play by the acclaimed playwright Molière.[3]

Louis XIV took it all in stride, but he had also seen Colbert's reports that at least 15 million pounds, enough to keep an army in the field for quite a while, had been unaccounted for in the royal treasury. Perhaps tucked away by the deceased Mazarin and certainly by Fouquet since he was the minister responsible for the realm's finances. No wonder that he could host lavish parties. He had even secretly fortified one of his fiefs at Belle-Isle to provide him with a safe haven. Worse, many officials in all government departments were on his payroll; some of them were at the royal palace and in the royal guard as well as the army at large, acting as spies, ready to report anything the King might do.

Dismissing and arresting Fouquet for corruption was no simple matter. He had his web of informants and was popular in many circles. Even certain Garde du Corps personnel were suspected of being in Fouquet's web and thus might warn him. A move against him might even cause a revolt. Yet he had to go. Louis thus turned to that part of the guard that could be most trusted

2-2 Jean-Baptiste Colbert, 1677. The discreet auditor to the king who rose to become one of history's most remarkable financial figures as minister of trade and commerce. He was one of the most powerful men in France and rival of Minister of War Louvois. Bust by A. Coysevox. Musée du Louvre, Paris. Author's photo..

---

3   Toudouze, *Le Roy Soleil*, p. 24. See also: Jean-Christian Petitfils, *Fouquet 1615–1680* (Paris: Perrin, 1998).

for loyalty and discretion, the *Mousquetaires du Roi* (King's Musketeers) under the command of Captain-Lieutenant D'Artagnan, a veteran of secret intrigues at the highest level. As the Duc de Saint-Simon recalled, it was known at the royal court that Musketeers were especially designated to make discreet arrests and guard important prisoners. On 4 September 1661, the King signed the secret *Lettre de cachet* – the order that instructed d'Artagnan to arrest Fouquet. Louis XIV and his ministers were then at Nantes. Following a meeting of the King with his ministers, Fouquet was arrested by d'Artagnan with his Musketeers and spirited away to the castle at Angers bordering the Loire River where he was detained until brought to Vincennes, near Paris, and eventually the Bastille, which served as a prison for political figures. He was guarded by a detachment of some 45 musketeers and, found guilty of embezzlement and of diverting state funds, was condemned to jail for the rest of his life; he passed away in the Alpine fortress and prison of Pignerol in 1680. This action certainly thereafter bolstered the loyalty of courtiers and officers at the royal court. Especially as the autocratic young king henceforth had the blind support of his royal guard. The Gardes du Corps, who were also usually involved in these secret operations, were also back in grace and assumed again such duties.[4]

2-3 Arrest of Fouquet at Nantes in 1661. Captain d'Artagnan of the King's Musketeers respectfully informs Fouquet that he is now in his custody by order of the king. A very strong detachment of the King's Musketeers is present to discourage any escape or rescue attempt. Print after Lix. Private collection. Author's photo.

Transforming the Army

The control of the armed forces was, to the Sun King, the largest equation to securing royal power. Traditionally, in times of war as well as in peacetime, the former king had basically abandoned the management of the armed forces to members of the high nobility. Only his royal guard, which was a small force that was really on duty at all times with a few permanent regiments made up a modest-sized standing army in peacetime. In wartime, it was multiplied by many units raised at the outbreak of hostilities and disbanded at the end of the war.

Young Louis XIV came up with a new plan: have a large standing army whose command was directly controlled by the King. By protocol, by tradition and by the laws of the kingdom, the king was the commander-in-chief and

---

4 *Mémoires de Louis XIV*, pp. 64–65; Louis XIV. *Lettres de Louis XIV aux princes de l'Europe…* (Paris et Francfort: Bassompierre, 1756), Vol. 1, pp. 50–58; *Dictionnaire historique, critique et bibliographique* (Paris: Menard et Desenne, 1821), Vol. 7, pp. 99–102; Rousset, *Histoire de Louvois*, Vol. 1, pp. 17–19; René Chartrand, *French Musketeer 1622–1775* (Oxford: Osprey, 2013), pp. 30–34.

the Sun King certainly meant to assume a very large role in the management and command the French armies on land and sea.

The first thing to do was to secure effective and direct command so that the military institution would truly become "the King's army". On 25 July 1661, the colonel general of French infantry, the Duc d'Épernon passed away. This was, for the Sun King, a most excellent opportunity. Only three days later, on 28 July, a royal ordinance signed by the King announced that, henceforth, the *mestres de camp* commanding regiments of infantry "being in the pay of His Majesty, will henceforth take the title of colonel and that they will immediately command them under the authority of His Majesty". The King further announced unequivocally that he "extinguishes and abolishes the said charge of colonel general, to be never revived or re-established in any manner and for whatever reason there could be: His Majesty has resolved to assume by himself" the functions that cover all infantry troops, that commanders would answer only to the king in the future and that he would establish the order and manner in which they would exercise their command.[5]

2-4 Bernard de Nogaret de La Valette, Duc d'Épernon, c. 1655. He was the powerful colonel general of French infantry who passed away on 25 July 1661. Louis XIV abolished the post the next day. Courtesy Anne S.K. Brown Military Collection, Brown University Library, Providence, RI, USA.

If this first paragraph surely caused grumbles from old-style conservative officers, the next provisions must have produced guarded amazement. The Sun King now announced that the colonel would be assisted by a lieutenant-colonel whose appointment and commission was henceforth solely the king's prerogative and not the colonel's. Previously, a lieutenant-colonel answered to the colonel general. Now he was the king's man in the regiment; he was appointed by the king and no longer needed to be a senior captain getting up the scale since Louis XIV had a habit of commissioning officers of merit that were not necessarily titled nor very rich, but very efficient in their service. By this loophole through the noble officers, more humble officers of obvious capacity could bypass the colonelcy and become general officers. Indeed, Marshal Turenne had convinced the young king to create the rank of cavalry brigadier on 8 June 1667 and, on 30 March 1668, the King enlarged the rank, eventually, to the whole army. This loophole in the system ensured the rise of Catinat, Vauban and many other officers of relatively humble origins. In the field, there could be rather novel and humorous situations whereas a brigadier would be commanding to his regimental colonel since he also kept his regimental rank.[6]

---

5   *Mémoires de Louis XIV*, p. 43; Quincy, *Histoire militaire*, Vol. 1, p. 254.
6   Rousset, *Histoire de Louvois*, Vol. 1, pp. 231–232; Jean-Philippe Cénat, *Louvois, le double de Louis XIV* (Paris: Tallandier, 2015), p. 121.

Once the "French" infantry was under direct royal authority, there was no pressing need to do the same in the foreign infantry, the cavalry and the artillery. Their colonel generals knew that the Sun King was now the effective supreme authority and that such nominations now wholly rested upon the king's royal pleasure. With the high command and protocol firmly in his hands, the Sun King moved to introduce "order" into his army during the following years.

An idea of the Sun King's ambitions for a better army is given in a letter he wrote to the Marquis de Monpazat in command of the troops at Gravelines in early 1663:

> I rejoice to [learn] what you tell me of the good state of my regiment and of the zeal of the captains of its companies; but that is not enough for me, if the lesser one is not as strong and as fine as the best one of all the other corps, without any exception and you must write them [the captains] of this conformity.

Why the King insisted on hitherto unseen control and discipline was surely because he foresaw the effects of the changes that would quietly but steadily take place in the art of war: the advent of larger armies that had to be increasingly mobile and needed effective logistical support; the progress in arms technology that resulted in greater firepower. A numerous, well-armed, well-organised, disciplined, state-of-the-art army was an essential instrument to establish France as the greatest European power.

The Strength of the Army, to the 1670s

Determining the strength of any European army before the 18th century is remarkably difficult. What data there appears to be is not necessarily exact. Modern studies regarding the Sun King's French armies do give some idea of the numbers of soldiers they mustered, but these are fraught with many contradictions.

Thus, the numbers we bring forward try to make some sense out of figures that are hard to believe. For instance, Colonel Belhomme's late 19th century study of Louis XIV's infantry gave suspiciously high numbers. He compiled, just for the infantry, 218,000 men in 1645 while Stéphane Thion's study of the whole French army during the Thirty Years' War allotted a strength of 186,000 men (164,000 foot and 22,000 horse) at that time. By 1648, Belhomme lists 273,000 infantrymen while Corvisier estimated 270,000 men theoretical strength and an actual strength of 130,00 men. Thion now had 44,000 (40,000 foot and 4,000 horse) for the whole army, but this was after many disbandment since the Thirty Years' War ended that year. Hostilities with Spain remained, but were not intense. The Fronde certainly mobilised more soldiers in various camps and the Spanish, who had lured the Prince of Condé to join them, were more warlike. However, by 1653, the Frondes were a thing of the past and the French royal army now stood at about 120,000 men. It was divided into six armies:

Army of Champagne under Marshal Turenne: 302 companies of infantry, 260 of cavalry

Army of reserve under Marshal La Ferté-Senectère: 372 companies of infantry, 256 of cavalry

Army at Calais under Marshal d'Aumont: 105 companies of infantry, 120 of cavalry

Army of Catalonia under Marshal d'Hocquincourt: 316 companies of infantry, 160 of cavalry

Army of Guyenne under Marshal d'Épernon: 367 companies of infantry, 123 of cavalry

Army of Italy under Marshal Grancey: 325 companies of infantry, 79 of cavalry

This only represented about 20,000 men per army, which made it stronger than the Spanish army, but not enough to give the French army the overwhelming advantage of a concentrated force. Corvisier estimated 160,000 theoretical strength and 110,000 actual strength for 1655. In the following years, the strength of the army appears to have hovered around 125,000 men until the 1659 Peace of the Pyrenees. This came to one soldier per 160 inhabitants. It then went down to 105,000 and kept declining for several years.[7]

In 1666, according to the King's notes kept in his desk drawers, the army's total strength was 72,000 men including 20,000 garrison troops. Maxime Weygand's history further stated that, in 1667, the strength had been raised to 70,000 infantry and 35,000 cavalrymen "at the beginning of the campaign" of the War of Devolution. By the end of the war in 1668, the army had about 134,000 men. Numbers went back down to about 70,000 men between 1669 and 1671, peace years, then crept back up.[8]

When the war with the Netherlands broke out in 1672, the periodical *Mercure Galant* mentioned in its March issue that the army now stood at 176,687 men. As will be seen in future volumes of this series, these numbers rose to amazing heights in the following decades, getting close to half a million by the early 18th century, or even surpassing that high number, depending on how one calculates the potential number of men under arms.

There also was, in addition to the above regular army, a very substantial reserve when one considers the various types of local regular troops, militias and volunteers in the kingdom. Some larger towns maintained small regular

---

[7] Stéphane Thion, *Les Armées françaises de la guerre de Trente Ans* (Auzielle: LRT, 2008), p. 79; Bély, Bérenger and Corvisier, *Guerre et paix dans l'Europe du XVIIe siècle*, p. 31; Victor Belhomme, *Histoire de l'infanterie en France* (Paris: Lavauzelle, 1892), Vol. 2, chapters 15 and 16. Belhomme's numbers from the late 1640s to the mid 1660s, while decreasing, remained high: 192,000 infantrymen in 1650, during the Fronde revolts, 156,000 in 1658 and, once peace had been agreed to in 1659, only 67,000 infantrymen. Further decreases until 1663 and especially 1666 when the infantry goes from 70,400 men to 155,000 men. There were tens of thousands of cavalrymen and gunners in addition not calculated by Belhomme that renders his compilation suspect. The 1653 list is from: R. Quarré de Verneuil, *L'armée en France depuis Charles VII jusqu'à la Révolution* (Paris: Dumaine, 1880), p. 181. The post-1659 figures are from: Philippe Henri de Grimoard, *Recherches sur la force de l'armée Française* (Paris, 1806), pp. 53–54.

[8] Bibliothèque du Ministère des Armées (henceforth cited as: BMA), Ms A1b, 1626, 'Tiroirs de Louis XIV'; Maxime Weygand, *Histoire de l'Armée française* (Paris: Flammarion, 1938), p. 150.

armed units of *hommes de guerre* (men-at-arms), halberdsmen and archer constables that were organised, armed and often uniformed like army troops. Nearly every town, big and small, had militia companies of varying sorts, the bourgeois militia being often very well appointed and acting as social clubs while a substantial coast guard militia was in place along France's coastline. The medieval vintage *ban* and *arrière ban* that supposedly gathered country squires and the "small" nobles at the King's call early in the reign were ineffective and later replaced by the royal militia that was a premonition of national conscription in later times. All these organisations probably mustered hundreds of thousands of men as potential soldiers, be they for temporary or more permanent duties. A December 1697 account in the *Mercure Galant* mentions that some 10,000 militiamen had been mustered for reviews in Bordeaux while its March 1701 issue related that some 6,000 were assembled in Toulouse. These auxiliary troops will be further presented in volume 4.

A Modern, State-of-the-Art, Army

Numbers are essential, but not the only factor for an effective army. Young Louis XIV certainly knew that he had, or could have, Europe's most numerous army. He also understood that, to succeed, his army had to be well organised, well supplied and well led. Up to the 1660s, the French regular army was probably only marginally better than other European armies. The young Sun King had far grander plans for his army. The French army had to become the most numerous, best-organised, best-disciplined, best-armed and best-equipped force in Europe. He had a profound sense of order and understood the importance of administrative control by central authority and the power of effective logistics. In the mid 1660s, he found the man who could carry out the reforms. It was Louvois, the son of Minister of War Le Tellier who gradually replaced his ageing father. Hard-working, talented, vain, brutal and utterly brilliant, Louvois espoused with passionate zeal the King's objective: create the largest and best army in Europe.

2-5 Michel le Tellier, 1661. Minister of War until gradually replaced by his son Louvois from 1662. He is shown wearing the robes of a state councillor, black lined with red and decorated with the Order of the Holy Spirit. Print after Robert Nanteuil. Rijksmuseum, Amsterdam. RP-P-OB-21.214.

Command

In the past, command and control of armies in the field were generally left to senior marshals and generals even if the king was present with the army on campaign, senior army officers were still in charge of strategic and tactical choices unless the king happened to be a good enough general that he would be the actual army commander. In France, this had not been seen since the reign of Henri IV, King of France from 1589 to 1610. The regency of Louis XIII was assumed by Queen Marie de Médicis until 1617, but Louis' personal

2-6 François-Michel le Tellier, Marquis de Louvois, c.1670. Louvois (1641–1691) was Louis XIV's genial and autocratic Minister of War from 1662 to his passing in 1691, which made him one of the most powerful persons in France. Library and Archives Canada, NL 15536.

reign did not make him a general in spite of his many portraits wearing armour. From Louis XIII's death until 1661, the Sun King was not in effective command and the army continued to be under the actual command of marshals and, for some administrative matters, the minister of war.

When, in 1661, Louis XIV took effective control of the nation's government as seen above, he also became the real commander-in-chief of the armed forces on land and sea. In an autocratic state, everything revolves around the sovereign with the consequence that military commanders have less independence. Having abolished the post of colonel general of the French infantry, he kept the other posts of colonel general for Swiss and other foreign infantry, for cavalry and for dragoons. These prestigious posts were still much sought after and noblemen paid great sums of money to fill them, but they became much less relevant in the actual command structure. While retaining their privileges, marshals and generals were much more subject to the King and Louvois' instructions – to ignore them would bring serious consequences. More orderly processes were introduced, notably a system to regulate promotions.

Control

The king was supreme and the minister of war had full authority to regulate, but always with royal approval, various improvements and discipline. With the King's approval, Louvois created inspectors that reported directly to him, incepted far better administrative controls over the army and militarised the artillery. There was a good deal of fraudulent activity going on in the army. An example was the widespread resort to *passe-volants* by countless captains when inspectors showed up to check if companies had the required number of men that were paid for. To fill the ranks, captains hired local men called *passe-volant* to be soldiers for a day and pocketed the pay of the non-existant soldiers. This also flawed what generals thought the strength of their armies were; it might have been substantially weaker than they believed from grossly inaccurate musters. Therefore, Louvois' inspecting officers now showed up unannounced and, from 1667, any detected *passe-volant* could be hanged while the officer could be jailed and condemned to pay a substantial fine or be dismissed. Detection of *passe-volants* was much better after soldiers who denounced their captain could leave the army if they wished with a 300 pounds reward (deducted from the captain's pay). Sometimes, even a *commissaire des guerres* (an inspecting officer) might pocket ill-gained funds. In 1671, one Aubert drew money from the garrison at Dunkirk by letting captains know when he would show up. Unfortunately for him, Louvois heard about it and, to quote Lewis, "Dunkirk knew Commissioner Aubert no longer." At Belle-Isle during 1675, the governor and the major were heavily fined while the captain was dismissed; these officers had jailed a sergeant who had denounced their resort to *passe-volants*. But, thanks to his web of informants, Louvois learned about it and further warned that any complaint from the sergeant for bad treatment would make their penalties far worse. These examples show the remarkable control, unthinkable before the 1660s, that Louvois managed to impose on the army.[9]

Discipline

The 1661 French army was no worse nor any better than other armies. The "rape and pillage" traditions of earlier ages were still to be seen and somewhat unchecked although Cardinal Richelieu had brought some consequences to such vile acts. Soldiers said to be guilty of such crimes were occasionally rounded up for multiple hangings on the nearest trees in front of the assembled troops. However, poor peasants in the war zones or, indeed, in any hamlet that an army might march through, considered their own soldiers nearly as awful as enemy troops. The Sun King resolved to have a much higher standard of discipline to stem such conduct; this was likely motivated more by his hatred of disorder than by overwhelming humanitarian concerns. Imposing orderly conduct equated to increasing central control.

To address these lacks of discipline, Louis XIV signed throughout his reign a stream of *Ordonnances du Roy* concerning all aspects of order and discipline in his armies. They could not and were not all followed to the letter, but woe to officers that were lax in their commands if Minister of War Louvois heard about it. Drill and precise movements became all-important. Thus, as years went by, order and discipline did get better and the routinely slovenly soldiers of yesteryears were seen less and less. In their stead were increasingly proper-looking men whose *esprit de corps* had clearly improved.

Officers were, up to the early 1660s, rather independent-minded insofar as their behaviour was concerned so that there was often considerable neglect. Many thought that showing up at court to obtain royal favours was far more important than managing their units and living with their soldiers. On this matter, a famous incident involving Louvois occurred when he encountered an officer at court and told him: "Sir, your company is in a very bad state." The officer answered "I did not know that." Louvois retorted: "But you must know it, sir; have you seen your company?" The officer answered: "No". Louvois pressed on: "You should have seen it." "I will give orders to see to it" was the officer's answer. The minister, close to rage, exclaimed: "The orders should have been given, because one must choose his own status, either to be a courtier, or perform his duty when an officer." One can imagine that the tone was given by this exchange in front of a crowd of courtiers, which appears to have occurred during the 1660s. Officers could not expect anything except

---

9   W.H. Lewis, *The Splendid Century, Life in the France of Louis XIV* (London: William Sloane, 1953 and New York: Anchor 1957), pp. 129, 132; Rousset, *Histoire de Louvois*, Vol.1, pp. 202–204.

reprobation from the king down through the administration if they did not take their commissions seriously. Purchase of rank was no longer enough.[10]

Logistics and Money

To maintain a large force, not only does one need a solid treasury with ample cash and credit, but an organisation that can feed, clothe, pay, arm and equip tens or even hundreds of thousands of men, be they on campaign and in garrisons. Heretofore, the relatively modest armies in Europe lived largely "in the field" when on campaign. From the time of the War of Devolution when the army largely exceeded 100,000 men, Louvois organised a centralised supply system capable of producing the millions of rations necessary to keep the men in the field. From the mid 1660s, thanks to a much more centralised chain of responsibility, the soldier's pay became more regular and, as seen above, knavish officers were no longer immune from severe condemnations if caught by intendants and commissaries that answered to ministerial authority. The line infantry's soldier's pay itself was certainly modest. As for the money supply, it was ample from the time Minister Colbert took over the government's financial responsibilities. This was the situation for the period covered by this first volume, but it became more problematic in the last decades of the reign, especially in the era covered in volume 4.[11]

10　C.-S. Viator, *Histoire de France* (Fontaine-sur-Saone: E. Robert, 1906), p. 100.
11　Voltaire, *Le siècle de Louis XIV*, pp. 534–535.

3

Foreign Intrigues and Adventures

Assisting Portugal

The Kingdom of Portugal had been absorbed into Spain during 1580 in what turned out to be a very unhappy union. In 1640, led by João, Duke of Braganza, the Portuguese rose in revolt and, on 1 December, annulled the union and proclaimed the duke as King João IV. The Portuguese raised an army of some 20,000 infantry and 4,000 cavalry, a surprisingly high number at that time especially for a small nation. The ensuing fighting was won by the Portuguese troops and a sort of status quo resulted for years, but without a formal peace treaty. The proud Spanish could not bear the notion of recognising Portugal's regained independence. Every once in a while, they would try to invade Portugal without success while other nations, including France, recognised Portugal as a sovereign kingdom.

In 1660, the Portuguese question came up at the royal court of France before Louis XIV assumed full powers. Peace had been made in 1659 between France and Spain by the Treaty of the Pyrenees. At that time, Donna Luiza, the Queen Regent of Portugal sent as ambassador the Count of Soure to seek military and financial help from France. A very important aspect to the Portuguese was to keep up the effectiveness of their army so as to be able to successfully resist the Spanish. The French had recently humbled the Spaniards. However, this was greeted without any interest by Cardinal Mazarin. He did not wish to upset the 1659 treaty so the ambassador was told he would have neither French generals or troops, but he might approach Marshal Turenne for suggestions of foreign officers in French service that might wish to go to Portugal. Turenne recommended Lieutenant-General Schomberg who accepted Soure's offer. Hearing of this, many French veteran officers and men of recently disbanded regiments wished to accompany him so that, on 13 November 1660, he arrived in Lisbon with some 200 officers and about 600 veteran troopers. They were early "military advisors" to modernise the Portuguese army with the troopers formed into a model regiment for the Portuguese cavalry. It is notable that, unlike Spain, Portugal has a long history of inviting in foreign expertise from the leading military

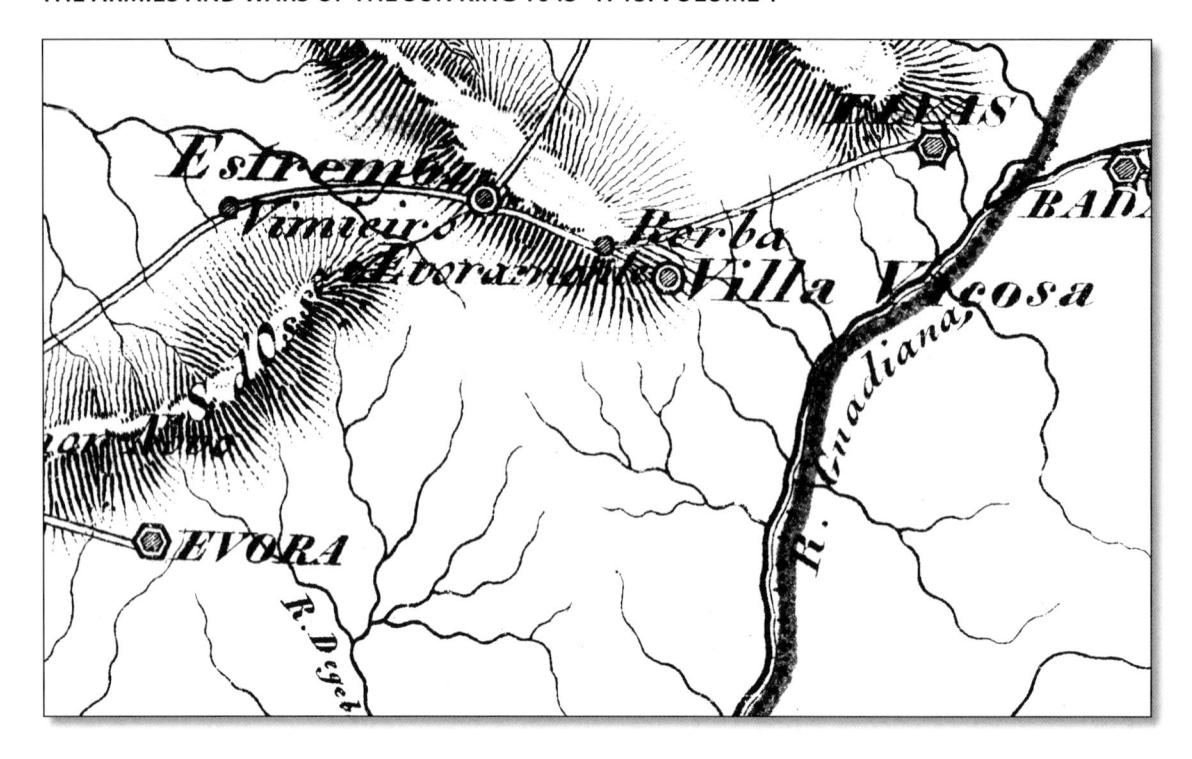

THE ARMIES AND WARS OF THE SUN KING 1643–1715: VOLUME 1

3-1 (above): Map of southeastern Portugal. This is the area where most of the fighting occurred during the early 1660s. The Spanish took Evora (lower left) in 1662, but it was retaken the following year by the Portuguese with help from French and British volunteers. The Spanish were decisively defeated at Vila Viçosa in 1665. The Portuguese fortress of Elvas faced that of Spanish Badajos, the frontier being the Guadiana River. Detail of a map in Luz Soriano. Private collection. Author's photo.

3-2 (opposite): Battle of Montes Claros (or Vila Viçosa), Portugal, 17 June 1665. Detail from an *azulejo* of the period. Courtesy Fronteira Palace, Lisbon.

nations when its armies were judged to be rather antiquated. For several years, Schomberg thus gradually transformed the small Portuguese army into a state-of-the-art force.

In June 1661 Portugal's oldest ally, England, had also heard the call for help and pledged veterans of its past civil war to fight the Spaniards. In France meanwhile, Mazarin passed away and the Sun King assumed full power. Although he had a queen from Madrid, the young king noted there had been some tacit underhanded infractions to the treaty by the Spanish. Helping Portugal seemed like a good idea to Louis XIV and his councillors, especially Marshal Turenne, since it would keep the Spanish militarily preoccupied in their own Iberian peninsula thus making it more difficult for them to reinforce Spanish Flanders. Should they succeed in conquering Portugal, argued Turenne, other nations might conclude that Spain's military power would again be supreme instead of France's. As a result, French money was sent and Schomberg assured the Portuguese of the Sun King's royal support. In 1662, some 3,000 promised English volunteers arrived in Portugal. The following year Schomberg assumed supreme command as a marshal of Portugal. There were now hundreds of Germans and other French soldiers who also arrived. By 1664 according to Dumauriez's history, the foreign troops consisted of Schomberg's guard company, the French model cavalry regiment, six companies of Chauvet's Regiment, three French companies, two Catalan companies, a French regiment of 1,100 men, two contingents of 300 men each recently arrived from France under officers named Maret and Briquemaut and of Clairan's (or Cléran's) German Regiment. The English brigade was made up of two infantry and one cavalry regiments. It was really a tripartite army.

FOREIGN INTRIGUES AND ADVENTURES

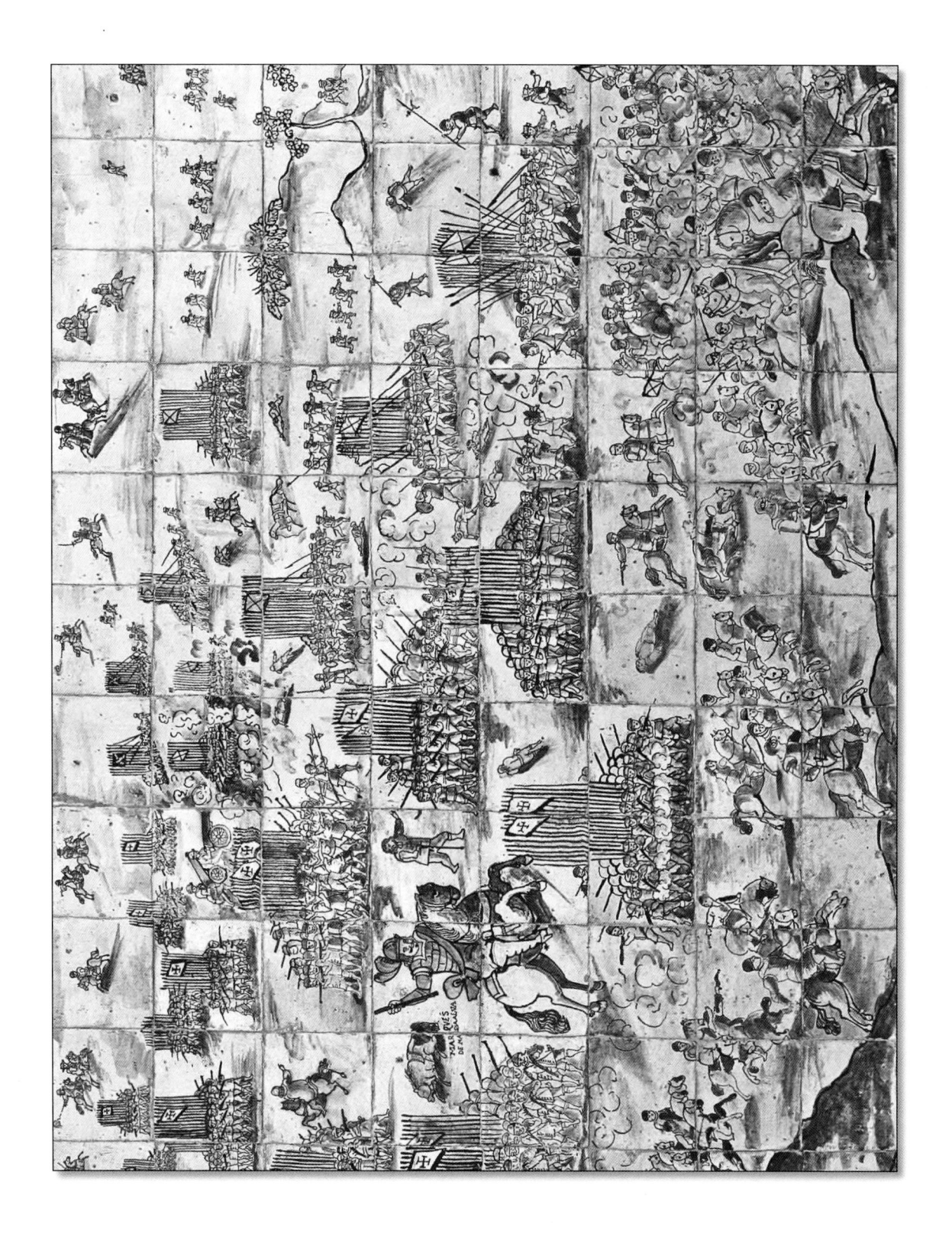

3-3 Lieutenant General Armand-Frédéric de Schomberg, c.1670. This talented officer went to Portugal in late 1660, reorganised the Portuguese army and won several battles against the Spanish. He went back to France in 1668 and was promoted to marshal of France in 1675. Courtesy Anne S.K. Brown Military Collection, Brown University Library, Providence, RI, USA.

An interesting aspect to these troops was that they wore uniform clothing. The British contingent had red coats lined with various colours. This had an effect on the rest of the army. A Portuguese account of 1664 revealed that in April of that year, Portugal's *Terço de Infanteria da guarniçao da Armada* (marine infantry) wore green coats lined with yellow, that the *Terço de Roque da Costa* (the unit led by Roque da Costa) had blue lined with red, and that the commanders (*Mestres de Campo*) and officers wore the same colours. Furthermore, this uniform dress fashion had been introduced in the Portuguese army by Marshal Schomberg whose own French troops all wore blue coats said to have been in the colours of the King of France, meaning blue coats lined red as per the royal livery. At least according to the Portuguese account. Frémont d'Ablancourt's memoirs mentions that the French regiment and Cléran's Germans were "clothed in grey, lined differently" although this could also mean only Cléran's was in grey.

Although the Spanish always enjoyed superior numbers, their repeated invasion attempts were repulsed with loss in 1663, notably at Ameixial and Evora, and in 1664 at Castel Rodrigo, but it was at Vila Viçosa (also named Montes Claros) on 17 June 1665, that they were crushed by a Portuguese army under the Marquis de Marialva. Thereafter Schomberg organised raids into Spain. With the 1667 outbreak of the War of Devolution and the French invasion of Spanish Flanders and Franche-Comté, the court of Madrid was overwhelmed. On 13 February 1668, Spain recognised the independence of Portugal and hostilities ended at last.[1]

The Ottoman Turk Equation

From the time of the Renaissance, France's policy towards the Ottoman Empire might be defined as one of subdued opportunism since it was also an opponent of the Hapsburgs' power. However, this was mixed with some hostile feelings to a rather distant and mysterious power that promoted

---

1   For accounts of Schomberg's foreign contingents in Portugal, see: Jonathon Riley, *The Last Ironsides* (Solihull: Helion & Company, 2014) and Charles François Dumauriez, *Campagnes de Maréchal de Schomberg en Portugal* (London, 1807). On the Portuguese, see: Simao José da Luz Soriano, *Historia da Guerra Civil* (Lisbon: Impresa Nacional, 1866), Vol. 1, pp. 176–178; a Carlos Selvagem, *Portugal Militar* (Lisbon: Impresa Nacional, 1931), pp. 433–452; Ferreira Martins, *Historia do Exercito Portugues* (Lisbon: Inquérito, 1945), pp. 161–168. On uniforms: Carlos da Silva Lopes, 'Contribuiçao para o estudio dos uniformes militares portugueses desde 1664 ate 1806', *Documentos e memorias para a historia do Porto, XIX, Exposiçao historico-militar* (Porto, 1958): 56–57 is the best source.

FOREIGN INTRIGUES AND ADVENTURES

3-4 Europe in the second half of the 17th century. Louis XIVs France was Europe's most populous nation. Germany then had about 300 loosely connected states in the Holy Roman Empire in which Austria was the leading member. Italy was also divided into several independent states. Holland and England were important trading nations, but with smaller populations. Spain was in decline, but still had the strategically and economically important Spanish Netherlands (basically present day Belgium). Further East was the Turks'# powerful Ottoman Empire whose vast domain then included the Balkans. Private collection. Author's photo.

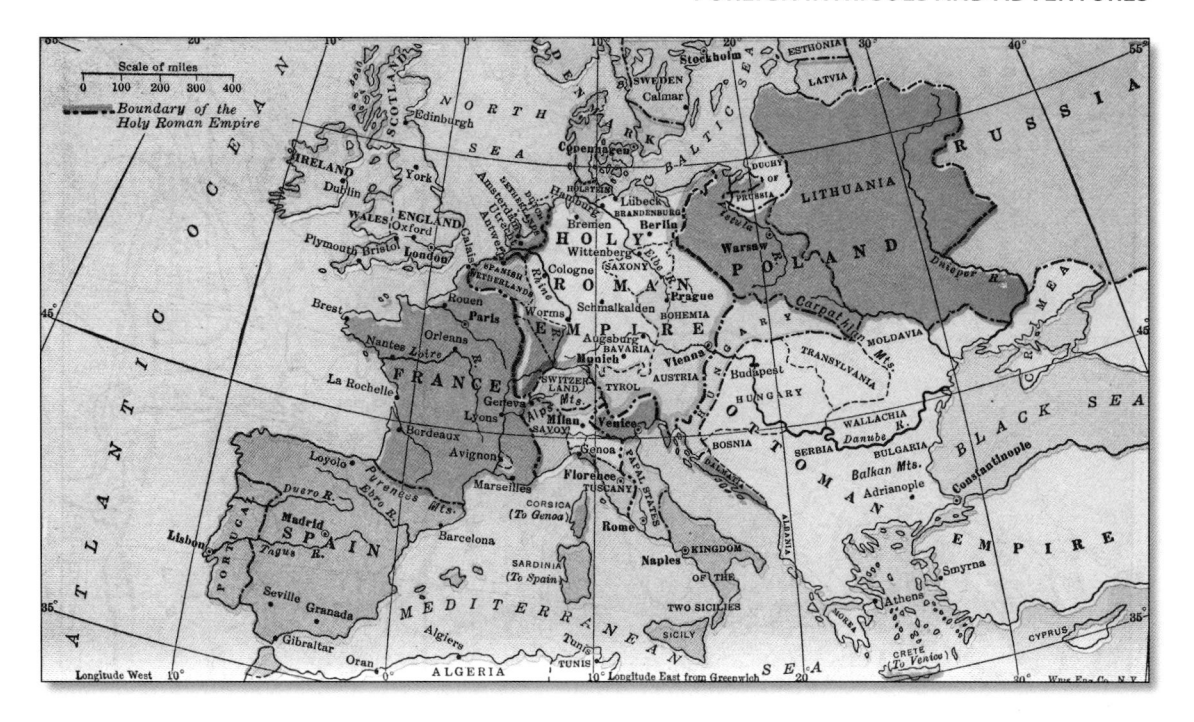

Islam. Turkey was the seat of this vast domain with the ruling sultans holding court in Istanbul, which Christians still called Constantinople. It consisted of a rather loosely federated empire in North Africa running from Algeria to Egypt, in the Middle East from Palestine to Syria, in Europe with substantial territories that included Greece, the Balkans, parts of Hungary and, eastward, along the shores of the Black Sea as far as the Sea of Azov. Its great cities besides Istanbul included Cairo, Alexandria, Bagdad, Damascus, Azov, Sofia, Athens and Belgrade. During the second half of the 17th century, this large empire's population may have numbered up to a hundred million souls.

Until the early 17th century, the Ottoman government was, on the whole, wealthy and well organised. Its armed forces were redoubtable although organised very differently than armies and navies in western Europe. Up to the 1660s, it was the only government in Europe that permanently maintained, in peacetime, a very large regular army. The Ottoman Turk land army's corps of Janissaries were the elite and had a standing somewhat akin to an imperial guard since they belonged to the sultan yet many served in far off garrisons or with armies in the field. During Louis XIVs reign, their strength hovered between 20,000 to nearly 70,000 men. By that time Janissaries were recruited amongst adult Muslim men and no longer by forcibly enlisting young Christian boys. The Ottoman army's artillery and engineers, which numbered about 5,000 men, enjoyed a good reputation for their efficiency; the pieces of ordnance, both for defence and offence, could be very large and some at the siege of Candia in Crete were said to have been cast in their camp. In siege operations there, their trenches had parallels, a technique that was not yet in general use in western European armies according to Voltaire's history. There were also cavalry divisions numbering about 17,000 troopers for a regular army of probably some 100,000 men and about 70,000 men in other infantry formations of various types, some of which were local levies for temporary service with the armies in the field or in forts. In 1670 it was estimated that in wartime, the army could muster about 248,000 men on service and over 300,000 if one included roops belonging to princes of the Balkans, the Middle East, Egypt, Tripoli, Algiers, and the Crimea. Camp followers were very numerous being estimated at one for every soldier.[2]

During the 17th century, the Ottoman Empire's economy and governance weakened. There was now a slow but gradual erosion of its financial and political power. From 1648, when Mehmet IV became sultan, an agressive conquest policy was implemented to reverse the decline by acquiring territories (and thus tax revenues) as well as to strengthen authority. High taxes were imposed to compensate for decreasing revenues, but these provoked revolts in various parts of the Empire. Towards the end of the century, serious rivalries between the Janissaries and other parts of the army weakened the quality of its command, its cohesion and its discipline. It nevertheless remained a formidable force. The Ottoman navy, consisting mainly of war galleys divided in three fleets, was manned by some 35,000 men in peacetime. It basically dominated the Eastern Mediterranean although it had substantial opposition from the Venetian and Maltese navies.

The immediate European opponents west and north of the Balkans to the Ottoman Turks were the Germanic Holy Roman Empire led by Austria, with, in addition, parts of Hungary and Poland. To the north-east and towards the Black Sea was "Muscovy" as Imperial Russia was then often called; it was not a serious threat to Turkey until after its somewhat forced modernisation by Tsar Peter the Great from the end of the 17th century. The Republic of Venice, although also in economic and military decline, more or less contained the Ottomans outside the Adriatic and maintained small but powerful fortresses and naval bases for its own sizeable navy along the Balkans and Greek coasts and also held the island of "Candie" (Crete). Venice was Sultan Mehmet IV's immediate target, and by June 1657 with assistance from Maltese and Papal galleys, the Venetian blockade of Ottoman ships in the Dardanelles was broken and some Venetian garrisons in the Aegean Sea had to be withdrawn.[3]

The other notable opponents was the Order of St. John of Jerusalem whose modest navy and knights were nevertheless a major irritant to Ottomans.

---

[2] Hulya Toker, 'Turkish Army from the Ottoman period to today', *International Review of Military History*, No. 87 (Ankara, 2007), pp. 105–108, 113–115; Gábor Ágoston. 'Firearms and Military Adaptation: The Ottomans and the European Military Revolution, 1450–1800', *Journal of World History*, XXV (2014), p. 113; Paul Ricaut, *Histoire de l'état présent de l'empire ottoman* (Paris: Mabre-Cramoisy, 1670), pp. 303–382 containing a detailed description of the Ottoman armies by the author who had been secretary of the British ambassador to Sultan Mahomet Han IV. Bély, Bérenger and Corvisier, *Guerre et paix dans l'Europe du XVIIe siècle*, pp. 141–145, 191. The enforced enlistment of young Christian boys taken notably in the Balkans largely ceased from the 1640s. The Muslim soldiers of the Janissaries were also valiant, but could marry, some 15,000 lived in Istanbul where they organised mutinies for better pay and were involved in harem intrigues to support (or impair) certain sons of senior concubines to be sultans or assume other highly powerful posts such as grand vizir. From 1656, Grand Vizier Mehmet Koprulu and later his son were brilliant administrators who, notably, put a stop to the Janissaries being involved in political matters. They were instead deployed to fight non-Muslims at the borders of the empire.

[3] David Nicolle, *Armies of the Ottoman Turks 1300–1774* (London: Osprey, 1983), pp. 20–27.

FOREIGN INTRIGUES AND ADVENTURES

The Order of St. John was also called the Sovereign Order of Malta because it was based on the strategically located island of Malta situated between Sicily and Libya. It was a powerful military organisation that had *commanderies* in most Christian countries of western Europe and especially in France (see orders of chivalry below) since over half of the knights were from that nation. During 1565, the Ottoman Turks had tried and failed to conquer Malta, which destroyed the then largely held European perception that they were invincible. Many more fortifications were added in Malta thereafter thanks to European subsidies, which transformed it into a near-impregnable fortress. In the 17th century, it was considered a formidable and necessary bastion protecting western Europe from any sizeable agression by the Ottoman Turks while also offering a certain protection against piratical practices out of North African ports.

Louis XIV's Early Ottoman Relations

During the early part of his personal rule, the Sun King was rather displeased with the Ottomans. Diplomatic relations had worsened between French ambassadors in Istanbul and the Ottoman Turkish rulers. The capture of French merchant ships by North African piratical corsairs were such that Louis XIV had sent a fleet to bombard Tunis, an action that resulted in the release of some 3,000 enslaved French sailors. While the Ottoman Turks had a rather loose control over their Arab subjects, their benevolent attitude to piracy was not appreciated by the Sun King. Yet another upsetting matter was that, traditionally, trade between Christian nations and the Ottomans was carried by French ships. However, ambassadors of the Italian Republic of Genoa were greeted in Istanbul to conclude a similar agreement for their own ships and it was a move that Louis XIV would not forget in later year regarding that Italian city state. In the short term, all this soured the Franco-Ottoman relations so that, during the 1660s, the King broke France's traditional neutral stance and committed royal army units in expeditionary corps to join other European troops in containing the advance of Turkish armies, first in Hungary and later on the island of Crete, then called Candia.

St. Gotthard (Hungary)

In the early 16th century, the Ottoman Turks conquered and occupied most of the Balkans and parts of Hungary. This led to henceforth very strained relations with Austria in particular as well as with other Christian states nearby. After various incidents, the Turks declared war in 1658, successfully invaded Hungarian Transylvania and, by 1663, had reached and occupied strategic points in Slovenia. Their force was reckoned at about 130,000 men. The road to Vienna was open and Austrian Holy Roman Emperor Leopold I called for a mobilisation of Christian states to push back the Ottomans. Through the League of the Rhine, a French-influenced group of German principalities, Louis XIV committed 6,000 French troops led by Comte Jean de Coligny-Saligny to join the international army of about 70,000 men gathering east of Vienna under the command of Austrian General Raymond, Count of Montecuccoli, one of the best tacticians of his era. The French infantry included the regiments of Espagny, La Ferté, Grancey, Turenne and

THE ARMIES AND WARS OF THE SUN KING 1643–1715: VOLUME 1

3-5 (left): Battle of St. Gotthard (Hungary), 1 August 1664. The French contingent under the command of the Comte Jean de Coligny is at right (F), the Austrian and German troops at the centre and left (E, G and H), the Ottoman Turks are at top (I and L). The generals at lower left are the Count of Montecuccoli (A), the Prince of Baden (B) and the Prince de Corenso. Although the Turkish artillery is shown firing, it was actually hardly engaged in the battle. Print after Joseph Waldtman. Courtesy Anne S.K. Brown Military Collection, Brown University Library, Providence, RI, USA.

Piémont, the cavalry gathering 26 companies. Both forces disposed their troops along a fairly lengthy front on the shores of the River Raab.

On 26 July 1664, a first Ottoman forward detachment attempted to cross to the western shore of the Raab River, but was repulsed by an Imperial detachment. The following day, the two main armies came with sight of each other marching along their respective shores as they approached St. Gotthard. For Coligny-Saligny and the French contingent, it was a new and fascinating vision to see the Ottoman army, sometimes at only 40 paces. Coligny-Saligny recalled that:

> We could see all their baggage and their camels marching. Never was there such an agreeable spectacle; in one instance we could see an entire world of men on foot; in another a forest of lances, followed by a crowd of cavalry, and succeeded by different other corps that made up their army, each troop with a multitude of flags, standards and pennants of various colours or bearing different figures and a quantity of hautbois, flutes and drums that made a rather pleasant harmony although the troops marched without any order nor regularity…

In the evening, they could see the Ottoman army's camp that, although the tents were very close to each other, occupied more "than a lieue and a half and the tents of the grand vizir could be seen in a very large park, filled with the tents of the grand vizir's household, which looked like high towers compared to the others in his camp." Coligny-Saligny further noted that the Ottomans had shown their "ignorance for war" because, although they had arrived first at St. Gotthard, they had not tried to cross it before the arrival of the allied army.[4]

Commanding Pasha Ahmet Koprulu determined to try crossing the Raab River again at St. Gotthard on 1 August with about 30,000 Janissaries and Spahis, his elite troops. If they could establish a position on the western shore, the rest of his numerous army could cross and, ultimately, march on Vienna. A first, the few thousand allied troops retreated before the Ottoman columns, but more allied reinforcements came up. Desperate fighting ensued, a breach at the centre of the allied army occurred, but was countered by an attack of the French corps followed by the rest of Montecuccoli's troops. The Ottomans wavered, some panicked and their retreat was sounded. French reports hailed Louis XIV's expeditionary corps as having been the

---

[4] Louis XIV. *Lettres*, Vol. 2, pp. 5–6, 9–10, 26–27, 49–52, 60–66, 73–78, 82–88; Jean, Comte de Coligny-Saligny, *Mémoires du Comte de Coligny-Saligny* (Paris: Société de l'histoire de France, 1841), pp. 91–93.

outstanding reason for the victory, which was certainly meant to please the Sun King. However, the memoirs of the Chevalier de Melvill, an obscure Scottish officer in the Austrian army, confirms this version. He wrote that:

> The disorder was so great in our army that no one doubted that it would have been totally defeated had it not been for the French troops that Louis XIV had sent to the emperor [Leopold I]. Coligny and La Feuillade who led them ... having broken [the Turks at St. Gotthard], forced them into the river where they almost all perished. This action brought peace. The Turks having lost the elite [troops] of their army asked to end the hostilities.

It was a success, hailed as a great victory at the time, but there were many recriminations on the allied side, notably due to heavy casualties – some 5,000 to 6,000 out of about 22,000 allies – as well as from Hungarians whose country had been ravaged and sacked by both the Christian and Ottoman armies. Turkish casualties may have been as much as 17,000. Emperor Leopold I quickly agreed to a peace with the Turks on 10 August that confirmed the status quo giving the rise of a party of "Malcontents" party in his Hungarian domains. Louis XIV was not pleased at this unilateral deal made by Leopold I with the Turks, viewing it as a veiled insult to him who had sent an expeditionary force. This further cooled his already tense relations with the Holy Roman Emperor.[5]

3-6 Admiral François de Vendôme, Duc de Beaufort. Print after Jean Nocroit. Courtesy Yale University Art Gallery, New Haven, CT, USA.

Algeria

To quell the piratical practices of North African harbour cities such as Tunis and Algiers, it was decided to occupy permanently a port on the Algerian coast to that would be a base for European warships. The sun King took the lead on this initiative and Admiral François de Vendôme, Duc de Beaufort sailed with a fleet for the Algerian coast with some 4,000 army troops on board under Lieutenant-General, the Marquis de Gadagne. The regiments of Picardie, Royal-Vaisseaux and Normandie with a detachment from the Gardes Françaises were part of the contingent. They were joined by Dutch and British squadrons as well as by seven galleys from Malta with 1,200 Maltese troops. On 23 July 1664, the expeditionary force landed at Djidjelli (also spelt Gigery or

---

5 Camille Rousset, *Hisoire de Louvois*, Vol. 1, pp. 37–81; E. de Langsdorff, 'Une armée française en Hongrie – Bataille de Saint-Gothard', *Revue des Deux Mondes*, Vol. 57 (1865); Coligny-Saligny, *Mémoires*, pp. 94–99; Quincy, *Histoire militaire*, Vol. 1, pp. 267–269; *Mémoires de Monsieur le Chevalier de Melvill* (Amsterdam: J. Desbordes, 1704), pp. 202–203; Sabbatai Sevi, *Histoire de l'empire ottoman* (La Haye: C. Johnson, 1709), Vol. 3, pp. 96–101, 112–114.

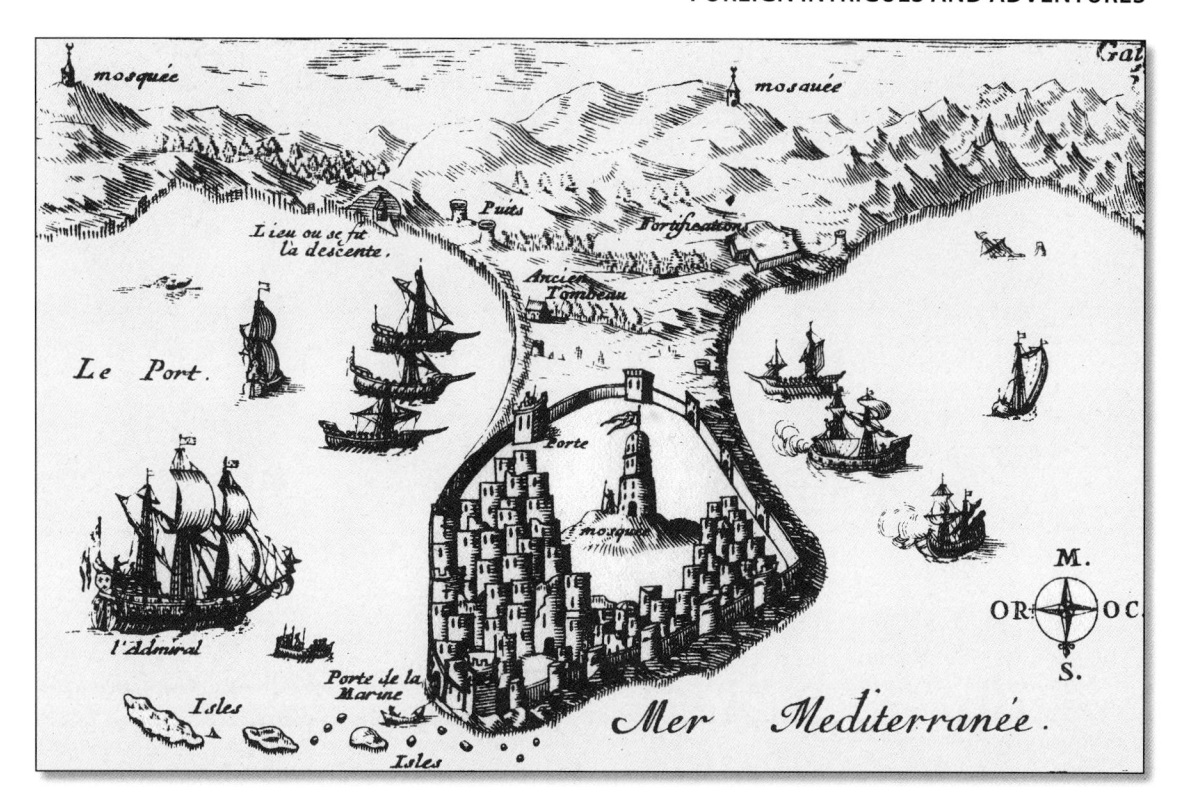

Gigelly), situated near Bone, east of Algiers, and easily took it. A dispute now erupted between naval and army officers over precedence of command while strong Ottoman forces gathered and ambushed some 700 French and Maltese troops, some of whom were killed and their heads cut off and displayed. By August, the local defenders were being reinforced by troops from Constantine and Algiers; some 11,000 Ottomans troops were in the area building trench lines around Djidjelli.

At the beginning of October, a corps of elite Janissary troops arrived. On 5 October, they attacked the French lines, but were repulsed after five hours of heavy fighting. Some very large cannons also arrived from Algiers and, once bombardment got under way, their huge cannonballs practically levelled the French redoubts and field works. Meanwhile the Duc de Beaufort had gone with his fleet to cruise off Tunis to try, with limited results, to bombard it. By 22 October, Lieutenant-General de Gadagne and his officers knew the situation at Djidjelli was hopeless; some 1,400 French and Maltese troops were dead or wounded. They evacuated their force including some 900 wounded and sick onto French ships nearby. The expedition's misfortune was further compounded when the warship *La Lune* stuck a reef off Toulon and went down with all hands including soldiers of the Picardie Infantry Regiment aboard, at total of about 700 men. Some of the failure was blamed on the early departure of the Dutch squadron, but a lack of good intelligence and detailed preparations for such expeditions were the main culprits. Certainly, landing relatively small expeditionary corps in North Africa with the presumption that they would sweep all before them proved near-disastrous and it was not attempted again. Piracy remained and the only somewhat effective solution

3-7 Capture of Djidjelli (Algeria), 23 July 1664. French and Maltese forces at the upper left – *Lieu ou se fit la descente*. After some fighting and establishing defence lines – *fortifications* – outside the town (upper centre). Print after E. Vouillemont. Private collection. Author's photo.

3-8 Ottoman Turk troops, mid 17th century. From the feft: an artilleryman, a back view of an infantryman of the elite Janissary Corps and a Spahi cavalryman. The appearance of the Ottoman troops did not vary much from the 16th to the early 19th centuries. Print after the Illustrated Naval and Military Magazine, November 1886. Private collection. Author's photo.

was for naval squadrons to cruise off the coast. De Beaufort did just that in 1665 and managed to take or destroy five Algerian Ottoman ships off Cherchell on 24 August. Still, nothing was really resolved and the Ottoman Turks were cheered by their victory at Djidjelli.[6]

The War of Candia (Crete)

Crete was a domain of the Republic of Venice. The Ottoman Turks repeatedly attempted to occupy it. Although Venice appealed to other Christian states for military help since it could not, by itself, contain the numerous Ottoman troops. Other Italian and German states thus sent volunteers as did the Knights of Malta. Even before Louis XIVs personal rule, Cardinal Mazarin had taken some measures to help the Venetians defend the island. In September and October 1646, a French squadron of some 10 ships under the command

---

6   Louis XIV. *Lettres*, Vol. 2, pp. 17–20, 23–25, 38–47, 93–95; *Gazette*, 16 and 28 August, 15 and 22 November 1664; H.-D. de Grammont, *Histoire d'Alger sous la domination turque* (Paris, 1887); Quincy, *Histoire militaire*, Vol. 1, pp. 2–3; Rousset, *Histoire de Louvois*, Vol. 1, pp. 78–81

FOREIGN INTRIGUES AND ADVENTURES

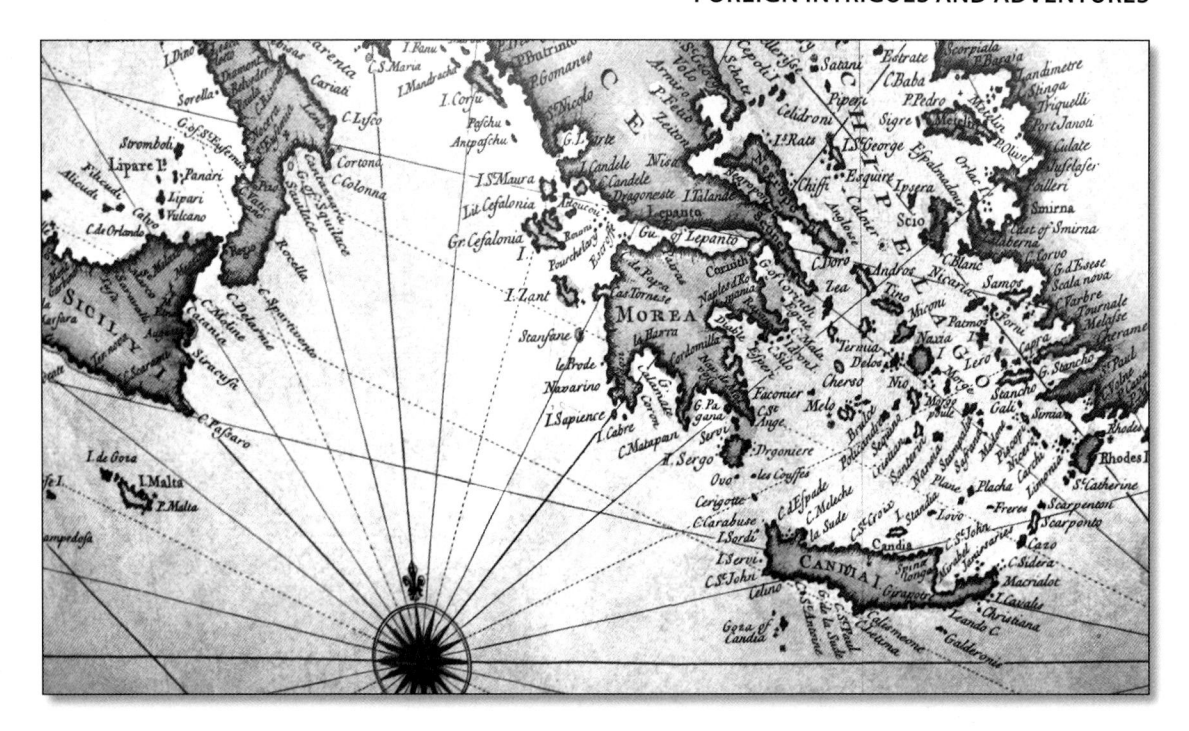

of François de Nuchèze, a French knight of Malta, had cruised in the area without achieving much. In 1660, Mazarin tried again with the dispatch of an expeditionary corps under the Italian Prince de Este. It landed on Crete in November, but was plagued with bad luck. The prince became ill and died. The French nevertheless took four forts from the Turks, but then ran into a large Ottoman reinforcement and were crushed losing several hundred men.

Thus, young Louis XIV inherited strained diplomatic relations with both Venice and the Ottoman court when he assumed direct power the following year. A few years went by until 1667 when he became convinced that, if nothing was done, the Venetians could not hope to hold on to Crete for much longer. Since 1645, Ottoman troops had managed to occupy much of the island's countryside, but the Venetians held on to major fortifications and, in particular, the fortress city of La Canea (Chania). In the spring of 1667 however, the Ottoman Grand Vizir Achmet Aga arrived in Crete with considerable reinforcements and siege operations of La Canea started. Thus, when the War of Devolution ended in May 1668, the Duc de La Feuillade was tasked with going to Crete with 200 gentlemen and 400 soldiers who volunteered to go led by the Comte de Saint-Paul, the Duc de Château-Thierry and the Duc de Roanez. In late October 1668 when they arrived in Malta, there were also some 800 men of the Lorraine Regiment led by the Chevalier d'Harcourt who also joined the expedition although it is not certain if all did arrive since some ships were still at sea. Impressed, Order of Malta Grand Master d'Aubusson, who was French and a relative of the Duc de Roanez, gave the French volunteers colours that bore the cross of the order with his coat of arms. The Lorraine Regiment already had colours bearing the coats of arms of Lorraine and of Venice. The Malta council also resolved to send 60 knights and 300 soldiers. The French contingent arrived at La Canea on

3-9 The south-eastern Mediterranean Sea, later 17th century. At lower right, the large Venetian island of Candia (Crete) where Louis XIV sent French troops that could not prevent its fall to the Ottoman Turks in 1669. Turkey and Greece at upper right and centre were then part of the Ottoman empire. The Venetians had a few Adriatic Sea island outposts such as Zante, Santa Maura and Corfu that were never taken by the Turks. At lower left, the fortress island of Malta and Italy above. Detail from *A Correct Chart of the Mediterranean Sea*. Costa Ship Lines collection. Author's photo.

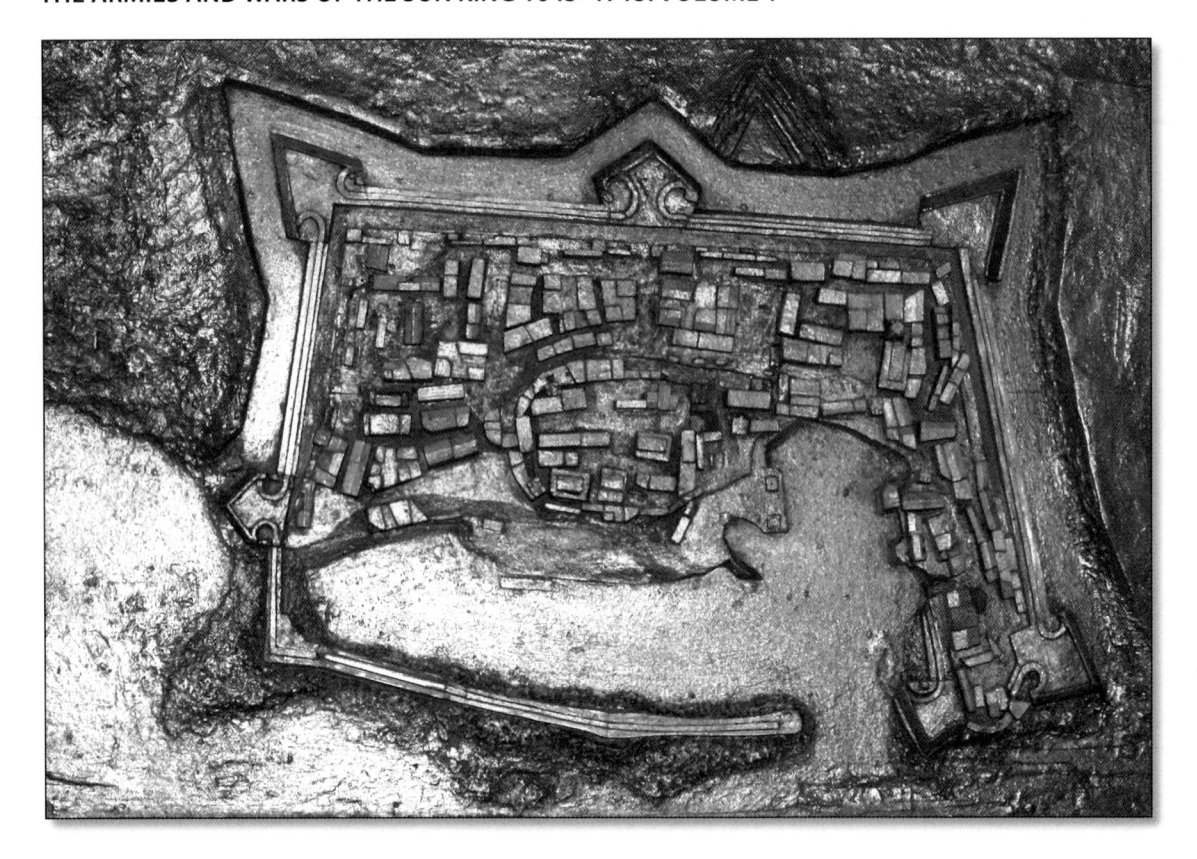

3-10 Topographic model of the Venetian fortress of La Canea (also called Candia) in Crete, 1614. Louis XIV sent reinforcement to the Venetian garrison there to resist the Turks in 1668–1669. Museo Storico Navale di Venezia, Venice. Author's photo.

3 November. They were organised into four numbered brigades under the Comte de Saint-Paul (later Duc de Longueville), the Duc de Caderousse, the Duc de Château-Thierry and the Comte de Villamont respectively; soon were engaged in robust skirmishes with the Turks culminating in a failed sortie on 16 December where hundreds were killed or wounded. Only 230 French volunteers survived and they were evacuated to Malta in January 1669.

The contribution of La Feuillade and his volunteers to the defence of La Canea had been minimal, but was nevertheless considered as heroic in France. Pope Clement IX weighted in with pleas to the Sun King for help. He had sent what Papal forces he could and so had Malta. Other European countries were strangely deaf to these pleas to save this strategically important Venetian outpost now being overrun by as many as 40,000 Ottoman troops. Perhaps Austria and Spain were not unhappy at seeing Venice humbled at last so they could take its place in the eastern Mediterranean.

The Sun King's vision was much broader and, in a sense, precursor to a pan-European approach to face invasions together; he was ahead of his times by three centuries. Nobody else joined in. Nevertheless, in January 1669, Louis XIV finally decided to send a large force to Crete under the command of the Duc de Beaufort, his most experienced naval officer in the Mediterranean. His fleet of about 40 ships and galleys carrying some 6,000 troops led by Philippe de Montault-Bénac, Due de Navailles was in sight of Crete on 19 June. On board were the following troops:

King's Musketeers 50 men
Gardes Françaises 3 companies
Espagny 4 companies
Saint-Vallier 4 companies
Lignières 4 companies
Montaigu 4 companies
Lorraine 4 companies
Rozan 4 companies
Bretagne 4 companies
Conti 2 companies
Grancey 4 companies
Montpezat 2 companies
Lyonnais (also called Vendôme) 2 companies
La Farre 2 companies
Château-Thierry 2 companies
Jonsac 4 companies
Rouergue 2 companies

There were also the guards of the Duc de Beaufort, three companies of cavalry and 232 extra officers formed in two companies.

Once in the fortress, both de Beaufort and de Navailles were anxious to attack the Turks by making a grand sortie that would drive them away and end the siege. Venetian General Francesco Morosini and his senior officers, who knew well the aptitudes of the enemy, were not so optimistic and recommended caution adding they could not risk losing their own meagre troops in such an action. The French commanders nevertheless decided to attack and, on the night of 24 to 25 June, some 5,400 men proceeded towards the Turkish lines. They were organised in four battalions with the Duke the Beaufort's with his guards at their left and initially overcame surprised Ottoman soldiers in their trenches. All was going well until a powder magazine exploded making a tremendous noise that

3-11 French and Maltese galleys and ships at the Venetian fortress of La Canea (also called Candia) in Crete, 1669. Print after Isabey. Private collection. Author's photo.

3-12 The Duc de Beaufort killed in action at La Canea (Crete) on 25 June 1669. Print after Cerlier in J. Trousset's *Histoire nationale de la marine*. Anne S.K. Brown Military Collection, Brown University Library, Providence, RI, USA. Author's photo.

woke up the whole Turkish army's camp. The French were somewhat startled by this explosion. They now came under robust counter-attacks by numerous enemy infantrymen and cavalrymen, panicked and ran back to the city, losing some 800 men including many officers, amongst them, the Duc de Beaufort. The Venetians had promised to assist, but when Louis de Buade, Comte de Frontenac (then a lieutenant-general in Venetian service and destined to become a famous figure in Canada) tried to rally them, only a few answered.

The loss of the experienced Duc de Beaufort was a serious blow and more misfortunes followed. The siege went on and, another sortie being unfeasible, a bombardment of the Ottoman camp by the French ships with Venetian, French and Papal galleys pulling them was attempted on 24 July. The Turkish gunners were well prepared for such an event, opened an effective fire on the fleet and disaster struck: *La Thérèse*, a 58 gun French ship-of-the-line, blew up. All 700 hands were lost and its falling debris damaged several nearby galleys killing or wounding some of their crews. After a disorderly retreat back to the town, disputes erupted between the Venetian and French officers. The latter had already lost at least 3,500 men; there were only about 2,500 still fit for duty. The French senior commander, the Duc de Navailles, decided nothing further could be done and sailed back to France on 31 August with the remnants of his forces. The fate of Crete was thus sealed and the Venetians capitulated on 6 September. Louis XIV publicly praised the officers and men for their outstanding efforts.

Privately however, he did not appreciate the way the operations had been carried out and he exiled the Duc de Navailles to his estates.[7]

The fall of Crete may have seemed like a major defeat for the Venetians in particular and European nations in general, but it was not as disastrous as it first looked. The Ottoman Turks had been at war with Venice and its supporters since 1645 and they had also suffered defeats, notably in Dalmatia. There were strong lobbies to end the war in Istanbul and in Venice. The sultan pressed Grand Vizir Achmet Aga to come up with a general framework for a peace treaty in the negotiations with general Morosini for Canea's surrender. The result was that the fortress of La Canea did indeed go to the Ottomans, but three other outlying citadels on Crete remained Venetian as did Clissa and the places taken by Venetians in Dalmatia. This treaty was approved in Venice and Istanbul ending a siege that had been vigorously prosecuted for 28 months and a war that was entering its 25th year.[8]

In all this, it must be recalled that, despite the above-mentioned operations, neither France nor the Ottoman Empire had declared war on each other. The Ottomans obviously did not wish to have powerful France as yet another opponent and the Sun King, in spite of his vacillating policy, had also been cautious. With the end of the episode in Crete followed by the peace treaty, he now took stock of the situation as it existed in his times and applied some *realpolitik* concerning the Ottoman Empire. It was worthy of the great German statesman two centuries later, Count Bismark, in what can be perceived as a total "turn around" in foreign policy towards the Middle East. Apart from the occasional French navy bombardments on piratical North African Ottoman ports such as Algiers or Tunis with some support for Malta, large corps of French land forces would no longer face Turkish armies.

The Sun King correctly determined that if he did not overly upset the Ottoman Empire, he would in fact have a very powerful de facto ally that could keep the Austrians and Germans mobilised to defend themselves in the Balkans. As following decades showed, the Ottomans in Istanbul obviously understood this as their many campaigns on the borders of Austria and Hungary would show. As a result, a sizeable proportion of the troops of the Holy Roman Empire had to be deployed to guard and defend their eastern borders against the Ottomans. Poland, although weakening politically, was involved as would be Sweden and, eventually, Tsar Peter the Great's Russia. This eastern geo-strategic situation made the western borders of the German

---

7 *Gazette*, 1668, pp. 1271; Ghyron François, Marquis de Ville, *Les mémoires du voyage de Monsieur le Marquis de Ville en Dalmatie et au Levant* (Amsterdam, 1670), pp. 134, 185, 191–192, 291–296; François Savinien D'Alquie, *Histoire curieuse du siège de Candie* (Amsterdam, 1671), 2 vols.; H.P. de Limiers, *Histoire du règne de Louis XIV* (Amsterdam, 1718), Vol. 3, pp. 244–246; Bruno Mungnai and Alberto Secco, *La Guerra di Candia / The War of Candia 1645-69* (n.p., n.d.: Soldiershop Publishing), 2 vols., Vol. 1, pp. 60–61, 72, 92, 97 (list of French troops), 114, Vol. 2, pp. 104, 111, 126; Özkan Bardakçi and François Pugnière, *La dernière croisade. Les Français et la guerre de Candie 1669* (Rennes: Presses universitaires, 2008), Chapter 3; Sevi, *Histoire de l'empire ottoman*, Vol. 4, pp. 267–270, 288–302.

8 Baptiste Nani, *Histoire de la république de Venise* (Amsterdam: Henri Schelte, 1702), Vol. 2, pp. 395–403; Rycaut, *Histoire de l'empire ottoman* Vol. 4, pp. 303–306. In the treaty's terms, La Canea's garrison and any inhabitants wishing to leave the fortress with all their belongings were allowed to depart, as well as all government and church property and even some artillery.

and Italian states, as well as those of Spain and the Netherlands, more vulnerable to their own neighbour: France.

On the whole and in part because of the geo-strategic outlook of the Sun King, the Ottoman Empire maintained much of its power during his reign. Although French forces would not be involved as they had been during the 1660s, the Ottoman Turks' military pressure in the Mediterranean and eastern Europe was certainly beneficial for Louis XIV's military endeavours. This important aspect, strangely, does not seem to have drawn much attention, but the further volumes of this study will mention the eastern campaigns and their benefits to France's armies.

Assisting the Dutch Ally

Since 1662, a treaty of alliance and trade was signed between France and the Dutch Republic. From March 1665, the Dutch were at war with Great Britain over trade conflicts and of course pressured France to join in since it was its treaty ally. Louis XIV saw no overbearing reason to declare war on Britain, but also felt somewhat obligated. Oddly enough, it was the German Prince-Bishop of Münster whot provided a way out when, during the fall of 1665, bands of warrior bandits fell upon three Dutch provinces which they ravaged and looted. A Dutch force was being gathered to deal with this small invasion and the United Provinces clamoured for French help. Louis XIV agreed to immediately send 4,000 infantry and 2,000 horse to the Netherlands to act in conjunction with the Dutch troops. Detachments of the royal guard formed part of this contingent. The news of this expeditionary corps considerably soured France's relations with Great Britain, some excited members of the British Parliament even calling for war against France, but nothing was done at the time.

Meanwhile, the French expeditionary corps gathered at Sédan under the command of Lieutenant-General the Marquis de Pradel. It then marched into Germany in November and caught up with the Bishop's marauders near an isolated place called Lochem. At the sight of the well-appointed and orderly French troops, many of these looters fled while about 400 infantrymen and 50 to 60 troopers put up a feeble resistance before surrendering. De Pradel later reported that they were in such a ragged and miserable state that he was ashamed to have drawn his sword against such paltry opponents!

The French expeditionary corps remained in the field for the rest of the winter and its relations with the inhabitants were not the best. The Dutch thought the French to be knavish and immoral while the French despised the Dutch for their narrow-mindedness and their incapacity to defend themselves even against such miserable enemies. Finally, the Bishop of Münster signed a peace treaty with the Netherlands on 18 April 1666 and the French expeditionary corps came back home.[9]

---

9   Louis XIV. *Lettres*, Vol. 2, pp. 78–81, 140–142, 152–153; Quincy, *Histoire militaire*, Vol. 1, pp. 271–272; Rousset, *Histoire de Louvois*, Vol. 1, pp. 86–92.

4

The Sun King's *Blitzkrieg*

The death in Madrid of King Felipe IV in September 1665 occasioned a complicated and lengthly diplomatic crisis between France and Spain due to the *Droit de Dévolution* (right of devolution) of Queen Marie-Thérèse who was the daughter of the deceased King of Spain by his first wife, Queen Élizabeth de Bourbon, sister of Louis XIII of France. As part of her dowry she had brought many of her fiefs, situated mostly in Flanders, such as the Duchy of Brabant, towns and cities such as Antwerp, Namur, Malines, Cambrai and many other places. She was the mother of Queen Marie-Thérèse who had married Louis XIV in 1660. Her own dowry consisted of 600,000 gold *écus* in return for which she agreed not to press for possession by devolution of her mother's territories, for Queen Élizabeth had kept her title rights, but granted their government and all their revenues to Spain. This was according to the laws of Brabant and other areas in Flanders. Time passed and Spanish gold coins still had not been paid to France when Felipe IV passed away.

After holding a "magnificent" memorial service to the deceased Felipe IV in Notre-Dame church, Louis XIV now pressed for a settlement of the dowry one way or another. Power in Madrid was now in the hands of Felipe IV's second wife, Regent Queen Mariana of Austria, daughter of Holy Roman Emperor Ferdinand III. She was a Hapsburg with little sympathy for the Bourbons and, through a lot of diplomatic shuffling in 1666, made it clear to the King of France that there would be no money and no devolution. Such a person as the Sun King certainly did not stand for what he perceived as a grave insult to his wife, himself and to the honour of France. He then announced publicly that he would seek justice by other means in response to the Spanish arrogant failure to respect agreed terms over the rights of the Queen of France, and therefore the rights of France itself. That, of course, meant going to war. Due to earlier treaties of alliance, the Dutch Republic would be France's ally while Great Britain would be Spain's. It was understood that the impact of the allies would be mainly at sea. At that time, the Dutch navy was the most powerful in Europe. With the assistance of the rapidly growing new French navy, there was little doubt that the Dutch navy could keep the somewhat decrepit Spanish navy from reinforcing Flanders and the indifferently led British navy at bay.

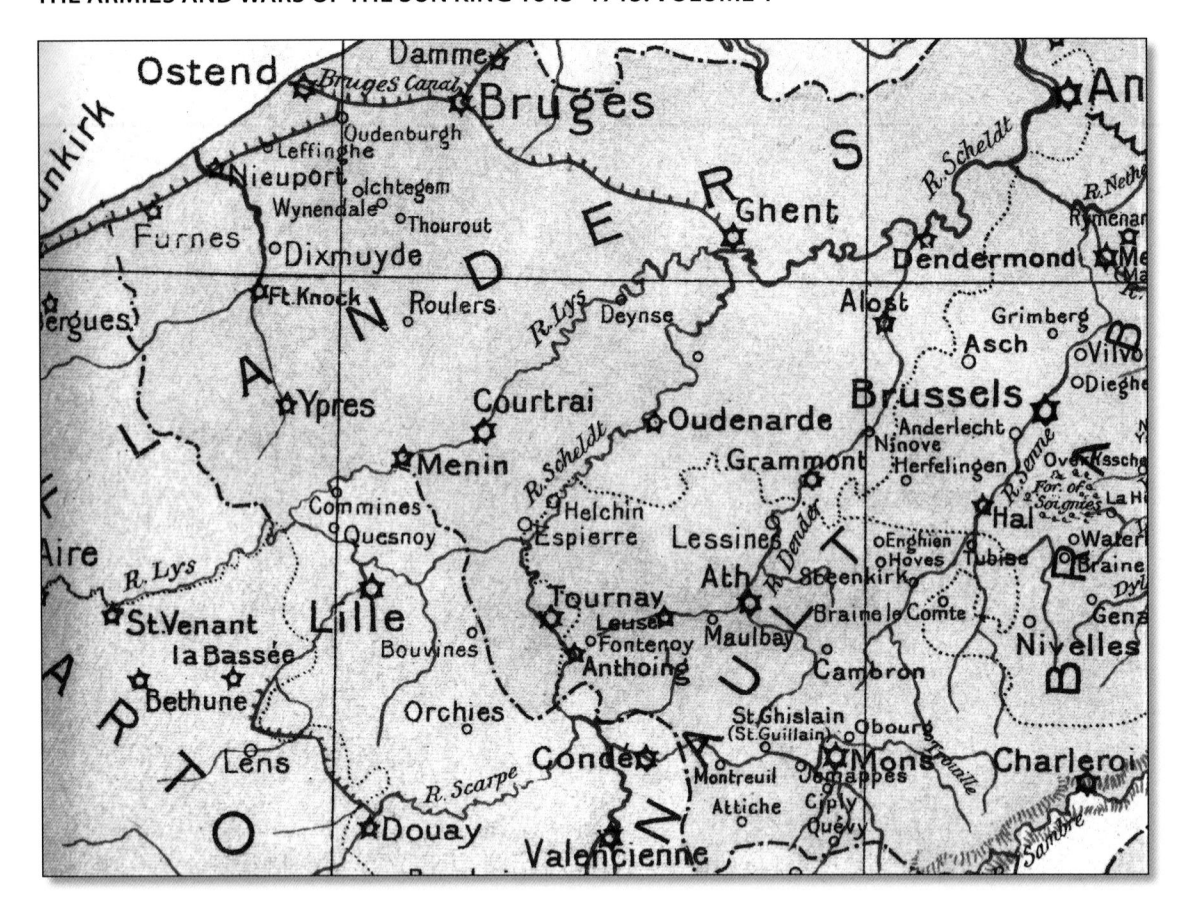

THE ARMIES AND WARS OF THE SUN KING 1643–1715: VOLUME 1

4-1 Map of Spanish Flanders. The fortresses are shown by six-pointed dots. Most were easily taken by the French army in Louis XIV's 1667 blitzkrieg. Detail of a map from Fortescues' *History of the British Army*. Author's photo.

The young Sun King would definitely march with his troops towards Flanders. He might have seen the whiff of powder from a distance during the Fronde, but this was the first time he went on a real campaign. He was very eager and determined to participate in person, and in early May 1667 left Saint-Germain-en-Laye palace to join his troops who were assembling at Amiens. While on the way, he received a dispatch from Spanish Flanders Governor and Captain-General the Marquis de Castel Rodrigo proposing more negotiations, being assured that the Queen Regent would make a reasonable agreement. For Louis XIV it was too little too late, and he felt that the Marquis de Castel Rodrigo was in fact terrified of the forces which were assembling to invade his territory. By 19 May, the King joined part of his army already in Amiens. The total mobilised for the campaign amounted to some 55,000 men. Due to the reforms introduced in the army by the Sun King and Minister of War Louvois, the French army was the best-trained, best-disciplined, best-equipped, best-organised, best-led and best-supplied force in Europe. Its morale was quite high.

To defend the Spanish Netherlands, Castel Rodrigo had only about 20,000 troops at most. He had arrived on 28 November 1664 to assume his post in Brussels, the capital and largest city of Spanish Flanders, escorted by a large suite that included his mounted guard wearing his green and silver livery, according to the *Gazette*. He had thereafter been practically starved of troops and resources from Madrid and, by the spring of 1667, could not

CHARLEROY.

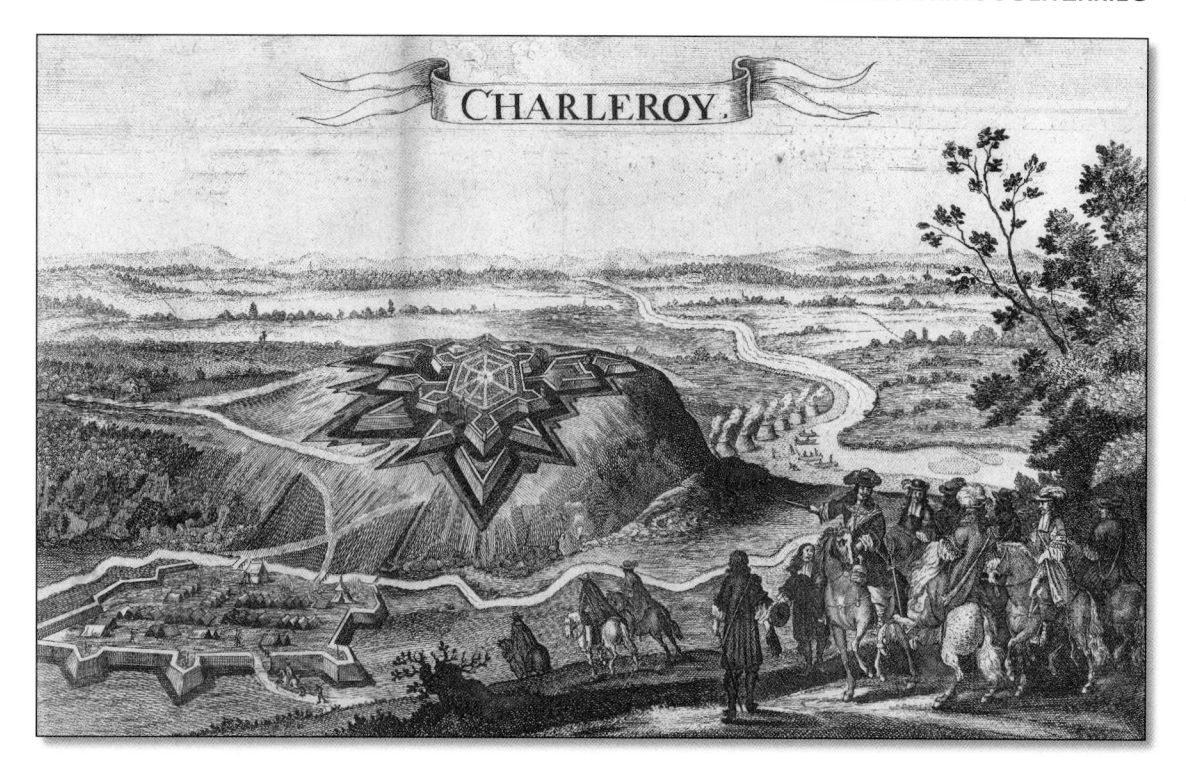

4-2 Charleroi, 1666. The town's fortifications were ordered upgraded by the Marquis de Castel Rodrigo, governor and captain general of Spanish Flanders during 1666. These works were not completed when Marshal Turenne arrived in sight of the town, which surrendered on 2 June 1667. Courtesy Rijksmuseum, Amsterdam. RP-P-OB-82.015.

expect reinforcements from Spain due to the naval blockade. With his spies telling him that more and more French troops were massing on the border, things looked very grim indeed.

The Sun King held supreme command of his army and Marshal Turenne was its chief of operations. An invasion plan was drawn up and agreed upon by senior officers. It called for a three-pronged simultaneous attack. The main corps of 35,000 men would march into the centre of Spanish Flanders; indeed, part of this corps led by Marshal Turenne had already invested Charleroi, which surrendered on 2 June, even before the King arrived, because its fortifications had not been completed by the Spanish. Chief engineer Vauban was asked to get them finished.

Another corps of about 10,000 men commanded by Lieutenant-General (later Marshal) de Créqui was detached to the south-east at Sierk, on the Moselle River, to watch whether German state troops of the Holy Roman Empire might want to intervene and outflank the French once in Flanders. It did not seem they would, but the Holy Roman Emperor in Vienna was a Hapsburg so Louis XIV and Turenne took no chances.

Meanwhile, Marshal d'Aumont at the head of some 10,000 men invaded northern Flanders and arrived at the fortress of Bergues which, after some hesitation, capitulated without a fight on 6 June. D'Aumont marched to nearby Furnes whose governor, Don Juan de Toledo, seemed to put up some resistance with a few weak sorties against the arriving French who soon counter-attacked and occupied the fortress' counterscarp. By 12 June, the siege's third day, French troops were nearing the main ramparts at which point the place surrendered. Marshal d'Aumont then occupied Armentières and its powerful Fort Saint-François which, Quincy recalled, offered "hardly any resistance." Shortly

THE ARMIES AND WARS OF THE SUN KING 1643–1715: VOLUME 1

4-3 (above): Louis XIV at the siege of Douai, early June 1667. The king is at the centre with, at left, the potrayal of an actual incident when an enemy cannonball hit a nearby Garde du Corps trooper's horse. Print after Charles Le Brun. Library and Archives Canada, NL 15533.

4-4 (below): Francisco de Moura y de Castelreal, Marquis de Castel Rodrigo, governor and captain general of Spanish Flanders from 1664 to 1668. He had to face the Sun King's blitzkrieg upon Spanish Flanders with insufficient forces to repeal the French armies. Print after Adriaen Millaert. Courtesy Rijksmuseum, Amsterdam. RP-P-1908-2476.

thereafter, he was asked by the King to detach 1,200 cavalry to watch the roads leading to Tournai and send 1,200 infantrymen to La Bassée on the other side of that city.[1]

The reason was that the Sun King wanted to take Tournai, one of Flanders' main cities. His army corps had first marched to Ath, abandoned by its garrison. It was surrendered on 16 June by town officials who asked for and were granted a French garrison. The King also ordered its fortifications revamped. A few days later, French troops started to invest Tournai. The King arrived on the spot on 21 June and, the next day, two false attacks by the Gardes Françaises and the Picardie Regiment were made followed by the Gardes Françaises taking the covered way led by Marshal de Grammont, the regiment's colonel. The King was on the spot "sharing the fatigues" of his troops and "spending a few nights in the bivouac" until the lines of circumvolution were built. On 23 June, the Spanish made a sortie that was soon repulsed. The trenches approached the curtain walls and the artillery pounded the fortifications night and day. Apprehending a general assault, negotiations were entered into that led to the surrender of the city on 25 June. Its defence, under the command

---

1   Quincy, *Histoire militaire*, Vol. 1, pp. 277–278

THE SUN KING'S BLITZKRIEG

of its governor, the Marquis de Tresigni, had been quite honourable. The Sun King entered it with pomp and circumstance escorted by his mounted guards wearing red and blue cassock and "a great number of princes of the blood and lords magnificently dressed" according to Quincy. To upgrade its defences, the King ordered that a citadel be built there.[2]

His army corps then went to Douai, which it invested on 1 July. The next day, a cavalry fight revealed that this city had a substantial artillery park so French batteries were built in record time, the troops being much encouraged by the King's presence. On 6 July, the Marquis de Castelnau led his regiment which attacked and took the covered way; this caused the governor to ask for a ceasefire. The capitulation was signed the next day.

Meanwhile, Marshal d'Aumont was asked to besiege Courtrai, which he reached on 15 July. It surrendered on 18 July. A detachment of the guards from the King's main corps under M. de Marigny went to take Aalst (Alost) that surrendered without resistance on 1 August. It was later reoccupied by the Spanish, but reoccupied by the French on 12 September who then

4-5 French troops attack a fortified town in Spanish Flanders, 1667. print after van der Meulen. Courtesy Anne S.K. Brown Military Collection, Brown University Library, Providence, RI, USA.

---

[2] Quincy, *Histoire militaire*, Vol. 1, pp. 279–280; Louis XIV. *Lettres*, Vol. 2, pp. 203–204.

razed its fortifications. Earlier, Oudenarde had capitulated on 31 July after a two-day siege.

At this point, there seemed nothing that could stop the French army in Flanders. It was certainly *blitzkrieg* 17th century-style. In less than seven weeks, Louis XIV's army had swept through areas that had not seen such overwhelming invasions since the Dark Ages. Earlier 16th and 17th century campaigns had been difficult and drawn-out bloody affairs for taking just one important town. Now, thanks to quick and disciplined movements, superior military doctrine and numbers as well as in innovative tactics for field and siege operations, the French army seemed invincible.

The Sun King now took a break to go back to France and, some days later, was on the way back to Flanders accompanied by the Queen and a huge suite since every courtier wanted to be part of the royal couple's triumphal tour which featured a lavish "galant and magnificent" reception for their entry into Douai whose inhabitants wished, Quincy relates, to "show their joy at becoming subjects of such a great prince" as Louis XIV. He was indeed more exciting and interesting than the Spanish Hapsburgs in remote Madrid.[3]

4-6 Marshal Antoine d'Aumont, 1663. He commanded the 10,000 French troops that invaded and overcame rapidly the northern part of Spanish Flanders. Courtesy Yale University Art Gallery, New Haven, CT, USA.

There was a slight reverse in the otherwise lightning campaign regarding Dandermonde, a town on the shores of the Escault (Scheldt) River. It had suddenly gained some importance to its location. If taken, it might open the way to Brussels. The Spanish managed to boost its garrison to 2,500 men and open the dikes around the town. The Comte de Duras leading a French detachment was too weak to attack it, especially with its surroundings flooded. Marshal Turenne then arrived on 3 September, appraised the situation, decided that it was not worth the effort and left two days later. This "failure" resulted in gossip that swept European courts that Dandermonde was a huge French defeat resulting in 6,000 French casualties; wags at the court in Vienna even made mock condolences to the French ambassador. The joking stopped when the Austrian courtiers learned that Lille was under threat.[4]

A crowning achievement to the campaign would be the capture of the great city of Lille if it could be done. By late August, Louis XIV's and Turenne's army corps was now weaker, having detached troops to garrison the newly conquered towns. Meanwhile, the Comte de Marcin who commanded Spanish troops in Flanders had assembled near Brussels a corps of 6,000 men with which he hoped to reinforce Lille's defences. Its garrison, commanded

---

3 Coligny-Saligny, *Mémoires*, pp. 123–124; Quincy, *Histoire militaire*, Vol. 1, p. 281
4 Rousset, *Histoire de Louvois*, Vol. 1, pp. 106–107.

by its governor, the Comte de Croui, amounted to 2,800 regulars (including 800 cavalrymen) with a large number of militiamen. Since it was a large city, the French army's siegeworks had to be very extensive to succeed in cutting it off from being reinforced. On 28 August, French troops started to surround the city. This time, progress was slower than usual since there were not enough men for the extensive siegeworks required. On 10 September, the King arrived to join his army still working on the lines of circumvolution that, once completed would be insufficiently garnished with troops, reported Vauban. The King therefore ordered Créqui to join him at once with his corps since there were no perceived threats on the Moselle. Meanwhile, the Sun King was always on horseback going from one place to another encouraging his men's work. The first trench line to advance towards the city walls was ready on the night of 18 September and soon reached the covered way. The Spanish made two unsuccessful sorties in as many days and, on 21 August, the French siege batteries opened fire. Four days later, the covered way was taken by the Gardes Françaises, Picardie and Orléans regiments. By now, the outer fortifications were in peril and a sortie to drive off the French was repulsed. On 27 September, it was clear that the French would soon overcome the defences and the Spanish surrendered. The next day, the French army entered Lille.

The King then learned that the strong body of Spanish troops under the Comte de Marcin was approaching Lille not knowing it had surrendered. Créqui and Lieutenant-General de Belfond were sent with a strong body of cavalry to intercept the Spanish. De Marcin now learned Lille had capitulated and turned back, but not fast enough because the French caught up with him near the Bruges Canal, attacked on 31 August, and took 1,500 prisoners, 18 colours and five kettledrums. It was a fitting triumph for an amazing campaign.[5]

At this point, since the King had been on campaign as a brave soldier, one may ask fairly: had he learned a great deal about the art of war? It must be answered that the *blitzkrieg* he had presided over, expertly carried out by Turenne and other fine generals with good troops, had surely given him a distorted view of warfare. Five cities had been occupied without resistance, six invested and besieged for five days or less; only the siege of Lille had been more involved and the only battle in the field had been the repulse of a Spanish relief force by French cavalry. Certainly, Louis XIV enjoyed going on campaign, especially since he did it with great luxury, but he saw his role

4-7 Marshal de Créqui, 1662. He led a French force of 10,000 men that was detached to the Moselle River to watch the German border. Courtesy Yale University Art Gallery, New Haven, CT, USA.

---

5   Rousset, *Histoire de Louvois*, Vol. 1, pp. 107–111; Quincy, *Histoire militaire*, Vol. 1, p. 281–285.

THE ARMIES AND WARS OF THE SUN KING 1643–1715: VOLUME 1

4-8 (left, top): The Sun King with his staff at the siege of Lille, August 1667. Print after van der Meulen. Courtesy Rijksmuseum, Amsterdam. RP-P-OB-83.303.

4-9 (left, below): Townsmen presenting the keys of their city to Louis XIV, c.1667. The keys to the gates of a town were symbolic of the entry and the "freedom" of the city. They were presented to a visiting dignitary figure or to a commanding monarch or general following a town's capitulation. Print after van der Meulen. Courtesy Anne S.K. Brown Military Collection, Brown University Library, Providence, RI, USA.

not so much as a general but as a strategist. Tactics would remain with the real generals although, in future wars, he would cross the line into more detailed tactical operations and decisions. For now the glories of a "military promenade" were the happy result of the *blitzkrieg*.

While the Republic of the Netherlands had been France's ally, its land forces were not engaged in campaigns against the Spanish or British in Europe. However the powerful Dutch fleet with the growing French fleet kept the Spanish and British fleets on the defensive. Of the several naval engagements, the most remarkable was certainly Admiral Michiel de Ruyter's raid up the Thames River on the Medway, which resulted in the loss of 15 warships of the Royal Navy including five capital ships. This disaster resulted in the peace treaty that the British signed at Breda on 31 July 1667. In France, Louis XIV was so pleased that he awarded the Order of Saint-Michel to Admiral de Ruyter.[6]

The Triple Alliance

By the autumn of 1667, the Dutch's attitude towards France became much more suspicious following the lightning success of the Sun King's armies. If the war went on into 1668, it seemed obvious that all of Spanish Flanders would be conquered and that mighty France would be the Dutch Republic's neighbour. In order to prevent this, the Dutch government masterminded a triple alliance with Great Britain and Sweden to come to Spain's help in defending its realm in Flanders. On 23 January 1668, the Triple Alliance agreement was sealed at the Hague between the Netherlands, Great Britain and Sweden to contain the power of France, particularly in the Spanish Netherlands. The final agreement was signed on 25 April. The Dutch army numbered up to 40,000 men, many of them mercenaries. Sweden promised an expeditionary corps of about 10,000 men and the British would also contribute troops. Added to the remaining Spanish troops in northern Flanders the opposition could now amount to as many as 70,000 troops, much more if the Germanic-Austrian Holy Roman Empire joined in. The whole French army was stronger at some 105,000 men, was certainly better organised and had some excellent commanders, but it was a tall order. It would have to be deployed on three fronts (Flanders, Spain and Italy). The situation was as if, in 1939–1940 when Germany invaded Poland and then

---

6   M. de La Neuville, *Histoire de la Hollande* (Paris: Libraires Associez, 1703), vol. 3, pp. 161–162.

4-10 Carriages with courtiers escorted by Gardes du Corps troopers arrive at a newly captured town in Flanders following the Sun King's 1667 Blitzkrieg. Grand parties and celebrations were then the order of the day. Print after van der Meulen. Courtesy Anne S.K. Brown Military Collection, Brown University Library, Providence, RI, USA.

northern France, there had been large Russian, American and British armies nearby ready to step in if the invaders got too close to Warsaw or Paris.

This triple alliance was, in effect, a major diplomatic reversal for the Dutch who, in effect, reneged the 1662 alliance with France. If French troops advanced further, they would now face a coalition on land and sea. The Sun King considered the Dutch to have betrayed him; he was deeply insulted and was not about to forget their double-crossing behaviour as future years revealed. However, he was quite calm when he learned of it in January. Taking stock of the new geo-strategic situation, he ordered a pause to the invasion of Spanish Flanders. Pursuing the *blitzkrieg* could end up in a costly attrition campaign so he put an end to it. Instead of marching on Brussels and further north, he agreed to an armistice in Flanders. What was unknown to all was that on 19 January 1668 a secret agreement had been signed in Vienna between France and the Holy Roman Empire to end the war in return for part of Flanders.[7]

---

7   Neuville, *Histoire de la Hollande*, vol. 3, pp. 170–176; Rousset, *Histoire de Louvois*, Vol. 1, pp. 124–128; Quincy, *Histoire militaire*, Vol. 1, p. 288; Bély, Bérenger and Corvisier, *Guerre et paix dans l'Europe du XVIIe siècle*, pp. 343–346. The secret agreement became known as the Grémonville Treaty.

Blitzkrieg Again

At that time the Sun King identified a new objective and served notice that he would invade the then Spanish province of Franche-Comté that was, he wrote, besides being compensation for his queen's heritage, "by its [French] language and by its rights, as justified as they were ancient, [it] should be part of this kingdom". Furthermore, it gave France a "door" to enter Germany while its occupation would secure that border area. Franche-Comté was not in Flanders but south of it, bordering Germany and northern Switzerland. It was, however, under the government of Spanish Flanders. Its regular Spanish garrison was very weak, perhaps a couple of thousand men.

To invade Franche-Comté, Louis XIV assembled some 18,000 troops in Dijon and southern Burgundy during January 1668. For this campaign, the Prince de Condé was chosen as the commander of field operations.

In early February 1668 the French army under the Prince de Condé entered Franche-Comté. By the 5th, it was in view of Besançon, the largest city and capital of the province. Prince Condé assured its inhabitants that they would retain all their rights and privileges if they capitulated. They accepted his offer rather than sustain a siege that was most unlikely to repel Condé's troops who accordingly took possession of the city and its citadel the next day. The same day, a French corps led by lieutenant-general de Luxembourg accepted the surrender of the town of Salins.

The Sun King joined Condé's army on 10 February. It had now reached the fortress of Dôle that chose to spurn the King's call to surrender. Accordingly, the city was invested and three trenches simultaneously started on 12 February and soon reached the glacis. The covered way was attacked and, although defended with valour by its Spanish defenders, was taken by the Gardes Françaises Regiment. The King reiterated that Dôle would retain its privileges while warning of the disastrous effects that a general assault could have on the inhabitants at the mercy of battle-crazed soldiers. With royal approval, in a very unusual and daring gesture, General Philibert, Comte de Gramont, approached one of the gates alone and called out joking with the Spanish soldiers on guard; amazed, they answered and exchanged jokes and teased each other. Four hours later, he was speaking pleasantly with the city's leaders of the Sun King's great and generous qualities as well as his redoubtable power. After reconsideration, the city's authorities capitulated on 14 February.[8]

Louis XIV and Condé then marched to the outskirts of the city of Gray and the French army immediately started work on siege trenches. Two days later, its inhabitants and garrison concluded they could not resist successfully and capitulated. At the same time, a detached French army corps under Lieutenant-General de Luxembourg attacked the large mountain citadels of Joux and of Sainte-Anne, both of which surrendered.[9]

---

8   Quincy, *Histoire militaire*, Vol. 1, p. 289; *Histoire populaire de la France* (Paris: Germer Baillière, 1882), Vol. 3, p. 203. Philibert de Gramont was a younger halfbrother of Marshal de Gramont.
9   Quincy, *Histoire militaire*, Vol. 1, pp. 289–290; Rousset, *Histoire de Louvois*, Vol. 1, pp. 133–138; Voltaire, *Le Siècle de Louis XIV*, pp. 145–149; Louis XIV. *Lettres*, Vol. 2, pp. 212–213.

4-11 The Comte de Gramont joking with the Spanish sentries at the gates of Dôle, 13 February 1668. This daring and risky gesture led to the capitulation of Dôle, which had offered stiff resistance until then. Print after Joliet. Private collection. Author's photo.

THE SUN KING'S BLITZKRIEG

4-12 French troops approaching the fortress of Gray in Franche-Comté, 1668. Print after van der Meulen. Library and Archives Canada, NL15534.

Thus, in three weeks, the whole of Franche-Comté was occupied by the Sun King's army. As for the King himself, he was back at Saint-Germain-en-Laye to preside, with Cardinal Vendôme, over the baptism of the Dauphin, his first-born son and heir to the throne of France. After this event, celebrated joyfully throughout the kingdom, came the tortuous peace negotiations with Spain and the countries of the Triple Alliance with, in the background, the Germanic Holy Roman Empire. Obviously, Louis XIV did not wish to prolong the war so, in substance, he agreed to evacuate his troops of Franche-Comté, but kept the real prize, which was all the places taken in Flanders which included the large city of Lille. In effect, about half of Spanish Flanders became French.

Nevertheless, in spite of showing public satisfaction, the King was privately very displeased. He severely blamed the powerful yet small Dutch Republic for its double-crossing Triple Alliance and two-faced diplomacy. Throughout his life, Louis XIV could show compassion and forgiveness in various matters, but was unflinching if he felt betrayed, abused or insulted. In such cases, he might react quickly or would bide his time. He did not forget. The Dutch probably thought he would after a while and they would be secure with the remaining Spanish Flanders as a buffer. But they were not dealing with an ordinary king; this was the Sun King whose vision was far grander and, for the Dutch, very dangerous; he was determined to break the Republic's power. In a broader perspective, the *blitzkrieg* had opened new visions to Louis XIV. He wondered why all French-speaking Catholic populations should not be part of France. For that matter, could not the Rhine River be France's "natural" border with Germany? The ancient Romans had for Gaul, so why not have that border now?

5

The Army's Command

France was an autocratic state and, in Louis XIV, it had a monarch who used as much as possible the powers to rule that a French king could exercise. It was not infinite power and he could not, for instance, condemn anyone to death; this was the duty of the courts of law although the king could issue a pardon as a sign of benevolence. In practice, the king's government depended on a large bureaucracy that had been gradually centralised since the later 16th century, but especially by Cardinal Richelieu, Louis XIII's prime minister, which is largely credited with creating the modern state. Thus, when the Sun King assumed personal rule in 1661, the royal government was already in a strong administrative position. All important matters were reported to Paris (later Versailles) and all important decisions were made at the royal court and in the ministries by senior bureaucrats. The 17th century saw advent of large and powerful bureaucracies in major western European kingdoms made up of clerks, secretaries, translators and accountants. In France, a minister depended on the *premier commis* (senior clerk – the relative equivalent to a deputy minister or an under secretary nowadays). These high-ranking civil servants were initially subject to being dismissed when ministers changed thus creating some havoc in their departments. This was changed by the King during the last quarter of the 17th century so as to promote a more stable and orderly senior civil service that would thus have more leeway to administer efficiently the myriad of issues they dealt with without undue political pressure.[1]

Outside of Paris and Versailles, army commanders, admirals, provincial or colonial governors and intendants ruled in the name of the king, but any measure they ordered was eventually double checked in Paris. Senior bureaucrats would brief ministers who would relay top issues to the King by outlining the most important parts of the correspondance or reports in the briefing papers; ministers and, at times, the King himself would dictate a reply in a memoir sometimes accompanied by an *Ordonnance du Roi* (royal ordinance) to rule on various matters. Many royal ordinances or orders

---

1   Marie-Ève Ouellet, *Le métier d'intendant en France et en Nouvelle-France* (Québec: Septentrion, 2018), pp. 45–46.

5-1 The Sun King introducing his son, the Grand Dauphin, to military affairs with the help of toy soldiers, c.1670. Print after JOB. Private collection. Author's photo.

did not in fact originate from the King but from government ministries or judicial courts. It was intellectually or physically impossible for the Sun King to have prepared, studied and signed at least 4,000 *arrest* (edicts) a year besides many hundreds if not thousands of orders regarding the army. There were at least 15 per day excluding Saturdays and Sundays for edicts alone; thus, only the most important matters were seen by the King.

The King's council, called *le Conseil d'En-Haut* (the upper council), consisted of just a few ministers such as the minister of war, of foreign affairs and of finance. A large part of its work concerned military matters. It was convened in the King's office three or four times a week from 9:30 to noon and, if the agenda was heavy, from 14:30 to 16:00. The Sun King sat at the head of the table and the ministers gave their advice, without being interrupted by the King, who agreed 95 percent of the time, but he alone decided and that was the end of the matter. Campaign strategy could be also raised or might, especially if the King was with the army, be discussed with senior officers. This became less frequent from the mid 1670s when campaign matters were increasingly decided by the King at Versailles.

Population, Religion and Nobles

Due to a myriad of jurisdictions in Old Regime France, the size of the bureaucracy is basically impossible to calculate except to affirm that it was surely huge. The country had about 18 to 20 million inhabitants, which infers hundred of thousands of petty government employees of all sorts, the great majority performing humble tasks. Of the realm's population, about 15 percent lived in towns and cities, the rest were spread in villages throughout the kingdom and most were peasants working the land.

Voltaire estimated that, before 1685, about one Frenchman or Frenchwoman in 12 was Protestant and most resided in the more southernly provinces. France's overwhelming majority was thus Roman Catholic and it was the state religion. There had been bitter religious conflicts in the 16th and early 17th centuries, which had left deep scars in French society. By Louis XIV's reign (he himself being a convinced Catholic), the Protestant community was somewhat tolerated by the rest of the populace and even less considered by the government – a situation that could be compared with Catholics in Ireland at that time. Judaic, Muslim and other creeds were minuscule and barely tolerated except that some Jews had a bit more leeway in business.

The Roman Catholic church held a large place in France since the Dark Ages and controlled vast estates, the country being divided into 126 dioceses (in 1680) led by many bishops and cardinals; there may have been about 160,000 members of religious orders. Their presence was everywhere, from the humble parish priests in every village and towns to influential bishops in town or city councils without forgetting about 90,000 monks and nuns working the land around monasteries and abbeys as well as running hospitals since the church, with the help of royal subsidies, ran what we now know as social services. The armed forces were also provided with chaplains as will be seen in volume 4. In a fiscal sense, the church had its own tax system to provide basic revenues, *la dîme*, which, unlike royal taxes, was to be paid by all although it seems the more humble individuals were the hardest hit.

The *noblesse* or persons of more or less noble birth may have numbered between 300,000 and 400,000 people proclaiming their blue blood. Of these, about 80,000 were of the "old" nobility. At the top of the structure was the *grande noblesse* that was made up by the richest and most influential families that nearly always had their noble roots going back several centuries. These often had important revenues from substantial estates passed on from one generation to another and the more wealthy might have a mansion in Paris and/or an apartment at Versailles. Far more numerous were the much humbler *petite noblesse*. They were almost invariably country squires with a modest revenue, some taking part in the management of their small estates. Be they grand or humble, the nobles were unanimous in proclaiming their warrior heritage from the days of medieval knights and their absolute belief that they had priority to be officers in the army. It went back to the Dark Ages division of society: the churchmen prayed; the commoners laboured; the nobles fought to protect the churchmen and commoners. In exchange for which nobles paid few or no taxes.

Nobles had certain privileges. Wearing a sword was restricted to noble and squired gentlemen in civil society; all others could be prosecuted and severely punished for transgressing this rule. However, non-nobles belonging to the armed forces were allowed to wear swords. Nobles sought the *emplois réservés* (reserved employment) especially in the army, but also in the church and at the royal court. They were expected to live in a gentlemanly style, have a certain education, know and use weapons efficiently, be good horsemen and never be seen in a low occupation performing manual labour. The guards (especially the Gardes du Corps) and all line regiments had reserved commissions that were meant for noble gentlemen so long as they could prove that they had *quatre quartiers* (four quarters) of noble blood, this even for the rank of lieutenant. Naturally, they clamoured that they should have all officer's commissions since there were never enough reserved posts for all the nobles, thus implying common *roturiers* were unfit for command. However, the Sun King, while humouring the nobility, actually sought military talent wherever he could find it as many of his appointments to higher command show. They could always be ennobled later on. So, there was something like a double system in place. By the early 18th century, possibly up to a third of line regimental officers were not noble or else of dubious peerage.[2]

Finances and Taxes

The ministry of war had two budgets that were identified publicly as military spending. The first one was the *ordinaires des guerres* (ordinaries of the wars) paid for the general officers, the royal guard, the Gendarmerie cavalry, the maréchaussée constabulary, the artillery and the upkeep of fortification. The second budget was the *extraordinaires des guerres* (extraordinaries of the wars) which funded the pay of all the other regular troops, additional expenses of the artillery, construction of new fortifications, rations for troops, hospitals and bedding. A deduction of three pennies for each pound of the military budgets went to the Invalides for its upkeep. On the other hand, the quartering and movement of troops, the embodied militias and local companies were paid for by provincial or town budgets although they might be recipients of a royal government subsidy.

The portion of the national budget devoted to warlike affairs is basically unknown since many military services were not directly provided by the ministry of war. For instance, engineering was an appointment and its recipient, even if he was an army officer, was expected to provide plans and supervise construction or repair, not only of fortifications, but also of churches, windmills, roads, and so on. Such expenses did not always appear in strictly military budgets. Some would be found in provincial and town budgets. A "king's gunner" responsible for artillery pieces and training in a garrison town was a supposedly non-combatant specialist like his engineer comrade and was not usually paid by a military budget. Indeed, a vast number of services and supplies for armies were not necessarily included in the War Ministry's budgets. Overseeing government property was the Marquis de Villacerf who was *Inspecteur Général des Bâtiments* – Inspector General of all government buildings, a post that came with important responsibilities at the War Ministry as well as in other departments, all of which made him one of the most influential civil servants in France.

Whatever budget the funds might be, Jean-Baptiste Colbert's fiscal measures kept large amounts of money flowing although this did not last as decades went by. Loans and pre-emptive taxes were sought by the 1690s leading

---

2   Bély, Bérenger and Corvisier, *Guerre et paix dans l'Europe du XVIIe siècle*, pp. 49–51, 417–418; Pierre Goubert and Daniel Roche, *Les Français et l'Ancien Régime, la société et l'état* (Paris: Armand Colin, 1984), pp. 124, 127

to skyrocketing interest rates. The whole financial system of the kingdom has been qualified as an inscrutable vacuum by historians André Corvisier, Pierre Goubert and Daniel Roche. They estimated that anywhere from 30 to 80 percent of the kingdom's revenues went into what could be termed military spending in the reigns of Louis XIV and Louis XV. An average from 1661 to 1682 came to 52 percent, and for later:

> 1683 (a year of peace): 65.3 million pounds; 56.7% of total budget; debt service 8.9%
>
> 1692 (a war year): 140 million pounds; 79.8% of total budget; debt service 8.8%
>
> 1699 (a year of peace): 74.3 million pounds; 16.5% of total budget; debt service 76.5%

Surprisingly, the tax burden on a Frenchman was lower than for an Englishman, but the taxation system in France was far less equitable. Thus, the poor became poorer and might actually starve while the nobility and the church were largely exempt of taxes. In 1695, a timid reform tried to address this iniquity, without success. This led Marshal Vauban to later propose a different system, but it was never adopted. Only in the rather desperate year of 1709 was a head tax brought in to shore up an empty treasury, but this was not a permanent measure and was naturally much criticised by the nobles.[3]

Royal Governance

This, then, was the government apparatus presided over by the King. Nowadays, it is often believed that if the Sun King had a good or a bad day in Versailles, its effects were soon felt in the remotest part of the realm. This could not be the case in such a large and complex administrative structure.

What Louis XIV did change, and this concerned primarily the armed forces, was that he alone, as the autocratic king, decided on the important issues and that he personally appointed ministers and other very senior officials, provided them with wide powers to perform their duties, but had complete authority over them. All power and all decisions revolved around him at court. All ministers, members of the royal family, senior officers and courtiers were to have absolute loyalty and attention to the King's royal pleasure. If this was not forthcoming, one might be banished from court to live in his country estate for a while or, in the worst cases, be taken away to prison or a convent by a party of the King's Musketeers or Gardes du Corps.

While the mass of noble courtiers soon elevated the Sun King to the status of an Olympian God, hoping that his rays might warm their fortunes, a meeting of one of them with the King might occasionally be a traumatic experience. Although renowned for his almost faultless politeness and kind remarks, the

---

[3] Goubert and Roche, *Les Français et l'Ancien Régime*, pp. 336–337; Thomas Piketty, *Le capital au XXIe siècle* (Paris: Seuil, 2013), chapter 2.

THE ARMY'S COMMAND

5-2 The Sun King having a heated discussion with Minister of War Louvois, c. 1685. There are few recorded instances of the royal temper flaring up. Print after Maurice Leloir. Private collection. Author's photo.

King might also lose his temper. During a 1669 meeting with Antonin Nompar de Caumont de Lauzun, the discussion became torrid and Louis XIV threw his cane out of the window so as not strike a gentleman with it! Needless to add that Lauzun did not obtain the post of grand master of artillery and was banished. Another time, while discussing heatedly with Louvois, the minister of war, *le roi s'emporta* (the King lost his temper) over some matter. Normally joyful at news of victories and stoic when learning of defeats, the King was so enraged by the loss of Namur in 1695, which was reportedly due to the lack of stamina and bravery of the Duc de Maine, one of his legitimised sons, that he lost his temper in front of a few courtiers. The Sun King had a strong volatile temper, but otherwise nearly always managed to keep it reined in. In public, he was the very example of calm and dignity.[4]

Choosing Commanders

In principle, the supreme command of an army in the field was entrusted to a prince of the very high nobility that was related to the royal family or to a marshal of France. The prince, especially if he was not an experienced commander like Prince Condé, always had a marshal to guide him through the complexities of strategy and tactics. An army commanded by a marshal

---

4 Toudouze, *Le Roy Soleil*, pp. 56, 58.

could also have another marshal as second in command. Several lieutenant-generals would command portions of the army. A *maréchal de camp général* acted as chief of staff and another *maréchal de camp* (both were major-generals) saw to battlefield dispositions of units in those days of linear tactics. A *maréchal de camp général des logis* saw to supplies, forage, pay, marches and encampments assisted by intendants and commissaries.

The King made the final choices in the spring of each year insofar as command of an army to take the field for the ensuing campaigns was concerned. He kept nominations in deep secrecy although individuals such as Louvois or his mistresses might make suggestions in private. Sometimes, the Sun King did nominate a suggested officer, but would eventually also impose his own choice to "assist" as second in command. Naturally there was much excitement at a royal court ripe with all manners of gossip that depended on observation as to which marshals had many meetings with the King. The appointed officers did not have much choice, rarely turned down commands and did not have much say as to who would be their second in command, how strong their army would be and which units made it up.

Reputation and battlefield performance played a big part in the choices made, but there was a certain criteria imposed even on the King. The advent of *l'ordre du tableau* in 1675, a promotion system that favoured seniority (see below) to which were added such factors as birthright, merit and just plain favouritism in nominations that invariably provoked endless debates amongst jealous courtiers. In 1688, Chamlay mentioned rather full of optimism that the King could pick whom he wanted thanks to a system that removed "any apprehension for the mediocre capacity" of the officer he entrusted with the command. For all that, it can be perilous for historians to conclude that there was a clear path to higher command according to a rigid criteria. The Sun King had his unpredictable side when it came to appointing army commandeers and elevating officers. Nobility was desirable, but nominations of rather humble officers such as Catinat and Vauban showed that the Sun King did as he pleased. Naturally their comrades at court proclaimed (amongst themselves) that the King was mistaken since only noble blood was worthy of a marshal's baton. The appointed officer, whatever his ancestry, certainly needed support at court while he was away (or even when on the spot). Usually, an officer having secured an army's command was henceforth fairly independent and secure; the hardest part was the lobbying to obtain the post. Once promoted, good results were naturally expected on the battlefield. A more or less talented or worse, a defeated general or marshal, could not expect much grace thereafter; an exception was Marshal Luxembourg whose loss of Philippsburg in 1676 put him on the retired list until called back in 1690 when good commanders were getting scarcer to find.[5]

All in all, the command choices by the Sun King were compromises between birth, seniority, merit and perceived competence to delegate authority while retaining control within the system in place to insure

---

5   Jean-Philippe Cénat, 'Chamlay (1650–1719), le stratège oublié de Louis XIV', *Revue historique des armées*, 263/2011. Online at: <http://rha.revues.org/7207>.

absolute loyalty. Outside influences played their part in the choices, but a greater difficulty was to find men who could hopefully truly do the job. So there was the luck, or ill luck, of the draw in this unpredictable bargain that has haunted all political war leaders since the dawn of history. Louis XIV had his good and not so good fortunes in his day. The worst period for the King is said to have been the War of the Spanish Succession, yet then too, a few good marshals made up for disasters brought on by incompetent creatures and a truly great marshal saved the day. A remarkable quality of the Sun King's system, soon largely copied by his opponents, was the stability enjoyed by the totally loyal and obedient senior military officers, which procured them wealth, power and prestige in the service of their country.

Another factor concerned the Sun King's perception of himself as a military leader. He did feel he was a good commander although never foolish enough to think that he could lead an army without experienced officers to do the tactical work. While he was actively engaged in the short War of Devolution and the early stages of the Dutch War, his presence leading armies was increasingly rare as time passed and age took its toll. He became convinced that he could run campaigns by sending flurries of instructions from the comfort of his Versailles office. The tempo of couriers galloping in and out of the royal palace thus much increased. It could not, however, equal presence in a war zone.

By the early 18th century, marshals would request approval to move the army from one place to the other to counter an enemy force, but by the time the answer was received, conditions had often changed. This was mainly true in Flanders, northern Italy and western Germany, but less so in distant Spain. Whether the disasters of the first half of the War of the Spanish Succession were due to a rigid command system depending on couriers galloping in and out of Versailles or the questionable choices of commanders or the combination of both cannot be known. At length, it seems that it gave pause for Louis XIV to reconsider aspects of his military leadership. Certainly, the successes of Marshal Berwick in Spain and the vigorous tactical moves made on the spot by Marshals Villars and Boufflers at Malplaquet may have brought about a gradual change of perception in Versailles. By 1712, the Sun King's grip had loosened and his freer field commanders gained decisive victories.

The King also appointed territorial commanders. Senior generals were granted postings as governor-generals of provinces and overseas territories. They were supreme commanders of all regular and militia troops in their jurisdiction. Under a governor-general were local governors, town majors and other town officers of a *place de guerre* (military fortress town or fort) formed the staff responsible for the welfare of the troops in garrison or passing through and the security of the place such as police, public works and fire prevention.

6

Senior Officials and Officers

A few high officials were responsible for the army's management. They were:[1]

Michel Le Tellier (1603–1685). He belonged to a Parisian family of administrators and lawyers going back to the early 16th century, was himself a prosecutor early in his career, then "intendant of justice" in the army in 1640. Cardinal Mazarin, impressed by his efficiency, appointed him minister of war in 1643. The army's administration was then weakened by corrupt practices of many officers who diverted royal treasury funds to their own pockets. Le Tellier largely ruined such practices by meticulous examination of accounts thus providing more control for royal authority. From the time he assumed personal power in 1661, Louis XIV fully supported Le Tellier with many royal ordnances that centralised army command and improved discipline. He also reorganised the War Ministry into five *bureaux* (offices or sections) that streamlined administration and required efficiency from administrators and officers. With his son François-Michel showing keen interest and remarkable administrative talent, Le Tellier gradually passed on his ministerial duties to him. He was appointed chancellor of France in 1677.

François-Michel Le Tellier, Marquis de Louvois (1641–1691). He was a brilliant man with a bad temper and would react strongly to any contradiction to his usually well-founded opinions. His father correctly saw that he could be a great administrator and, in 1666 with royal approval, devolved powers that made Louvois the effective minister of war, which was formalised when he became a member of the king's council in 1671. Up to the 1660s, orderly behaviour by soldiers was not a hallmark in any large armies, be they in Europe or elsewhere. This, from Louvois' perspective, was one of the main results of the somewhat lax performance of the army that he was responsible

---

1 These short biographies of official, members of the royal family, marshals and generals are based mainly on: Voltaire, *Le Siècle de Louis XIV*; Corvisier, *Dictionnaire d'art et d'histoire militaire*; L. Dussieux, *Les grands généraux de Louis XIV* (Paris: Victor Lecoffre, 1888); Vieux Caporal, 'Les maréchaux de France 1185–1791', *Petite histoire de l'armée française* in *Crapouillot*, No. 25 (1954), pp. 23–35; *Dictionnaire historique, critique et bibliographique*, Vol. 17, p. 112. The *États de la France* registers often have genealogical notices on the marshals.

for. In Louis XIV he was blessed to have, a sovereign deeply interested in orderly procedures; these were only possible by strong impositions carried out by administrators that were responsible to him. Louvois, always with the approval of the King, proceeded to implement ideas and practices that were then quite novel. He imposed a regime of hitherto unknown rigorous discipline in the French army. He worked hard, was devoted to his king and very often travelled to visit army units and camps in order to see what was actually happening and bring corrections when appropriate. With Vauban and Chamlay, he supported the creation of the *Pré-Carré* web of fortresses to defend France's borders.

His achievements were remarkable. He suggested the system of *L'Ordre du tableau* for promotions of officers (see below), came up to maintain in the field an army of up to 380,000 men that was efficiently supplied; thanks to good logistics, it was one of the most mobile and best-armed forces of its time. There was, regrettably, a darker side to Louvois' character. He could be cruel at times and ordered devastation and "scorched earth" by the conquering French troops in enemy areas that stubbornly resisted; perhaps even worse, he often turned a blind eye to the terrible abuses made by troops – notably dragoons – on French Protestants even before the 1685 Revocation of the Edict of Nantes and on conquered populations in the Netherlands and Germany that provoked enormous sufferings. He is nevertheless generally remembered as one of the greatest military administrators of modern times.

Louis-François-Marie, Marquis de Barbezieux. He was the son of Louvois whom he succeeded in 1691. Shrewd and promising young man who might have done well, but his personal values were very different than his father's. As Voltaire put it, he was much more interested in "pleasures and in feasting than in work." However, the King kept him as minister. He passed away in 1701 while in office, aged 33.

Michel Chamillart (1652–1721). Succeeded Barbezieux as minister of war in 1701 when he was already comptroller general of finances since 1699. The weight of the two portfolios in the difficult times of the Spanish Succession War were nearly overwhelming for the "mild and modest" man he was, according to Voltaire. The national debt was out of control and the army experienced major defeats. Unfortunately, some of the officers he recommended to the King for senior command proved nearly disastrous. At length, he had to warn the King that opponent nations would eventually be in a position to dictate to France terms to end the war. The old Sun King did not waver, but the weight of two ministries crushed Chamillart who wanted to retire in 1706, resigned as comptroller general in 1708 and was dismissed as minister of war on 10 June 1709.[2]

Daniel Voysin de La Noiraye (1655–1717). Initially an intendant of Hainault,

---

2 See also much more details the study by G. Esnault, *Michel Chamillard, contrôleur général des finances et secrétaire d'état de la guerre (1699–1709) correspondance et papiers inédits* (Le Mans: Edmond Monnoyer, 1884).

he became a state councillor and, in June 1709, was handed the portfolio of minister of war at a time when the army was seriously affected by shortages of supplies. He did what he could under the circumstances, but could not fully solve these problems. He was dismissed by the Regency Council in September 1715.

Jules-Louis Baule, Marquis de Chamlay (*c*.1650–1719). He inherited from his father the venal and rather vague field officer's rank of *maréchal général des logis aux camps et armées du roi* that, in his case, led him to be an appreciated chief of staff in Condé's and Turenne's armies. He was recommended to Louvois who was impressed by his sharp mind, excellent memory and outstanding strategic and political outlook, Introduced to the Sun King in 1689, who henceforth kept him at Versailles to be a private councillor. After Louvois passed away in 1691, the King first offered Chamlay the post of minister of war, but he declined, feeling it should go to Louvois' son, the Marquis de Barbezieux. He remained, however, very influential and continued to have, as before, private meetings to discuss military matters with the King thus being in fact his de facto chief of staff. Chamlay obviously preferred not to be in the limelight although his influence is said to have been considerable and, on the whole, very good. Much of his work consisted of writing a lengthly memoir during the winter outlining the campaigns planned for the upcoming year; his proposals would be discussed by the King with the minister and senior commanders. Not everything was approved of course, but it was an invaluable guide and it is likely that the wars of the League of Augsburg and of the Spanish Succession would have been worse for France had it not been for Chamlay. He was a proponent of offence in warfare more than defence while fully supporting fortifications in strategic planning, especially as he was also a gifted cartographer. His private ideas, which he shared with the King, included tolerance for Protestants, respect for civilian populations (he was against the sacking of the Palatinate) and, like Vauban, a better taxation system.

Jean-Baptiste Colbert (1619–1683). Born in Reims, the son of a cloth merchant, he developed a keen interest in economy and finances. In spite of his humble origins, his hard and intelligent work was recognised at the highest level when Cardinal Mazarin made him his personal intendant. Before his death, Mazarin recommended Colbert to Louis XIV. Following the demise and arrest of the corrupt superintendent of finances Fouquet in 1661, the Sun King recalled Mazarin's advice and entrusted Colbert with almost everything involving the French economy. This included the military budgets for the army and the navy. He was a rather different type of person compared to nearly all the gilded individuals who haunted the royal court seeking favours at the expense of the royal treasury. Colbert, who was guardian of the treasury, had a severe appearance, looking serious and cold. He dressed modestly and was utterly devoted to his duties that, rumours said, might make him work at times some 16 hours a day. Yet, he rubbed his hands in satisfaction when he sat at his desk to start a new day every morning.

Those noble courtiers and generals who had to curry him for certain favours nicknamed him "the man of marble." They rightly feared him and those who dared ask for some favour would indeed get the cold shoulder with Colbert not even listening. This attitude was exemplified by an incident when a lady of the court knelt before him exclaiming "I plead that you listen to me!" So, Colbert knelt in front of her and answered: "And I, my lady, beg of you to leave me alone!" All this made great gossip at court. He simply wanted to get his work done.[3]

Colbert saw better than anyone the extraordinary economic powerhouse that France could be with some good management. The reorganisation of the country's financial system and the reforms he brought to trade, industry and agriculture soon made France the leading economic power in Europe. Under his guidance royal revenues multiplied during the 1660s. It was largely thanks to his work that the means to create Europe's largest army were provided as well as a very powerful fleet. Up to his dying days, Colbert wrote countless memorandums to the King advising moderation in his lavish spending. The Sun King did not heed many of Colbert's warnings and lived to experience the consequences.[4]

Members of the Royal Family as Army Commanders

Members of the royal family and "princes of the blood" could and did hold high command posts. The most famous was the talented Prince de Condé, some of the others being the Dauphin, the Duc de Bourgogne, the Duc de Chartres and the Prince de Conti. Like marshals, they carried the blue velvet command baton sprinkled with gold lilies.

Louis de France (1661–1711). Called also the *Grand Dauphin* and *Monseigneur*, he was the eldest son of Louis XIV and Maria Teresa of Austria, Queen of France. He was the heir to the throne, called in France the Dauphin, just as Britain's heir to the throne is called the Prince of Wales. In his case he was the *Grand Dauphin* and addressed at *Monseigneur* (My Lord) in the pinnacle of court etiquette. As a child, Louis XIV first introduced him to military affairs with the help of toy soldiers and, as a teenager, the King often brought the Dauphin with him on campaign so he could see and learn the various aspects of the art of war. He also served in the King's Musketeers as a youth. He grew to be quite robust and stout. Generally described as a rather bland character, he was quiet, good-humoured and rather self-effacing, but could be very determined in his opinions although he would often choose silence rather than discuss matters, perhaps because he could not greatly influence his father. For instance, it is known he was against the revocation of the Edict of Nantes and the persecution of Protestants. Hunting bored him although he was a good horseman and his interests seem to have been mainly devoted to good

---

3   Viator, *Histoire de France*, pp. 99–100.
4   *Dictionnaire historique, critique et bibliographique*, Vol. 11, pp. 243–250; *Cours d'histoire de France* (Montreal: Beauchemin, 1919), p. 92.

food and collecting porcelain and silver. As heir to the throne and son of one of the more warlike rulers of Europe, he showed middling interest with military matters. Nevertheless, like most Bourbons, he had qualities in military leadership, but was in a delicate position, always having to be reserved when in command. His birth made him the protocolary second in command of the armed forces and his formal portraits show him in armour holding the baton of command. He was also the colonel-in-chief of any army unit that had the name of Dauphin, but did not command them personally. During the 1680s, he was old enough to be given command of an army, albeit under the guidance of the King's marshals and within control of the royal court. His first success was the siege of Philippsburg in 1688 and he was noted during the War of the League of Augsburg for bravery under fire. All his campaigns were successful if not outstanding. He had three sons by Princess Marie-Anne of Bavaria: Louis, Duc de Bourgogne (1682–1712); Philippe, Duc d'Anjou (1683–1746) for whom the Grand Dauphin put forth with great vigour his son's rights to be the King of Spain as Felipe V. As with Charles, Duc de Berry (1686–1714), his health appears to have degraded in the early 1700s and he died in 1711.

6-1 Louis de France, *c.*1688. Louis XIVs son and heir to the throne. This portrait by H. Rigaud is from a larger painting showing the Dauphin at the 1688 siege of Philippsburg. Rhode Island School of Design, Providence, USA. Author's photo.

6-2 Louis, Duc de Bourgogne, *c.*1700. He was the son of the Dauphin. Painting by H. Rigaud. Count Vitetti Collection, Rome. Author's photo..

Louis, Duc de Burgogne. Son of the *Grand Dauphin* born in 1682, he was said to have been rather arrogant and rough in his manner, but thanks to the brilliant cleric Bossuet, he also became charitable and devout. Allowed to attend the King's highest council from 1702 so he would learn of secret state matters, he showed modest interest in governance. He was nevertheless trusted with army commands in 1708 jointly with the Duc de Vendôme. They faced the Duke of Marlborough and Eugene of Savoy leading the allied armies and the result was the disastrous rout at Oudenarde for which he was largely blamed. Back at court in Versailles, he was the hope of reformers who argued for a less absolute monarchy. Fate decided otherwise. In February 1712 a smallpox epidemic swept the palace of Marly that on 12 February first carried off his wife, the sparkling and very popular Marie-Adelaïde de Savoie, Duchesse de Bourgogne, followed six days later by her husband and by their five-year-old son, Louis, Duc de Bretagne, a month later. It is proper to add here that the King was nearly shattered with grief.

Philippe, Duc d'Anjou. Second son of the *Grand Dauphin*, he was chosen at 17 as successor to the Spanish throne by its dying king, Carlos II, on 2 October 1702. This was contested by Austria, Great Britain, Holland, many German and Italian states and Portugal, all of whom supported Archduke Charles of Austria, Emperor Leopold I's brother. In spite of a civil war within Spain and with very substantial French support, the difficult War of the Spanish Succession confirmed Felipe V as "King of Spain and the Indies" as well as maintaining a great influence on southern Italy. The Spanish overseas empire was basically unscathed by the war and Felipe V fostered increased administrative efficiency in the Indies as well as in Spain itself, a result of the positive aspects that French influence had on the country's antiquated bureaucracy, armies and education. Felipe V died in 1746.

Charles, Duc de Berry. Third son of the Grand Dauphin born in 1686. He was not involved in any notable military duty and passed away in 1714.

Philippe de Bourbon, Duc de Chartres and later d'Orléans. Born in 1674, he was the grandson of Louis XIII and the son of the Duc d'Orléans, called *Monsieur*, Louis XIV's younger brother (1643–1701) who was generally recognised as being basically uninterested in military or state matters. However, Philippe liked soldiering and distinguished himself in several battles during the War of the League of Augsburg, but this raised jealousies with the other princes, his rivals at court. The King, not approving of his great love of girls and parties, put him aside after the war. In 1701, his title changed to Duc d'Orléans following the death of his father. He was called to command in Italy during the War of the Spanish Succession, which went relatively

6-3 (above): Philippe, Duc d'Anjou, *c.*1702, second grandson of Louis XIV. Print after Jean François de Troy. Rijksmuseum, Amsterdam. RP-P-1904-1429.

6-4 (below): Philippe de Bourbon, Duc de Chartres and later d'Orléans, *c.*1690. Courtesy Anne S.K. Brown Military Collection, Brown University Library, Providence, RI, USA.

well until, shunning the advice of his senior officers, Marshal Marchin in particular, the French army was crushed at Torino in 1706. Marchin having been killed, d'Orléans and his officers put the blame on the dead marshal and it would take Napoleon himself a century later to point to the disaster's true culprit: d'Orléans. Smooth and experienced courtier that d'Orléans was, his military talents were sought again by the King and he became commander of French armies in Spain where the Duc de Berwick won the strategic victory of Almanza just before he arrived. D'Orléans was much upset as he could not claim its glory. He took Tortosa in 1708, but was eventually passed over by the King as actual commander due to rumours of his intrigues in Versailles, notably about poisoning rivals (which appear to have been unfounded). His most important office came in 1715 when he was made Regent of France, which he assumed with competence as well as heralding a welcome era of relaxed behaviour and risqué parties after the rather puritan last years of the Sun King. He died in 1723.

6-5 Louis Auguste de Bourbon, Duc de Maine, c.1690. Musée Condé, Chantilly. Author's photo.

There were also "natural" and legitimised children fathered by the Sun King. Some of the sons had military appointments:

Louis-Auguste de Bourbon, Duc de Maine (1670–1736). The legitimised natural son of Louis XIV and the Marquise de Montespan. Colonel general of the Swiss troops from 1674 to 1710 when the post was assumed by his ten-year-old son Louis-Auguste. Most of all, from 1694, he was appointed grand master of the artillery, which assumed until his death. Thus, all the brass cannons cast between 1694 and 1737 bore his name.

Louis-Alexandre de Bourbon, Comte de Toulouse (1678–1737). He was made Duc de Penthièvre in 1697 to which were added the duchies of Arc, Châteauvillain and Rambouillet in 1711. Was *Amiral de France* (admiral of France, the senior protocol rank in the navy) from 1683 to his death. Although a lieutenant-general in 1697, he served mainly at sea and the fleet he nominally commanded inflicted heavy casualties on a British fleet off Malaga in 1704.

Princes of the Royal Blood

Louis de Bourbon, Prince de Condé (1621–1686), was an elder cousin of Louis XIV and a scion of the most powerful noble families in the country, being also related to such families as the Enghien and the Montmorency of the *grande noblesse*. Furthermore he was one of the best commanders of his times and, even as a youth, showed extraordinary aptitude for the art of war's strategy and tactics. Given "honorific" command of the Army of Picardie in 1642, he quickly assumed actual command and won the decisive battle of Rocroi against the Spanish in 1643. He victoriously led armies in Germany and Spain in the following years, then in Flanders where his success at Lens against the Holy German Empire brought about peace to France's advantage in 1648. Condé was not an astute politician when he joined the revolt of the nobility, the 1650 *Fronde des Princes*, and had to flee into exile seeking refuge with, ironically, the Spanish in Flanders. Pardoned by Louis XIV at the advent of the 1659 peace treaty, he accepted a minor command that he turned into his 1668 outstanding three-week *blitzkrieg* conquest of Franche-Comté. In Holland, he beat William of Orange at Senef in 1674 and successfully campaigned in Alsace the following year. But he was now sickly and retired to his chateau at Chantilly. Received by the King and his court, his rheumatism pains made his ascent of the great stairway slow and he excused himself to Louis XIV for making him wait. To which the Sun King made one of his more famous replies: "my cousin, when one is weighted down by laurels as you are, one can only walk with difficulty."[5]

6-6 Coat of arms of Louis de Bourbon, Prince de Condé. Blue with gold lilies and a red baton. From a mural painting. Musée Condé, Chantilly. Author's photo.

Henri-Jules de Bourbon-Condé (1643–1709). Son of the Great Condé, he was therefore a legitimate prince of the blood and was in the army as a cavalry brigadier (1668), major-general (1672) and lieutenant-general the following year serving as chief of staff of the army on the Rhine. However, he had no appreciable military talents, was known as *Condé le Fol* (the crazy Condé) and neither the King nor Louvois could trust him with a real command. He was much more successful outside the army in elaborate financial manoeuvres later on.

François de Bourbon-Vendôme, Duc de Beaufort (1616–1669). He was a grandson of King Henri IV and thus a cousin of Louis XIV. He was only 12 when he accompanied a French army and was at several sieges during the Thirty Years' War. He also took part in plots against Cardinals Richelieu and Mazarin and even killed his brother-in-law, Charles Amédée de Savoie-Nemours in a 1652 duel over a political argument. The following year, he rallied to the royal party following the Fronde and was eventually named superintendent general of navigation, which made him a senior admiral. In 1664, he led a fleet at Djidjelli, beat an Algerian Ottoman fleet off Cherchell on 24 August 1665 and was killed in action at Crete on 25 June 1669.

---

5   Viator, *Histoire de France*, p. 104.

Louis-Joseph de Bourbon, Duc de Vendôme (1654–1712). Born into the powerful and very wealthy Vendôme family, he was a legitimised great-grandson of King Henry IV and therefore of royal blood as well as being related to the Duchess Regent of Savoy, the Queen of Portugal and Austrian Marshal Prince Eugene who was his cousin. It should be added that Vendôme was gay and one of his main lovers was an Italian priest who later became a cardinal, which reveals the remarkable tolerance for individuals at the pinnacles of society. Although holding several protocolary command posts such a general of the king's galley fleet (1659–1694), he went into the army at 18 where he was revealed to be a fine tactician and became lieutenant-general in 1688. He distinguished himself during the War of the League of Augsburg at Steenkirk and Marsaglia, then in command of the invasion army of Catalonia, he captured Barcelona in 1697. During the War of the Spanish Succession, he was sent to command in northern Italy following Marshal Villeroy's capture at Cremona, won the field at Cassano in August 1705, then defeated his cousin Prince Eugene's Austrian army at Calcinato the following year. Put in joint but somewhat subordinate command of the Duc de Bourgogne's army in Flanders. Vendôme was far more experienced and a better tactician so both commanders quarrelled and he could not prevent the disastrous defeat at Oudenarde on 11 July 1708. Disgusted, he retired to his estates, but the old Sun King was desperately looking for good commanders and he was sent to Spain to command King Felipe V's Hispano-French armies. On 8 and 10 December 1710 at Brihuega and Villaviciosa, he defeated the opposing allied armies which absolutely secured Louis XIV's grandson as King of Spain. Vendôme died of natural causes in Spain on 11 June 1712 and a grateful Felipe V had his remains interred in the royal vault in the Escorial palace.

6-7 Louis-Joseph de Bourbon, Duc de Vendôme, c.1710. Following Berwick's successes in Spain, his 1710 victories confirmed the Sun King's grandson as king of Spain "and the Indies". As can be seen in this print after Maurin, he wears the Spanish Order of the Golden Fleece with the French Order Saint-Esprit. Private collection. Author's photo.

Marshals and Generals

As in any army, only a few of all the marshals and generals listed below were outstanding commanders and remembered as recognised contributors to the art of war in all its aspects. However, Turenne, Catinat and Villars are still remembered as some of the best and, most of all, Vauban, the great engineer known the world over.

Originating in the Middle Ages, the rank of *Maréchal de France* (marshal of France) had become, by the 17th century, the highest for a non-royal family officer commanding an army. It should not be confused, as it routinely is by non-French authors, with a *maréchal de camp* or *maréchal général des logis*, both of which were major-generals, or still with a cavalry *maréchal des logis* which was and still is a senior sergeant in francophone armies. Between 1668 and 1709, 36 marshals were appointed by the Sun King. Marshals were allowed the highest honours such as being made peers of the kingdom and were to be addressed as *Monseigneur* (My Lord). Their command batons were covered with blue velvet embroidered with golden lilies. Drums beat and trumpets played when they came by and troops presented arms only to them and to members of the royal family.

Lieutenant-generals were more numerous. There were 54 in 1650 and numbers kept rising thereafter as did the number of major-generals. Between 1661 and 1715, some 307 lieutenant-generals (including 10 in the navy) and 544 major-generals (including one in the navy) were appointed. Their command baton was of varnished wood without any decoration. Drums beat when they came into camp, but their honours were far fewer than for marshals, and knightly orders might or might not be awarded.

Until 1 August 1675, promotions for generals were granted. Senior officials, ministers and the King himself were thus permanently subject to demands for promotions. This took a lot of time and tact with results that did not necessarily make anyone happy. The more suave and smooth courtiers, some of whom were favourites at court, might be advantaged while their military qualities did not really equate to a promotion. Some 20 promotions to lieutenant-general were made this way, over half of them (55 percent) termed as exceptional.

To solve at least in part this situation, the Sun King approved *L'Ordre du tableau* that was used from August 1675. Henceforth, all general officers were inscribed on a list by seniority – the *tableau* – with promotion now being tied to seniority. This, as Voltaire pointed out, no longer made noble birth a factor for promotion. Possibly its most bitter critic was the Duc de Saint-Simon who felt that it encouraged ignorance and a lax attitude since promotions were somewhat automatic, but one must not forget that Saint-Simon was himself a mediocre colonel who never made it to general. The system was not hermetic and the King could and sometimes did tamper with the list, often on advice of ministers and senior officials. There was still room for "exceptional" promotions although these decreased greatly following 1675 while the number of lieutenant-generals greatly increased:

1 August 1675 to 24 August 1688: 41 including 8 exceptional (19.5%)
24 August 1688 to 29 January 1702: 92 including 4 exceptional (4.3%)
29 January 1702 to 1715: 154 including 19 exceptional (12.3%)

With regard to higher command, the leadership of armies was still entirely a political and royal decision with regard to which marshals or royal princes would lead an army. This resulted, especially later in the reign, in some very poor choices being made. One thinks here of marshals La Feuillade, Villeroi and the Duc de Bourgogne. The War of Devolution had seen such talents as Condé and Turenne, the Dutch War involved the same two with Luxembourg, the War of the League of Augsburg had Luxembourg again with Catinat and the War of the Spanish Succession Vendôme and Villars with, we would add as near seconds, Boufflers and especially Berwick who is often forgotten because he was mainly in Spain. Most of these later marshals had risen as generals through the *Ordre du tableau* system.

The system, which became more rigid from 1688 to 1702, thereafter was relaxed somewhat, due to the imperatives of a difficult war. Whatever its shortfalls, the system provided sufficient numbers of experienced senior commanders for an army that mustered several hundreds of thousands of men – something unseen since the days of Imperial Rome. It was thanks to these now largely forgotten generals of all grades whose quiet, unknown yet relentless service maintained the fighting qualities of the army and ensured its cohesion. That was easy enough in victorious wars, but its real test came in the early 18th century when the French army, mauled by opponents whose commanders were often superior to its own leaders, never collapsed as an institution and, indeed, rose again and again, and on to victories when well led.[6]

With regards to staff officers, French princes, marshals and lieutenant-generals commanding armies were always seen on campaign with numerous subaltern officers as well as their personal guard unit. These staff officers would include a *maréchal de camp* acting as chief of staff, a *maréchal des batailles* responsible to line up units for combat and a *maréchal général des logis* who looked after camps and logistics, all of whom were usually major-generals. There might also be present a *maréchal général de l'infanterie* and a *maréchal général de la cavalerie* who were major-generals looking after the infantry and cavalry units respectively. They were assisted by *aides-majors* while *commissaires des guerres* were responsible for supplying and paying the troops. Senior engineer and artillery officers were also attached to the general staff. Marshals were allowed four aides-de-camp, lieutenant-generals in command of an army three and other lieutenant-generals two. Aides-de-camp had the rank of captain and were only allowed when the general officer was on campaign. They were chosen by the general and were usually, like today, ambitious young officers seeking promotions by serving on the staff. They were often from the general's family or circle of friends, sometimes supernumerary officers and very rarely officers detached from line units.[7]

Effective communications between the commander of an army and the head of state demanded an effective system of couriers. There had been royal household couriers until 1608 when King Henri IV, unsatisfied by their lax service, privatised the service. It was organised as a private monopoly company administered by the *Ferme des Postes*, which charged for the mail services. This

---

6   André Corvisier, 'Les généraux de Louis XIV et leur origine sociale', *XVIIe siècle*, (1959): 23–53; Léon Hennet, *Notices historiques sur l'État-Major* (Paris: L. Baudoin, 1892), pp. 1–10, 30–33, 49–50, 115–117, 149.
7   Hennet, *Notices historiques sur l'État-Major*, pp. 102, 115–117; Corvisier, *Dictionnaire d'art et d'histoire militaires*, p. 282. As seen above, until the War of Devolution, commanders of brigades were chosen from colonels and appointed for a limited time. From June 1667, the rank of brigadier of cavalry was made permanent by the Sun King and permanent infantry brigadiers created from May 1668. This rank was not purchased, was also accessible to lieutenant-colonels and allowed the king to reward meritorious officers without regards to birthright or money. The rank of brigadier thus became the first rank as general officer and opened the way to higher grades. This important innovation in the structure of higher command was copied in all armies.

monopoly became total even in the army in January 1629 when lieutenant-generals and other officers were ordered to use only the ordinary postal service. At times, officers were detached for exceptionally important news such as a major defeat or victory, but, otherwise, the carrying of dispatches between the battle zones and the royal court was usually performed by *chevaucheurs* (horse riders) who officially became *Maîtres de Poste* (postmasters). This system remained basically the same until the French Revolution.[8]

Marshals of France Appointed During the Reign of Louis XIV

Listed below are the generals who became marshals from 1638, the year Louis XIV was born. Some 36 were nominated from the time Louis XIV assumed full power during 1661. In fact, he waited some years and it was not until 1668 that he started appointing marshals and this eventually included five for the navy who were in fact admirals. The year of appointment is given after the marshal's name.

Also, we must stress that for even the highest-ranking general officers, this was an age different from our own on an essential point. Nowadays, generals are to be found in command centres or vehicles far from the heart of the battlefield and their safety is a major concern. In the age of the Sun King, a senior officer's honour rested upon his presence on the battlefield and he shared dangers with his men. It was dangerous business as proven by Marshal Turenne being killed by a stray cannonball. Five other marshals perished in action during Louis XIV's reign. Marshals Boufflers and Villars were both wounded at Malplaquet. And where was Villars three years later at his great victory of Denain? Leading his men in a charge. Which says it all. There were enormous social and class differences between a marshal and a private soldier but, unlike today, they equally faced death and glory together.

Charles de La Porte, Duc de la Meilleraie. 1639. Was considered the best French general to carry out siege operations during the Thirty Years' War. Highly educated and a friend of philosopher Descartes. Died in 1664.

Antoine, Duc de Gramont. 1641. Served in Italy, Flanders and Germany. Sent by Louis XIV to Spain to negotiate the King's marriage to the infanta Marie-Thérèse. Died in 1678.

Jean-Baptiste Budes, Comte de Guébriant. 1642. Campaigned during the Thirty Years' War, killed in action at Rothwell, Germany, in 1643. Very esteemed as a soldier; buried in pomp at Notre-Dame.

Philippe de La Mothe-Houdancourt, Duc de Cardonne. 1642. Campaigned mostly in Catalonia during the Thirty Years' War. Died in 1657.

---

8   Frémont, *Les payeurs d'armées. Historique du service de la Trésorerie et des Postes aux armées* (Paris: Plon, 1906), pp. 62–64.

THE ARMIES AND WARS OF THE SUN KING 1643–1715: VOLUME 1

6-8 (right): Marshal Antoine, Duc de Gramont. Antoine III de Gramont, c.1666. Rijksmuseum, Amsterdam. RP-P-BI-7520.

6-9 (below) Marshal Charles de La Porte, Duc de la Meilleraie, c.1662. Made marshal in 1639. Print after Robert Nanteuil. Rijskmuseum, Amsterdam. RP-P-OB-21.206.

6-10 (below right): Marshal Jean-Baptiste Budes, Comte de Guébriant. Promoted marshal of France in 1642, but killed in action at Rothwell, Germany, in 1643. Chateau de Bussy-Rabutin, Burgundy. Author's photo.

SENIOR OFFICIALS AND OFFICERS

Francois de l'Hospital, Comte du Hallier. 1643. Campaigned during the Thirty Years' War and notably played a distinguished role at the Battle of Rocroi in 1643. Died in 1660.

Henri de La Tour d'Auvergne, Vicomte et Prince de Turenne. 1643. Born in 1611 at Sédan, son of Vicomte Henri de Turenne. Early years in Dutch army fighting the Spanish under his cousins Maurice and Henry of Nassau; to French service in 1630; campaigns during the Thirty Years' War revealed him to be an excellent tactician; major-general in 1634 and marshal at 32 years old. Initially with the Fronde in 1649, defeated at Rethel by Choiseul (1650) and rallied to the royal camp; defeated Condé and secured Paris (1652); defeated Condé leading the Spanish at Arras (1654), beaten at Valenciennes (1656), but won the decisive Battle of the Dunes (1658). He was influential in diplomatic affairs relating to military matters during Cardinal Mazarin's government and in the early years of Louis XIV's rule. Led the French army in Flanders during the War of Devolution. Compelled to withdraw from the Rhine in 1673 by General Montecuccoli, but won at Sinsheim and Entzheim in Alsace (1674); by an audacious manoeuvre through mountains in winter, he defeated the Elector of Brandenburg's army at Turckheim (5 January 1675) which compelled the Elector's withdrawal across the Rhine. This campaign has remained a classic example of the war of movement initiated by Turenne. But his reputation was somewhat tarnished because he let his troops ravage the Palatinate in 1674. Killed by a cannonball at the battle of Salzbach on 27 July 1675. His opponent, General Montecuccoli could not prevent an orderly retreat of the French army. Turenne was one of the greatest field commanders of his era, undoubtedly one of the Sun King's greatest marshals and some say the best. His great strategic and tactical eye was actually the result of assiduous observation computed by an agile and sharp mind. Hard intellectual work was required from his staff officers. Like all great commanders, Turenne prepared with great care his battle plans while nevertheless leaving options for the inevitable surprises during an engagement. As a person, he had a humble outlook in an age of ostentatious luxury and pride; his lifestyle was more reserved than other marshals and generals. Andrew Ramzay in his biography of Turenne mentioned that when he spoke of his victories, he always said "our victories" in deference to his soldiers. He had the "common touch" and was beloved by his soldiers and by the people of France for whom he became a legend. When, in 1793, French revolutionaries shattered the royal family coffins at Saint-Denis, they came upon his remains there and carefully protected then. One of his greatest admirers, Napoleon, had them transferred to the Invalides.

6-11 Coat of arms of Marshal Henri de La Tour d'Auvergne, Vicomte et Prince de Turenne. Quarters 1 and 4 silver tower and gold lilies on blue, quarter 2 red balls on gold, quarter 3 red and gold, escutcheon half red tipped green on gold and silver bar on red. From a mural painting. Musée Condé, Chantilly. Author's photo.

Jean, Comte de Gassion. 1643. Campaigned during the Thirty Years' War in Germany under Gustavus Adolphus of Sweden and, back in France, introduced Swedish tactics in the French cavalry with decisive results at Rocroi in 1643. Killed at Lens in 1647.

Josais, Comte de Rantzau. 1645. A Danish officer who first served in Sweden and in the French army during the Thirty Years' War. Very brave and suffered many wounds at Dole, Arras and Honnecourt, became Catholic and made marshal at 36, but in 1649 Cardinal Mazarin suspected him of wrongdoings, had him jailed, which is where he died 11 months later.

César, Duc de Choiseul, Comte du Plessis-Praslin. 1645. Campaigned in Catalonia during the Thirty Years' War taking Rosas in 1645; a skilful tactician who, during the Fronde, defeated even Turenne at Rethel in 1650 during his short service with the princes. Later taught the art of war to young Louis XIV who appreciated his tutor enough to tell him that "what is impossible for others is only difficult for you." Became a diplomat in the later 1660s and negotiated the British alliance against the Netherlands. Died in 1675.

Nicolas de Neufville, Duc de Villeroi. 1646. Campaigned during the Thirty Years' War; superintendent of young Louis XIV in 1646. Awarded many honours and assumed high court functions including chairman of the royal board of finance in 1661. Died in 1685. His son François de Neufville, Duc de Villeroi became marshal in 1693.

Hans Ludwig Erlach, 1650. Also known as Jean Louis Erlach, he was born in Bern in 1595, first served in Germany and entered the French army in 1630. His services were such that they drew admiration from the Prince of Condé and Marshal Turenne, arguably amongst the greatest tacticians of the time. In January 1650, he was elevated to the rank of marshal of France, but sadly died a few days later. He was the only Swiss soldier to attain the dignity of marshal of France and it occurred during the reign of young Louis XIV.

Antoine de Rochebaron. Duc d'Aumont. 1651. Fought at Rethel in 1650, governor of Paris in 1662. Led an army corps and took several fortresses during the 1667 War of Devolution. Died in 1669.

Jacques d'Étampes, Seigneur de La Ferté-Imbault. 1651. Ambassador to England in 1641, campaigned in Flanders in 1646–1648. Died in 1668.

Charles de Monchy, Marquis d'Hocquincourt. 1651. During the Fronde, he contributed to Turenne's defeat at Rethel in 1650, which earned him the rank of marshal, but was beaten by Condé at Bléneau in 1652. Then went to command the army of Catalonia. Later joined Condé and surrendered to him the towns of Ham and Péronne which Condé sold back to the royal government. Now in Condé's Spanish army, he was sent to defend Dunkirk attacked by French and British troops in 1658 and was killed in action there. "He was not very bright", recalled Bussy-Rabutin.

6-12 Marshal Hans Ludwig Erlach, 1650. Also known as Jean Louis Erlach, the only Swiss general to achieve the rank of marshal of France. His crest was red with blue chevrons on silver. Print after Burthard Mangold. Private collection. Author's photo.

Henri de Senneterre, Duc de La Ferté. 1651. Distinguished himself at La Rochelle in 1628. Commanded the right of the French army at Rocroi where he was wounded by two pistol shots and two sword blows, had two horses killed under him and nevertheless led his men in the thickest fighting that overwhelmed the Spanish. Remained loyal to the crown during the Fronde. Took Chasté, Miirecourt, Vaudrevrange, Montmedy and Gravelines between 1651 and 1658. Died at 82 years old in 1680.

Jacques Rouxel de Médavy, Comte de Grangey. 1651. Born in 1603 and took part in all campaigns during Louis XIII's reign; lieutenant-general in 1644, defeated Spanish in Piemont in early 1650s; governor of Thionville in 1662. Died in 1680.

Armand-Nompar de Caumont, Duc de La Force. 1652. Campaigned during the Thirty Years' War, notably at the capture of Corbie in 1636. Died at 95 in 1675.

Philippe de Clérambault, Comte de Palluau. 1652. Born in 1606, entered the army at 16, and campaigned during the Thirty Years' War; lieutenant-general in 1648; governor of Berry province in 1661. Died in 1665.

César-Phoebus d'Albret, Comte de Miossens. 1653. A courtesan close to the Queen Mother and Cardinal Mazarin; governor of Guyenne province. A man of much wit "and even more of intrigue" according to the Duc de Saint-Simon; "esteemed in war" and an early lover of Madame de Maintenon according to Voltaire. Died in 1676.

Jean de Schulemberg, Comte de Montdejeu. 1658. Of Prussian origin. Campaigned during the Thirty Years' War; defence of Arras in 1654. Died in 1671.

Marquis de Castelnau-Maurissière. 1658. Campaigned with distinction during the Thirty Years' War and the 1650s war with Spain; mortally wounded at the Battle of the Dunes and awarded the rank of Marshal of France on his deathbed.

Abraham de Fabert. 1658. Entered the army in 1614 when he was 14 years old; noticed for valour at the 1628 siege of La Rochelle. Campaigned with distinction during the Thirty Years' War, remained with the royal army during the Fronde; lieutenant-general in 1651; took Stenay in 1654 with young Louis XIV present; was a remarkable engineer and introduced parallels and cavaliers in siege trenches. He was remembered as a brilliant officer of great courage, loyalty and humanity. He was uninterested in politics and declined participating in plots against Cardinals Richelieu and Mazarin. According to Voltaire, it was said that Cardinal Mazarin asked him to spy on other officers to which he replied: "Perhaps a minister needs brave men and knaves; I can only be of the first type." He was the first *roturier* (non-noble) to become a marshal of France. He died in 1662.

6-13 Marshal Abraham de Fabert, c.1660. Print after Edelinck. Private collection. Author's photo.

Bernardin Gigault, Marquis de Bellefond. 1668. Governor of Valogne (Normandy) in 1643, in the royal troops during the Fronde in 1649; favourite of the young king; lieutenant-general in 1655, distinguished service at Tournai in 1659; eight wounds during campaigns of War of Devolution; during the Dutch War, he disobeyed Marshal Créqui thus gaining a victory as a result in 1672 and refused to apply the 1673 order for evacuating Dutch fortresses – two happy instances of disobedience according to Chateaubriand – but banished by the King to his estate; back in grace, he took Gerona in Catalonia in 1684. He died in 1694.

Louis de Crevant, Duc d'Humières. 1668. Well-connected courtier of the King and friend of Louvois; governor of French Flanders; refused to serve under Turenne in 1672. Grand master of artillery in 1685. Died in 1694.

François, Chevalier de Créqui. 1669. He was also Marquis de Marines. Créqui (1625–1687) fought against Condé during the Fronde and the 1650s Spanish war. Campaigned in the 1667 War of Devolution and defeated the Spanish attempting to relieve Lille besieged by an army led by Louis XIV. Regarded as a brilliant officer, he was a rival of Marshal Turenne and was briefly exiled to his estate for refusing to serve under him in 1672; ironically, Créqui replaced Turenne after he was killed in 1675. Créqui participated in the captures of Fribourg and Khel; successful invasion of Luxembourg (1684). Was a tutor of future Marshal Villars to whom he once said: "Young

SENIOR OFFICIALS AND OFFICERS

man, if God preserves your life, you will have my place [as marshal] sooner than anyone."

François-Henri de Montmorency-Bouteville, Duc de Luxembourg. 1675. His father, the Comte de Luxembourg, was quite the swordsman and duellist who sent many an opponent to Heaven; he then disobeyed King Louis XIII's order to stop it and was beheaded as a result. Thus, when François-Henri was born, his father had departed six months earlier and he was raised in a rough and ready way, barely a teenager and said to be humpback when he joined the army. During the Fronde, he was with Condé, but rallied the royal camp; he campaigned hard and rose in rank to lieutenant-general, his keen tactical eye and his leadership qualities with his men being appreciated by nearly all. Minister of War Louvois, however, was less appreciative and managed to get Luxembourg accused by proxy into the "Poisons affair" from which he was cleared of any wrongdoing, but was nevertheless somewhat retired from the army following his loss of Philippsburg in 1676 until the War of the League of Augsburg. Louis XIV, increasingly looking for good general officers, entrusted him with the command of armies in the north-east where Luxembourg won the battles of Fleurus (1690), Steenkirk (1692) and Neerwinden (1693). Some battles were close calls, the allies also claiming success, but the flow of captured enemy colours going to Paris was such that he was nicknamed the *tapissier de Notre-Dame* (roughly translated, the decorator of that famous church). Not only was Luxembourg one of Louis XIV's best marshals, he could also be quite the wit. When told that William of Orange had loudly uttered, "Will I never be able to beat this damned humpback", Luxembourg replied: "How does he know I am a humpback? He never saw my back!" He passed away in 1695.

François d'Aubusson, Duc de La Feuillade. 1675. As a youth, he campaigned against the Spanish and the Turks, took part in the conquest of Franche-Comté and was a fanatic admirer of the Sun King, to the point of demolishing buildings in Paris to create the Place des Victoires featuring

6-14 Coat of arms of Marshal François de Créqui. Red on gold. Made marshal in 1669. From a mural painting. Musée Condé, Chantilly. Author's photo.

6-15 Marshal François-Henri de Montmorency-Bouteville, Duc de Luxembourg, 1694. Promoted to marshal in 1675. His 1690s victories brought so many captured colour to Paris that he was popularly nicknamed the decorator of the great Notre-Dame church. Print after Hyacinthe Rigaud. Rijksmuseum RP-P-OB-15.698

the equestrian statue of Louis XIV, an initiative that cost him a fortune. He was also quite rich. According to Saint-Simon, La Feuillade was an "authentic brigand" who once had seized for himself part of the church treasure held by the Bishop of Metz. Died in 1691.

Louis-Victor de Rochechouart, Duc de Mortemart et de Divonne. 1675. He was more of a naval officer than an army general, commanding the fleet that bombarded Algiers and appointed general of the galley fleet in 1669, but was also wounded when with the army during its 1672 crossing of the Rhine. He was obese, a witty courtier and a woman-chaser so that he was called *le gros crevé* (bursting fatness) by Madame de Sévigny's daughter. She perhaps knew more of his character than most because, after his 1688 death, she wrote that he was just as rotten in his soul as in his body.

Armand-Frédéric de Schomberg. 1675. Born in 1615 in the German Palatinate of a German father and a British mother (Anne Dudley), Schomberg was soon recognised as an exceptionally talented officer, first in Dutch and then French service in 1635 and served under the outstanding Marshal Turenne during the Thirty Years' War. Remained loyal to the crown during the Fronde. In the 1660s, he was sent to Portugal where he decisively defeated the Spanish. Later, in 1675 during the Dutch War, he was made marshal of France by Louis XIV following his capture of Fort Bellegarde. Being of the Protestant faith, he was forced to leave France in 1685 following the revocation of the Edict of Nantes. Rightly recognised as one of the best general officers in the French army, he was greeted with open arms being given overall command of the Brandenburg and, from 1688, of the British armies by William III who also made him duke and a knight of the Order of the Garter. Campaigned in Ireland and killed at the battle of the Boyne in 1690.

Philippe de Montault de Bérac, Duc de Navailles. 1675. Page to Cardinal Richelieu, loyal to Mazarin and the King during the Fronde; governor of Amiens; commanded French contingent to Crete in 1669 that failed to prevent the Ottoman Turks from taking Candie, and exiled for three years by the King; skillful courtier appointed to be *Premier gentilhomme de la chambre* (first gentleman of the chamber) and finance superintendent to the Duc de Chartres (future regent of France). Died in 1684.

Godefroi, Comte d'Estrades. 1675. Initially actually a secret agent of Cardinal Richelieu in several countries and a diplomat that also served in the army; governor of Dunkirk and of Aunis province; command of the French army in Catalonia where he defeated the Spanish in 1655. Negotiated the restitution of Dunkirk to France in 1659 and the 1678 peace of Nijmegen. Died in 1684.

Jacques-Henri de Durfort, Duc de Duras, 1675. Nephew of Turenne, campaigned during the Thirty Years' War; joined Condé who made him lieutenant-general during the Fronde, but went over to the royal forces in 1657 with that rank; governor of Flanders and Franche-Comté. Died in 1704.

Plate 1

(L–R): Gardes du Corps guardsman, *c*.1645–1656; Guard of the Duc de Beaufort 1660s; Gardes du Corps guardsman, 1st (Scottish) Company, *c*.1667–1668

(Illustration by Ed Dovey, © Helion & Company)

See Colour Plate Commentaries for further information.

Plate 2

(L–R): Officer, Gardes Suisses, *c*.1665–1670; pertuisanier, Gardes Françaises, *c*.1660–1670; pikeman, Gardes Suisses, mid-1660s to mid-1670s

(Illustration by Ed Dovey, © Helion & Company)

See Colour Plate Commentaries for further information.

Plate 3

(L–R): Gardes Françaises, private, *c*.1679; Gardes Françaises, sergeant, 1679; Grenadier à Cheval de la Garde, trooper, 1677–1678

(Illustration by Ed Dovey, © Helion & Company)

See Colour Plate Commentaries for further information.

Plate 4

(L–R): Gardes Françaises, sergeant, *c.*1695; Guard of the Prince of Conti, *c.*1690; 1st Company of the Mousquetaires du Roi (King's Musketeers), trooper, late 17th century

(Illustration by EdDovey, © Helion & Company)
See Colour Plate Commentaries for further information.

Plate 5

(L–R): Cent-Suisses de la Garde, guardsman fifer, *c.*1700; Gendarmerie de la Garde, trooper *c.*1704–1714; Marshal Villars' Bodyguard *c.*1704–1714

(Illustration by Ed Dovey, © Helion & Company)

See Colour Plate Commentaries for further information.

Plate 6

Louis XIV feigning sleep as militiamen of the Fronde pass by his bed on the night of 5–6 January 1649. Queen Mother Anne of Austria is at his side. This humiliating incident profoundly marked Louis XIV for the rest of his long life.
Print after Maurice Leloir. Private collection. Author's photo.

Plate 7

Young Louis XIV summons and disolves the Paris Parliament, March 1655. He is said to have proclaimed *l'état c'est moi* (I am the state) before dissolving the assembly.
Print after Maurice Leloir. Private collection. Author's photo.

Plate 8

Above: the Battle of the Dunes, 14 June 1658. French and British troops (wearing red coats) attack and overcome a redoubt defended by Spanish troops. This outstanding victory by Marshal Turenne led to a peace treaty.
Print after Maurice Leloir. Private collection. Author's photo.

Right: The French army in trenches during the siege of Tournai in late June 1667. At the right foreground, a royal servant wearing a blue livery coats hold the Sun King's white horse. The king is hazily seen in the background standing above the trench.
Painting by van der Meulen. Musée Magnin, Dijon. Author's photo.

Plate 9

Plate 10

The Dauphin de France as commander of the army in Germany, *c.*1688. This print gives a view of a senior commander's office in the field, that was suitably luxurious for enduring the rigours of a campaign.

Anne S.K. Brown Military Collection, Brown University Library, Providence, RI, USA. Author's photo.

Plate 11

Trooper of the personal guard of Marshal Luxembourg with a royal page, 1685. Luxembourg's guard (foreground right) was dressed in the very colourful livery shown, buff lined with blue and featuring multicoloured sleeves. The royal page (left) wears the king's blue livery lined with red and heavily decorated with royal livery lace.

Print after Alfred de Marbot. Canadian War Museum, Ottawa. Author's photo.

Three members of the royal guard, *c.*1660. Left, the ceremonial unit of Gentilhommes Ordinaires de la Garde was nicknamed *à Bec de Corbin* due to the ornate axe that distinguished it. Centre, a Garde du Corps wearing a blue cassock with the badge of an embroidered cross formed by 12 lilies and four royal crowns. At right, an archer of the Gardes de la Prévôté de l'Hôtel in the red, white and blue embroidered hocqueton surcoat.

Print after Alfred de Marbot. Canadian War Museum, Ottawa. Author's photo.

Plate 12

The Sun King's personal palace guards. At left, a member of the elite Garde de la Manche of the Gardes du corps and, at right, a guardsman of the Cent-Suisses. Guardsmen from these select units were always close to the king, day or night.
Print after Alfred de Marbot. Canadian War Museum, Ottawa. Author's photo.

Plate 13

Left: a member of the Gardes du Corps, *c*.1675. The unit was now clothed in the blue and red hues of the royal livery. It is difficult to tell if an officer or a trooper is shown since all were noblemen although the cane might indicate a command function. The bandolier is blue and silver indicating the 2nd (1st French) Company.

Anne S.K. Brown Military Collection, Brown University Library, Providence, RI, USA. Author's photo.

Right: a trooper of the Gardes du Corps, *c*.1675–1685. The bandoleer is yellow, which would indicate the 4th (3rd French) Company. The barrel of his rifled musket is shown as remarkably long.

Print after H. Bonnart's Recueil des modes de la cour de France. Courtesy Los Angeles County Museum of Art. M.2002.57.103.

Plate 14

Plate 15

Above: Trumpeter and kettle drummer of the Gardes du Corps, early 18th century.
Print after Alfred de Marbot. Canadian War Museum, Ottawa. Author's photo.

Left: Gardes du Corps troopers, palace guard duty, early 18th century. Both are dressed and accoutred for palace service on foot. At right the uniform worn in the last years of Louis XIVs reign and the early years of Louis XV's; the yellow and silver bandolier indicates de Lorges 3rd Company. At left, a member of the elite squad of the Gardes de la Manche (guards of the [king's] sleeve) wearing its magnificent and distinctive surcoat that was part of the of the 1st (Scottish) Company.
Watercolour by Lucien Rousselot. Courtesy Anne S.K. Brown Military Collection, Brown University Library, Providence, RI, USA.

Plate 16

Plate 17

Above: Personnel of the Cent-Suisses de la Garde, early 18th century. From the left: a captain in ceremonial dress; a subaltern officer wearing the scarlet officer's uniform laced with gold – note the polished steel gorget worn by Swiss officers in French service; a guardsman wearing the traditional so-called Swiss costume garnished with royal livery lace and a more modern tricorn.

Print after Alfred de Marbot. Canadian War Museum, Ottawa. Author's photo.

Left: Annual grand banquet of the Order of the Saint-Esprit, 1640s. The banquet was part of the annual meeting of the order that occurred yearly on 31 December and was presided over by the king. For the event, knights wore an elaborate 16th century-style white costume that was covered by the luxurious black velvet cloak embroidered with gold with the order's full gilt and enamel collar. A black cap with a plume completed their dress. The clergy members kept their own habits (upper left) and only had the sky blue neck ribbon for their badge. Bearded guardsmen of the Cent-Suisses wearing the royal livery serve the meat dishes to the knights under the scrutiny of their maître d'hôtel holding a halberd with a gilded head.

Detail from period painting. Power Corporation Art Collection, Montreal. Author's photo.

Plate 18

Left: Colour of the Cent-Suisses, early 18th century. Throughout the reign, details on this elaborate and complex colour vary depending on the sources. This reconstruction is mainly based on Hermand's and Delaistre's plates.
Private collection. Author's photo.

Right: A company colour of the Gardes Françaises Regiment, early 18th century. The gold lilies in the blue quarters were disposed upright from the early 18th century.
Anne S.K. Brown Military Collection, Brown University Library, Providence, RI, USA. Author's photo.

xviii

Plate 19

Left: A Garde de la Porte (left) with a trooper of the Garde du Corps, c.1688. The Garde du Corps trooper is from the 3rd Luxembourg's company, which had a green bandolier, and is shown for palace duty on foot. Print after Alfred de Marbot.
Canadian War Museum, Ottawa. Author's photo.

Right: Gardes de la Porte, early 18th century. From the left: a guard and an officer. Print after Alfred de Marbot.
Canadian War Museum, Ottawa. Author's photo.

Plate 20

Above: Gardes de la Prévôté de l'Hôtel, early 18th century. From the left: a guard and an officer. Print after Alfred de Marbot.
Canadian War Museum, Ottawa. Author's photo.

Right, top: Troopers of the Chevau-Légers de la Garde and Gendarmes de la Garde, 1660.
Print after Alfred de Marbot. Canadian War Museum, Ottawa. Author's photo.

Right, bottom: Captain-Lieutenant of the Gendarmes de la Garde and trooper of the Chevau-Légers de la Garde, 1694.
Print after Alfred de Marbot. Canadian War Museum, Ottawa. Author's photo.

Plate 21

Plate 22

Plate 23

Left: The Mousquetaires du Roi, 1663. At left, a trooper of the 1st Company recognizable by the red flames at the cross on his cassock; at right, a trooper of the 2nd Company distinguished by golden yellow flames.

Below: The Mousquetaires du Roi, 1676 and 1688. The cassock became very cumbersome as seen in the 1676 figure at left. Radical improvement came in 1688 with the introduction of the sleeveless *soubreveste* jacket.

Both prints after Alfred de Marbot. Canadian War Museum, Ottawa. Author's photos.

Left: Detail of Pierre-Denis Martin's rendering of the Lit de Justice ceremony at the Paris Parliament, 12 September 1715. The scarlet-coated troopers have black cuffs and thus belong to the Gendarmes de la Garde. The blue-uniformed infantry with white and silver lace belongs to the Gardes Françaises. Most of the carriage's footmen wear the blue king's livery, but a few have red coats and buff or yellow livery coats that may indicate the dukes of Maine or Vendôme and the princes of Conti or Condé.

Musée Carnavalet, Paris. Author's photo.

xxiii

Above: Trumpeter and kettle drummer of the Mousquetaires du Roi, early 18th century.
Print after Alfred de Marbot. Canadian War Museum, Ottawa. Author's photo.

Right, top: Colour of the 1st Company of the Mousquetaires du Roi, early 18th century. Colours were used when serving on foot.
Anne S.K. Brown Military Collection, Brown University Library, Providence, RI, USA. Author's photo.

Right, bottom: Colour of the 2nd Company of the Mousquetaires du Roi, early 18th century.
Anne S.K. Brown Military Collection, Brown University Library, Providence, RI, USA. Author's photo.

Plate 25

xxv

Plate 26

Above: Trooper and captain-lieutenant of the Grenadier à cheval de la Garde, early 18th century.
Print after Alfred de Marbot. Canadian War Museum, Ottawa. Author's photo

Right: Drummer and brigadier NCO of the Grenadier à cheval de la Garde, early 18th century.
Print after Alfred de Marbot. Canadian War Museum, Ottawa. Author's photo.

Plate 27

Right: Drummer of the Gardes-Françaises Regiment, early 18th century. His coat is garnished with the king's grand livery lace that also covers the drum collar. The drum is shown as plain but would have the royal coat of arm painted thereon.

Print after Alfred de Marbot. Canadian War Museum, Ottawa. Author's photo.

Left: Gardes- Françaises, enlisted men, 1685. On 24 March 1685, the regiment paraded before the king wearing its new uniform, blue lined with red. Some two centuries later, the great military illustrator Richard Knötel reconstructed what the soldiers might have looked like in 1685 by adapting figures in Mallet's 1684 *Travaux de Mars*, which gives an idea of the men's appearance according to the fashions of the mid-1680s.

Anne S.K. Brown Military Collection, Brown University Library, Providence, RI, USA. Author's photo.

Plate 28

Left: Grenadier of the Gardes Françaises Regiment, *c.*1696. Print after JOB based on the 1696 drill book prints.
Private collection. Author's photo.

Right: An ensign and a company officer of the Gardes Françaises Regiment, *c.*1696.
Print after Alfred de Marbot based on the 1696 drill book prints. Canadian War Museum, Ottawa. Author's photo.

Plate 29

Above: A pikeman and a musketeer of the Gardes Françaises Regiment, c.1696. The pikeman holds the pike and sword drawn, ready to receive an enemy's charge while the musketeer loads.
Print after Alfred de Marbot based on the 1696 drill book prints. Canadian War Museum, Ottawa. Author's photo.

Left: Gardes Suisses Regiment pikeman and musketeer with a sergeant wearing the royal livery, c.1667.
Print after Alfred de Marbot. Canadian War Museum, Ottawa. Author's photo.

Plate 30

Left: Officer of the Gardes-Suisses Regiment, *c.*1696–1700. His spontoon is of course shortened to fit the image.

Print after JOB copied from small images dating from the 1690s. Private collection. Author's photo.

Right: Pikeman of the Gardes Suisses Regiment, *c.*1690.

Print after JOB copied from contemporary small images. Private collection. Author's photo.

Plate 31

Five individuals from the Gardes Suisses Regiment
All courtesy Anne S.K. Brown Military Collection, Brown University Library, Providence, RI, USA.

Above, left: company officer, early 18th century. Company officers were armed with spontoons. Centre: sergeant, early 18th century. Right: *trabant*, early 18th century. The *trabants*, which were peculiar to Swiss regiments, wore the livery of their colonel. In the case of the Gardes Suisses, the king was the colonel and its trabants wore the king's royal livery of blue lined with red decorated with the royal livery lace.

Left: drummer, early 18th century. He is shown wearing the royal livery and its lace, the king being the regiment's colonel.

Right: fusilier, early 18th century. He is presenting arms as per the 1703 drill.

Plate 32

A rare view of the Sun King's era regimental colours of the Gardes Suisses at the Lit de Justice ceremony at the Paris Parliament, 12 September 1715. Until 1715, these colour has seven wavy flames of blue red and yellow in each quarter. Thereafter, a black wavy flame was added in each quarter. This formal event mobilised large detachments of the guard for a very crowded event including at least a company of the red-coated Gardes suisses.

Detail of a painting by Pierre-Denis Martin. Musée Carnavalet, Paris. Author's photo.

SENIOR OFFICIALS AND OFFICERS

Louis d'Aloigny, Marquis de Rochefort. 1675. Initially a guards officer, first with the Prince of Condé's bodyguards, then in Hungary in 1664 where he was wounded in the face and scarred for life; served with Turenne at nine sieges during the War of Devolution, brigadier, governor of Ath in 1667, major-general (1668), lieutenant-general (1672), campaigned in Holland and Germany, commander-in-chief on the Moselle (1676), died from wounds that year.

Guy-Aldonce de Durport de Duras, Duc de Lorges. 1676. Served with Turenne and credited with effecting an orderly retreat that saved his army after Turenne was killed at Salzbach on 27 July 1675. In command of the army in Germany from 1690 to 1696; victorious at Pforzheim were he captured the Prince Charles of Württemberg (17 September 1692) and took Heidelberg (1693). Died in 1703.

6-16 Coat of arms of Marshal Louis d'Aloigny, Marquis de Rochefort. Marshal in 1675. Silver lilies on red. From a mural painting. Musée Condé, Chantilly. Author's photo.

Jean, Comte (and later) Duc d'Estrées. 1681. First served in land armies during the Thirty Years' War, the Fronde, lieutenant-general in 1657, and the War of Devolution, but had disagreements with Louvois and went over to the navy in 1668 in which he had a distinguished if chequered career. Died in 1707.

Anne-Hilaron de Cotentin, Comte de Tourville. 1693. Was first a knight of Malta and campaigned against the Ottoman Turks in the Mediterranean. Entered the French navy as a captain in 1666 where he became one of the noted admirals. Died in 1701.

Louis-François, Duc de Boufflers. 1693. Served with Condé and Turenne in his youth; distinguished as colonel général of dragoons during the Dutch War (1672–1678); fought at Mayence (15 October 1688), Fleurus (1690), Furnes (1693), captured by King William III at Namur (5 September 1695 – see illustration caption). During the War of the Spanish Succession, commanded the army in Flanders (1702) and led the Gardes du Corps in the difficult retreat from Oudenarde (1704); defence of Lille (1708) and continued resistance with the citadel for four months after the town itself had been taken, finally surrendering on order from Louis XIV; commanded with great skill the retreat of the French army at Malplaquet (1709) in which he was wounded, but not as gravely as Marshal Villars whom he replaced; he not only saved the army including all its artillery, but also brought back some 30 colours taken from the enemy. Also intervened in Paris without an escort to successfully calm an angry mob thus ending sedition (see illustration in Vol. 4). He was renowned for his concern for the humble, and Saint-Simon noted of him that he excelled at good "order, exactitude and vigilance" .Although somewhat maligned by historians, one can also add

6-17 (right): Marshal Louis-François, Duc de Boufflers. Promoted to marshal in 1693. Courtesy Anne S.K. Brown Military Collection, Brown University Library, Providence, RI, USA.

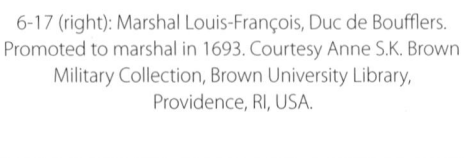

6-18 (left): Marshal Anne-Jules, Duc de Noailles. Promoted to marshal in 1693. Courtesy Anne S.K. Brown Military Collection, Brown University Library, Providence, RI, USA.

that Boufflers was a good marshal often placed in unlucky situations from which he made the best decisions to save his men and their honour from nearly impossible situations. Died in 1711.

Claude de Choiseul, Marquis de Francières. 1693. Joined the army in 1649, campaigns of the Fronde with the royal forces and the Spanish War, became one of the young king's staff officers, governor of Langes (1658); participated in the battle of St. Gotthard (Hungary) against the Ottoman Turks (1664); brigadier and took part in three sieges during the War of Devolution (1667); major-general and defence of Candie in Crete (1669); distinguished at Senef (1674), with Marshal Luxembourg's staff and took Cologne (1676); served in Germany during League of Augsburg War (1688–1698). Retired and died 1711.

Anne-Jules, Duc de Noailles. 1693. Captain of Noailles' company of the Gardes du Corps (1661), siege of Marsal in Lorraine (1663); impeccable courtier and named aide-de-camp to the King, present at conquest of France-Comté (1668), siege of Maastricht (1673), major-general (1677), lieutenant-general (1681); repression of Protestants in Roussillon from 1685, which he is said by some to have done with some clemency while others claim that he was without pity in executing Louvois' cruel orders; in action with his cavalry regiment in many engagements of the War of Augsburg League in Italy and Spain, named viceroy of Catalonia (1694), resigned due to sickness. Died in 1708.

6-19 Marshal François de Neufville, Duc de Villeroy. Promoted to marshal in 1693. Print after H. Rigaud. Courtesy Anne S.K. Brown Military Collection, Brown University Library, Providence, RI, USA.

François de Neufville, Duc de Villeroi. 1693. One of Louis XIV's schoolmates, accomplished courtier; wounded at St. Gotthard in Hungary (1664); in many engagements in War of Devolution and Dutch War; ambassador to Venice (1668); brigadier (1672), major-general (1674), lieutenant-general (1677). A favourite of the King, he was named marshal without having sufficient high command experience; ordered the useless bombardment of Brussels (1693) and his tactical ineptitude could not stop King William III from retaking Namur (1695). Sent to Italy at outset of War of the Spanish Succession, beaten by Prince Eugene at Chiari (1701) and captured at Cremona the following year (see illustration caption in Vol. 4). Defeated at Ramillies (1706) by the Duke of Marlborough losing his artillery, colours and baggage, he was relieved of command by the King who is said to have comforted Villeroi by telling him that "at our age, we are no longer happy." After Louis XIV's death, Villeroi was president of the Finance Council and "governor" of young Louis XV, but after some years, the Regent Duc d'Orléans was displeased and, in 1722, exiled him to his estates. He died aged 86 in 1730.

Nicolas de Catinat de La Fauconnerie. 1693. Initially a lawyer, he joined the Gardes Françaises in 1660 and was noted by Louis XIV for valour at the 1667 siege of Lille; gravely wounded at Senef (1674) where Condé appreciated him enough to write him that "there are so few persons like you; we lose too much when we lose them." He recovered, served with distinction in 1676–1678; major-general in 1680 and lieutenant-general in 1688; took part in siege of Philippsburg (1688) and won at Staffarde (1690) and Marsaglia (1693). Defeated by Prince Eugene at Carpi (1701). Disgraced by the King, he was made second in command of the army in Italy under Marshal Villeroi and managed to lead the army to safety after its defeat at Chiari (1701). Thereafter retired from the service, read philosophy and died "as a sage" at his Saint-Gratien estate in 1712. He had previously turned down Louis' offer to elevate him to the Order of the Holy Spirit.

6-20 Marshal Nicolas de Catinat. A brilliant officer esteemed by Condé and promoted marshal in 1693 following several notable victories. Perhaps too harshly scolded by the king following his not disastrous defeat at Carpi by Prince Eugene, he retired to his estate, read philosophy and refused further honours. Print after C. Vermeulen. Courtesy Anne S.K. Brown Military Collection, Brown University Library, Providence, RI, USA.

Jean-Armand de Joyeuse, Marquis de Grandpré. 1693. Battle (1650) and siege (1652) of Rethel and Stenay (1654); commanded left wing of French army at Neerwinden (1693) where he was wounded; later governor of Metz, Toul and Verdun. Died 1710.

Louis-Hector, Duc de Villars. 1702. Initially a page at the royal court (1670); in the King's Musketeers (1671); colonel of Villars Cavalry Regiment; diplomatic missions in Bavaria and Austria during 1687–1688; *Commissaire Général* of cavalry (1688); lieutenant-general (1693), commanded cavalry in Germany and Italy during War of League of Augsburg. In Germany during 1702 and victorious at Neubourg and Friedlingen where his delirious troops proclaimed him marshal on the battlefield, a "field promotion" approved by the King; wins at Hochstadt (1703); replaced Marshal Montrevel in southern France, negotiated an end of hostilities with the Camisards; made Duc de Villars (1704–1705); commanded with Marshal Boufflers at Malplaquet (1709) where he was badly wounded; commanded French army at decisive victory of Denain (1712) that led to the collapse of the front held by the allied army led by Prince Eugene; negotiated a truce with Prince Eugene at Rastadt in November 1713 leading to the end of the war on 6 March 1714. His outstanding military and diplomatic leadership earned Villars a reputation as one of France's greatest soldiers.

Noël-Bouton, Marquis de Chamilly. 1703. With royal troops during the Fronde; siege of Valenciennes (1656); Flanders and Battle of the Dunes (1658); expeditions to Portugal (1660–1667) wounded at Candie (Crete) in 1668; distinguished at defence of Graves (1674) and promoted lieutenant-general; later governor of Poitou, Saintonge and Aunis provinces. Best known for his 1669 *Lettres Portugaises* that related his torrid affair with a fiery and passionate Portuguese nun, Mariana Alcaforada, which became a bestseller in France and brought him fame. It was suggested that his elevation to marshal at age 67 was due to his *Lettres* as much as to his warlike deeds. Died in 1715.[9]

Sébastien Le Prestre, Marquis de Vauban. 1703. Initially a "poor" young gentleman with Prince Condé's forces during the Fronde; incorporated into royal army by Cardinal Mazarin who had noticed his ability; his great interest in fortifications and technology soon made him a recognised engineer and he was breveted as such in 1655 while keeping his commissions in the infantry, which was then the practice for engineer officers. Over the years, Vauban was made brigadier (1674), major-general (1676), commissioner general of fortifications (1678); lieutenant-general (1688) as well as governor of Lille (1668 and 1684), Douai where he was wounded by a bullet hitting hitting him on the left cheek (1680), and Brest (1694). Although he participated in the campaigns of the wars of Devolution, of Holland and of the League of Augsburg, he did not especially wish to be a marshal, but the King, on whose staff he often was during sieges, nevertheless bestowed the rank in 1703. Vauban was constantly travelling throughout France and its frontiers; he is said to have had repaired and upgraded at least 300 forts and fortresses and also had 33 new ones built on his plans. This was partly the result of his and Chamlay's advice to Louis XIV. The borders needed coherent fortifications systems made up of fortresses built at strategic sites that could interact with each other. He also revolutionised the conception of fortification design of which there were three successive versions (see Volume 4 of this series for a more detailed discussion of Vauban's systems as well as military engineering in the era of the Sun King). Vauban also wrote political studies, notably his study of the harmful effects of the Revocation of the Edict of Nantes (1685) and his *Dîme Royale* memoir which argued for a tax system for all Frenchmen according to their income. It was published in 1707 and it has often been said that Louis XIV was angered by this work and that the Paris Parliament had it burned. According to Saint-Simon, the privileged were very upset and the king disgraced him. All this was unfounded rumour. In fact, the king had read the memoir in 1700 and not acted upon it. Seven years

6-21 Marshal Louis-Hector, Duc de Villars. Promoted to marshal in 1702. He is shown wearing the Order of the Golden Fleece awarded by King Felipe V of Spain. The wide silk ribbon over his breastplate would be sky blue denoting the Order of the Holy Spirit. Frontispiece engraving from his memoirs. Private collection. Author's photo.

---

9   *Lettres portugaises traduites en françois* (Paris: Barbin, 1669) and many reprints as well as two cinema production in 2009 and 2014.

6-22 (left): Marshal Sébastien Le Prestre de Vauban. Promoted to marshal in 1703. Arguably the greatest military engineer of modern times. The large black dot on his left cheek is the mark of a wound from a spent bullet. Print after a circa 1705 sketch by Lebrun. Château de Bazoches-du-Morvan, Burgundy. Author's photo.

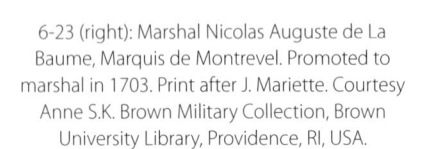

6-23 (right): Marshal Nicolas Auguste de La Baume, Marquis de Montrevel. Promoted to marshal in 1703. Print after J. Mariette. Courtesy Anne S.K. Brown Military Collection, Brown University Library, Providence, RI, USA.

SENIOR OFFICIALS AND OFFICERS

later Vauban was very ill and had quietly retired to his Château de Bazoche in Burgundy where he passed away on 30 March, only two months after the publication of the memoir. Reforming France's ancient and inefficient tax system was surely beyond the possibilities of the ageing Sun King and his government now engaged in a very difficult war. Vauban, however, obviously retained the esteem of his royal master.

Nicolas Auguste de La Baume, Marquis de Montrevel. 1703. As a young officer, he was fond of duels enough to be exiled for a while after bringing down two opponents in the 1650s; wounded during the War of Devolution; one of the first to cross the Rhine into Holland (1672); Luxembourg (1684); lieutenant-general (1693), campaigns in Flanders. Sent to repress Protestant Camisard revolts in Cévennes in 1703, had 466 villages burned, but this only spread the revolt even more and Montrevel was recalled. Montrevel did not impress the Duc de Saint-Simon who felt he was an idiot as well as a "base and miserable courtier." Died aged 70 in 1716.

Ferdinand, Comte de Marchin. 1703. His name is sometime given as Marsin. Courtier, commanded the Gendarmes de Flandres in late 1680s; wounded at Fleurus (1690), major-general (1693); campaigns in Flanders during the War of League of Augsburg, notably at Neerwinden and Charleroi; lieutenant-general (1695); ambassador to Spain (1701–1702); at Blenheim (1704); sent to Italy to serve with Philippe, Duc d'Orléans and Lieutenant-General de la Feuillade whose army was surrounded at Torino and totally defeated; Marchin was wounded 7 September 1706 and died at 50, two days after having been made prisoner. The defeat of Torino was conveniently blamed on him instead of other senior officers still alive, notably the Duc d'Orléans and the incapable La Feuillade (who was the son-in-law of Minister of War Chamillart). He was rehabilitated by no less a general than Napoleon, who was experienced in Italian campaigns and who had studied Marshal Marchin's tactics. Napoleon blamed instead Philippe, Duc d'Orléans who would not listen to his marshal's advice thus resulting in the 1706 disaster in Italy.

Camille d'Hostun, Duc de Tallard. 1703. First served in the cavalry; distinguished service during the 1670s Dutch War; major-general in 1688; lieutenant-general in 1693; served in Germany in War of League of Augsburg until sent as ambassador to London (1695–1697). Early successes on the German Rhine front in War of the Spanish Succession; commanded the Franco-Bavarian army with Elector of Bavaria that was defeated by the allied army led by the Duke of Marlborough and Prince Eugene at Blenheim in 1704. Taken prisoner and held at Nottingham until November 1711. Made Duc d'Hostun (1712); other administrative non-military posts until his death at 76 in 1728.

Louis-François Rousselet, Marquis de Châteaurenault. 1703. Initially served in the army in the late 1650s and distinguished himself at the Battle of the Dunes (1658). Joined the navy in 1661 where he earned laurels in many battles; knight of the Order of Saint-Lazare and Mont-Carmel in 1681 and

THE ARMIES AND WARS OF THE SUN KING 1643–1715: VOLUME 1

6-24 (above): Marshal Camille d'Hostun, Duc de Tallard. Promoted to marshal in 1703. Print after J. Mariette. Courtesy Anne S.K. Brown Military Collection, Brown University Library, Providence, RI, USA.

6-25 (below): Coat of arms of Marshal Ferdinand, Comte de Marchin. Made marshal in 1703. Quarters 1 and 4 red fish on silver, 2 and 3 blue crosses on gold and silver crosses on blue. From a mural painting. Musée Condé, Chantilly. Author's photo.

its grand prior for Britany in 1687; lieutenant-general of naval armies in 1689; captain-general "of the Ocean Sea" for King Felipe V during War of the Spanish Succession. Died aged 78 in 1716.

René de Froulay, Comte de Tessé. 1703. Initially an aide-de-camp to Marshal de Créqui in 1669; friend of Minister of War Louvois; distinguished himself as dragoon commander in Roussillon (1674); major-general (1688); colonel general of dragoons (1692); ravager of the Palatinate (1689); commander-in-chief of French troops in Spain (1704), defeated Portuguese at Badajos (1705); abortive siege of Barcelona (1706); repulsed allied siege of Toulon (1707). Later ambassador to Rome and to Madrid. Died in 1725.

Victor-Marie, Duc d'Estrées. 1703. Born in 1660, d'Estrées came from a long-standing noble family and had several marshals as his forbears. He was rather unique in that he was both a competent land army commander, being promoted to Marshal of France in 1703 for his land services in Flanders, Italy and Spain, and equally at ease as fleet commander in Europe and the West Indies; Vice-Admiral of the Ponant, one of the top ranks in the French Navy, in 1684 and made "general of the seas of Spain" for his contribution to victory at Velez-Malaga (24 August 1704). He co-presided the regency council of France from 1715. Died in 1737.

Conrad de Rosen, Comte de Bolweiller. 1703. Of Swedish origin like his uncle and father-in-law who had been lieutenant-generals in French service, he was a talented young officer who fled to France following duels in Sweden; repulsed the enemy at Cambrai (1671); battle of Senef (1674); became Roman Catholic (1681); lieutenant-general (1688); with French expeditionary corps in Ireland where King James II made him Marshal of Ireland; *Mestre de Camp* of cavalry (1690). Died at 87 in 1715.

SENIOR OFFICIALS AND OFFICERS

Nicolas de Blé, Marquis d'Huxelles. 1703. Initially a churchman, he joined the army following the 1669 death at Crete of his brother; friend of Louvois; governor of Châlon; Dutch War, sieges of Cambrai, Ghent, Ypres and Valenciennes and battle of Saint-Denis; Luxembourg (1684); lieutenant-general and wounded at siege of Philippsburg (1688); surrender of Mayenne for which he was heckled in Paris, but Louis XIV comforted him by saying: "you defended the place with all heart and capitulated as a man of spirit"; thereafter became more of a diplomat and had a part in the negotiation of treaties such as Utrecht (1713); responsible for foreign affairs in Regency Council (1715–1718). D'Huxelles was well known for being gay, which tells us something about a relative tolerance in the days of the Sun King. Died in 1730.

Henri, Duc d'Harcourt. 1703. Entered the cavalry in 1673 and was aide-de-camp to Marshal Turenne, Germany (1676), sieges of Valenciennes, Cambrai and Fribourg in 1677; Germany (1678) and Luxembourg (1684). Lieutenant-general in March 1690 and took Huy in July; Neerwinden (1693), commanded army on the Moselle until 1697. Ambassador to Spain and made Duc d'Harcourt in 1700. Voltaire mentions that he was largely responsible for fostering closer ties between France and Spain that culminated in the ailing King Charles II of Spain designating a grandson of the Sun King to succeed him on the Spanish throne. Died in 1718.

Jacques de Fitz-James, Duc de Berwick. 1706. He was the natural son of King James II of Great Britain and Arabella Churchill, the Duke of Marlborough's sister; his father made him Duke of Berwick in England, later also had duchies in France and Spain. First campaigned in 1686 with the Austrians when he was 16 against the Ottoman Turks in Hungary. Back in England, he witnessed the "Glorious Revolution" of 1688 and accompanied his father into exile, campaigned in Ireland and finally went to France in 1691 where he joined the French army. Came to France with the court of James II, revealed to be a very competent officer in the French army with a good sense of strategy and tactics, serving in many campaigns and sieges in Flanders under Marshals Luxembourg and Villeroi. Promoted lieutenant-general in 1693. Three years later, he was also made captain-general of Irish troops in France by James II. Appointed lieutenant-general in command of French troops in Spain in 1704; decisive victory over Austrian, British and Portuguese troops at Almanza in 1707 that secured Spain for Felipe V; successfully protected France's southeastern border with Italy during 1709–1711; took Barcelona in 1714. Killed at 64 at the siege of Philippsburg in 1734. He had been awarded the British Order

6-26 Marshal James FitzJames, Duke of Berwick. He was one of the outstanding generals in the later reign of Louis XIV and, on 15 February 1706, was elevated by the king to the rank of marshal of France. His victorious campaigns in Spain, followed by those of Vendôme, are largely considered to be the main reason that secured the throne of King Felipe V and made that country a Bourbon kingdom. Portrait at La Granja royal palace, Spain. Author's photo.

of the Garter (1688), the Spanish Order of the Golden Fleece (1704) and the French Ordre du Saint-Esprit (1724).

Charles-Auguste de Goyon de Matignon, Comte de Gacé. 1708. Known as Marshal de Matignon. Served at the siege of Lille in 1667, in Crete in 1669, the Netherlands, Flanders and Germany until 1684. Took part in the 1689 expedition in Ireland, the sieges of Mons (1691) and Namur (1692). Lieutenant-general in 1693. Served in Flanders and took Huys in 1705. Commanded the troops for the abortive expedition to Scotland in 1708. Died in 1729.

Jacques de Bazin, Comte de Bezons. 1709. With Marshal Schomberg in Portugal in 1667; in Crete in 1668; crossed the Rhine in 1672 with his cuirassiers, wounded at Senef (1674); brigadier in 1688; at Steinkirk (1692) and Neerwinden (1693). Campaigned in Italy 1701–1706 and Spain 1708–1711; from 1711, commanded the army in Germany with Marshal Harcourt. Was part of the regency council after Louis XIV's death. Besides the French awards, he was inducted into the Spanish Order of the Golden Fleece in 1710 by King Felipe V. Died in 1733.

6-27 Marshal Pierre de Montesquiou, Comte d'Artagnan. Promoted to marshal 1709. Print after a portrait by N. Laguillière. Musée des Beaux-Arts d'Arras.

Pierre de Montesquiou, Comte d'Artagnan. 1709. Born 1640, cousin of the famous d'Artagnan of the "Three Musketeers"; royal page in 1664, served in King's Musketeers from 1665 to 1688 when promoted major-general; made governor of Arras and Artois province after announcing to the King the victory of Neerwinden in 1693; lieutenant-general in 1696; was in many campaigns and battles since his youth. At Malplaquet in 1709, his actions were partly responsible for the orderly retreat of the French army. As a courtier, Saint-Simon noted that he was skilled at intrigue and that he discreetly informed the King of many matters, which, it must be added, was also a secret duty of a King's Musketeer officer. Died in 1725.

And a Few Generals

Bernard de Nogaret de La Valette, Duc d'Épernon, colonel general of the French infantry. Born in 1592, the Duc d'Épernon succeeded his father into the powerful venal post of colonel general of French infantry at the death of his father in 1610. Although he protected the famous playwright Molière, he had a rapacious, brutal and ruthless character. He was rumoured to have poisoned his first wife Gabrielle, a natural daughter of King Henri IV, in

1627, and brought much grief to his second wife while he lavished attention on his mistress. He participated in many campaigns, not all successful, and was not a notable tactician. However, he was especially talented when it came to the repression of popular revolts, notably in south-western France in 1637 and at Bordeaux in 1650 when its parliament joined the Fronde. His royal troops quickly put an end to it and burned the chateau of the Bordeaux parliament's president. Soon after Épernon's death in July 1661, young Louis XIV, who seemingly disliked the man rumoured to have killed his aunt, abolished the post of colonel general of the French infantry.

Charles de Sainte-Maure, Marquis and later Duc de Montausier. He was a talented young officer serving under the Duke of Saxe-Weimar's Swedish army in Germany and campaigned in the French army from 1636 eventually achieving the rank of *maréchal de camp* (major-general) and later became governor-general of Saintonge and of Artois. He was even better known as an outstanding literary figure so that in 1668 Louis XIV appointed him to be *gouverneur du Grand Dauphin* (responsible for the crown prince's education). The King was obviously pleased with his son's tutor and raised his noble standing to a duchy. Born a Protestant in 1610, he converted to Catholicism in 1645 and passed away in 1690. Finally, he was reputed to carry cleanliness to absurdity and, in an era when everyone one helped each other into a common soup tureen with his own spoon, he was rather disgusted by the practice and invented an item now seen in every home: the soup ladle.

6-28 Charles de Sainte-Maure, Marquis and later Duc de Montausier, c.1670s. General, man of letters, educator, sophisticated courtier and inventor of the soup ladle. He is shown wearing the coveted Order of the Holy Spirit embroidered on the breast of his coat. Statue by L.-P. Mouchy. Musée du Louvre, Paris. Author's photo.

Victor-Marie, Comte de Broglie. Of Italian origin from the Piemontese family of Broglio. Campaigned in Flanders (1667), Franche-Comté (1668), Holland (1672–1678) and Alsace. Also involved in the repression of Protestant uprisings in the Cévennes in southern France which he is said to have carried out with cruelty. Made a marshal of France in 1724, the year of his death.

Louis d'Aubusson, Duc de la Feuillade. Commanding the French army in Italy, he was beaten by Prince Eugene at Torino in 1706, which was such a disaster that it led to the evacuation of French

6-29 (left): Lieutenant General Charles-Amédée de Broglie, c.1700. Print after Hyacinthe Rigaud. Courtesy Rijksmuseum, Amsterdam. RP-P-OB-15.687.

6-30 (above): Lieutenant General Jacques François de Chastenet de Puységur. An intellectual soldier noticed by the Sun King, he also served with distinction during the War of Spanish Succession. He was promoted marshal of France in 1734, but his lasting fame was due to his treatise on the art of war (L'Art de la guerre). Musée de l'Armée, Paris. Author's photo.

6-31 (left): Charles Auguste D'Allonville, Marquis de Louville, 1708. His portrait by Hyacinthe Rigaud depicts him in the dress of a senior officer wearing armour and the white sash of France. Worcester Art Museum, Worcester (Massachusetts), USA. Author's photo.

troops from Italy. An angry Louis XIV disgraced and exiled him. Came back in grace after the Sun King's death and the regency government appointed him ambassador to Rome. Made Marshal of France in 1724. Died in 1725.

Jacques François de Chastenet de Puységur. Born in 1656, he was noticed by Louis XIV during the 1690s as a promising field officer. He had entered the Régiment du Roi at 17, was now its lieutenant-colonel and showed an academic interest in strategy and tactics. The king sought his advice occasionally, recognising his outstanding intellectual qualities, qualities that were not always the hallmark of his senior officers in the later part of his reign. He promoted Puységur to lieutenant-general in 1706 while he served in Spain participating with distinction at the 1714 siege of Barcelona with Marshal Berwick. He was made marshal of France in 1734, but his outstanding fame came from the publication, three years after his death in 1743 of his treatise on the art of war (*L'Art de la guerre*) which is still read.

Charles-Auguste D'Allonville, Marquis de Louville. Born in 1664, he was initially a captain in the Régiment du Roi rising to colonel of the Lombardie Infantry Regiment and later to major-general. A courtly soldier of many talents, he was appointed to the service of the young Philippe, Duc d'Anjou, supervising his education from 1690; ten years later, D'Allonville accompanied d'Anjou to Madrid when he became Felipe V, King of Spain. By that time he was deeply involved in diplomatic affairs. In France from 1703, he was governor of Courtrai and later of Navarrenx as well as on the staff of the Louis de France, Duc de Bourgogne and, after his death in 1712, to Charles, Duc de Berry. D'Allonville died in 1731.

Antoine-Gaston-Jean-Baptiste de Roquelaure. Served in many campaigns during the reign of Louis XIV; pacification of the Cévennes in southern France (1704), repulsed a British seaborne attack on Cette (1710). Made Marshal of France in 1724. Died in 1738.

Eugène-Maurice de Savoie, Comte de Soissons. He is an example of the high nobility filling important diplomatic and military posts. He was the son of Thomas de Savoie, Prince de Carignan and Marie de Bourbon, made colonel general of the Swiss troops in 1657, ambassador to Great Britain in November 1660, became Duc de Carignan in 1662, lieutenant-general on 15 April 1672. He served in the army during the 1650s, the War of Devolution and the Dutch War. Died on 6 June 1673 in Germany. He was the father of the famous Prince Eugene of Savoy (1663–1736), the great general of the Austrian Imperial troops.

Louis-Charles-Auguste Fouquet de Belle-Isle. He was the grandson of the corrupt superintendant Fouquet jailed by Louis XIV. Served in the War of the Spanish Succession when he was revealed to be a very talented young officer, later duke, marshal in 1741, served as a senior officer in the Imperial Austrian army, back in France and minister of war from 1758 until his death in 1761.

7

The World of Senior Officers

Travelling in Style

French army senior officers were usually renowned for their ostentatious suites that seemed to satisfy their every desire to make life easier to bear. This was as true in a fortress as it was amongst an army in the field. It was even enhanced when the Sun King was present since he travelled in unrivalled luxury equipped with magnificent tents, attended by a huge number of his household's servants and escorted by a large detachment of, usually, his guard cavalry. It was camping out in the very best style. Not to be outdone while respecting that the king was to have the most luxurious train, princes, marshals and generals also had their horse guards (of which more below) and their suites that made their lifestyles rather remarkable. A marshal or a senior general was allowed a numerous personal guard unit, the numbers of which varied according to rank. There were also numerous servants of all types. Alternately, when a senior officer was in command of a province and/or of a fortress, there was also a luxurious protocol to be observed. He was, after all, the king's direct representative. In theory, when a governor-general stepped out of his chateau to take a somewhat formal walk about town, drums rolled when he came out of his residence's gate, soldiers stood at attention as he passed by and he was escorted by a sizeable detachment of his guard with servants acting as ushers to clear the way forward and more in the back to close the mini-procession.

An idea of the phenomena is given in an August 1667 letter from Bussy-Rabutin to de Coligny-Saligny regarding the royal tour of the King and the Queen at the newly conquered cities in Flanders. They were joined by a multitude of courtiers and officers who travelled in style: "…the magnificence of Salomon and the grandeur of the King of Persia is not comparable to the pomp that accompanies the king during his voyage [in Flanders]. On the streets, one only sees plumes, gilded coats, chariots and donkeys superbly harnessed, parade horses, housings embroidered with fine gold. All the courtiers, officers and volunteers left [Paris] with sumptuous equipages..." that required about 30,000 horses to draw them![1]

Protocol and social values of the 17th century dictated that all this was important for dignity, prestige and respect. Servants were also liable to being exposed to warfare because of the military functions of their master and there were even occasions when they were unwilling combatants or subject to bombardments. An idea of their number is given in Audiger's 1692 *La maison réglée* (the regulated household) which recommended what was considered correct for a more or less noble *seigneur* (lord). A bachelor *seigneur* needed at least 37 servants, five of whom were senior (each of them having their own personal attendant), 14 carriage horses and 16 riding horses with plenty of straw for their "amusement" and bedding. All this should have cost a mere 1,600 *louis d'or*. Marriage added 16 servants and every child required another seven servants. So, a well-to-do couple with two children had 67 servants. And most of the men wore their master's livery, all also being fed and lodged. These were the *domestiques à gages* or *de livrée* (paid servants) who would also get regular pocket money from a proper seigneur's family. There could also be others not *à gages* that hung around the estate to perform some minor service in return for a tip. The above now seems incredible in our times with mechanised appliances; even the rich and powerful have hardly any household help. Yet, a mere 350 years ago, a large following was considered necessary for anyone who held a privileged and/or a leadership post. Indeed, even a trooper of the royal guard cavalry had at least one servant.[2]

General Officer's Dress

All general officers from marshal down did not have uniforms. Paintings of the period often show them wearing blue or scarlet coats with gold lace as the usual favourite. This does not indicate that generals had a de facto uniform or were required to wear one. When the Duc de Villeroi was promoted marshal in February 1695, he wore, according to Madame de Sévigné, an "extraordinarily magnificient" blue velvet coat that was surely covered with embroidery. Marshal Bouffler was seen in a black velvet coat laced with gold at the seams in 1698. Marshal d'Huxelles had a plain grey coat with gold buttons in 1703. Marshal Villars liked to wear a buff leather waistcoat under his coat when in battle and his clothes collected some 17 hits (without harm to the wearer) in 1691. He was wounded in 1709 at Malplaquet, but entered the entrenchments leading his men at Denain in 1712, wearing his buff leather waistcoat. Whatever their dress, general officers were to wear the shoulder silk sashes of the orders of chivalry to which they belonged. For national recognition, they wore white silk waist sashes. From 1676,

---

1 Coligny-Saligny, *Mémoires*, pp. 123–124.
2 Audiger, *La maison réglée et l'art de diriger la maison d'un grand seigneur et autres* (Paris: Le Gras, 1692), pp. 1–2, 9, 76–77. I – t also has recipes to make liquors, some of which were tasted by the King, jams, tea, coffee and even ice cream; W.H. Lewis, *The Splendid Century, Life in the France of Louis XIV* (London: William Sloane, 1953 and New York: Anchor 1957), p. 197.

7-1 A senior general officer and a personal guard of Colonel General, the Duc d'Épernon, mid 17th century. Generals at this time still wore some armour. The guardsman wear a cassock of the Épernon family's green livery with a white cross. Print after Alfred de Marbot. Canadian War Museum, Ottawa. Author's photo.

Louis XIV wanted general officers and cavalry officers to wear cuirasses for protection, but this was not universally accepted. Villars, when a general in 1677, refused to obey such an order telling his staff officers that he did not think his life was more precious than any of his brave men whom he led into battle. All the same, it was not an unreasonable request from the King and some paintings occasionally show marshals or generals wearing cuirasses over or under their coats; the murals of the 1670s at the Invalides often add shoulder and arm armour that would seem much less likely to have been actually worn.[3]

There was also a peculiar garment that was granted as a favour by the king, which was called a *justeaucorps à brevet*, being a coat that could only be worn by those high officials and courtiers that were granted a royal certificate to do so. Its origin was a 1644 edict that forbade courtiers, some of whom would ruin themselves for luxurious costumes, or have gold or silver embroidery on their coats unless they had the king's permission by way of a *brevet* – a certificate – signed by him. This was thereafter neglected, but it was reissued by the Sun King on 16 January 1665. The Sun King thereafter used it to honour certain individuals such as the Prince de Condé on 4 February. The recipients were often high-ranking officers although the number of brevets were limited, there being only 40 in 1686. As Voltaire later wrote, the permission to wear it was a

---

[3] Louis-Hector, Duc de Villars, *Mémoires du Maréchal Villars*, M. de Vogüé, ed., (Paris: Renouard, 1884), Vol. 1, p. 138, Vol. 3, p. 155 and Vol. 6, p. 170; Louis de Rouvroy, Duc de Saint-Simon, *La Cour du Régent*, ed. Henri Mazel (Paris, 1930), p. 99.

THE WORLD OF SENIOR OFFICERS

great favour to men ruled by vanity. But less ostentatious notables might have it too since Louis XIV was keen to reward the truly deserving individuals. Thus, Lieutenant-General (later Marshal) Villars was also honoured with a *brevet* in 1692. This coat was blue lined with red and covered with elaborate and very beautiful embroidery in mostly gold with some silver. These prestigious coats finally went out of favour after the King's death.[4]

Marshals' and Generals' Bodyguards

In royal France, high-ranking officers were allowed their own personal bodyguard to escort them. These usually consisted of mounted units whose size varied according to the importance of the officer they escorted. A royal order of 25 July 1665 specified that lieutenant-generals could "enter [towns] with their guards carrying their rifled carbines and [wearing] their livery cassocks, together with their gentlemen and others of their suite."

A marshal of France and a lieutenant-general commanding an army in the field each had a guard of 50 men; a subordinate lieutenant-general was allowed a guard of 30 men. Other lieutenant-generals, who were also often governor-generals of provinces, each had 20 men commanded by a captain, a lieutenant and a cornet. Therefore, from the 1660s to 1714, there were some 9,000 guardsmen led by at least 1,000 officers either attached to armies or serving in the provinces all over the kingdom. These bodyguard units were

7-2 Rear view of finely dressed French senior officers at the siege of Aardenberg, June 1672. From left, violet cloak with red scarf; blue coat with red cuffs richly embroidered with silver and red ribbons; red coat and stockings with blue cuffs, breeches and ribbons, silver embroidery; the mounted trumpeter at right in a brown coat with silver and red livery lace, red breeches and housings and has his instrument with its white embroidered gold banner slung over the shoulder. Unsigned c.1675 painting. Amsterdam Museum, Amsterdam. Author's photo.

---

4   Voltaire, *Le Siècle de Louis XIV*, p. 422; *Mémoires du Maréchal de Villars*, Vol. 6, p. 170.

THE ARMIES AND WARS OF THE SUN KING 1643–1715: VOLUME 1

7-3 An army commander with his senior officers and staff during a battle, c. 1690. As can be seen, there was no uniformity in the dress of senior officers. The commander wears a cuirass with an all blue coat and red breeches while other officers have coats of red, buff, brown and so on. Detail from a contemporary mural painting. Musée Condé, Chantilly. Author's photo.

the marshal's and general's own and, while subsided by royal funds, were not listed as part of the army. They were the men-at-arms of the marshal or the general. As such, they were under his authority and wore the colours of his family's livery. They served on foot and mounted. The officers could also have certain staff duties as additional unofficial aides-de-camp.

Earlier in the 17th century, these guardsmen wore cassocks in the livery colour edged with lace and bearing at front and back their master's coat of arms or a cross. From the 1660s, coats were worn of the livery colours, which were often a ground hue contrasted by lining (and cuffs) of a different colour. While servants, trumpeters and drummers had multi-coloured silk lace, troopers appear to have had their coat laced with gold or silver lace that was frequently applied on all seams. The guards were armed with a sword, pistols and, usually, with rifled carbines. Their were thus often termed as *carabiniers*. The shoulder bandoliers on which their carbines were hooked were usually of the livery colour edged with lace. They might have a metal badge bearing the officer's coat of arms.[5]

---

5   The 21 July 1665 order in quoted from: M. de Lamont, *Les fonctions de tous les officiers de l'infanterie* (Paris, 1669), p. 338; Gabriel Daniel, *Histoire de la milice françoise* (Paris: Jean-Baptiste Coignard, 1721), Vol. 2, pp. 18–19; Émmanuel Bourrrassin, 'Les gardes des reines-

THE WORLD OF SENIOR OFFICERS

7-4 A marshal commanding an army, *c.*1690. He holds the command baton with gold lilies and wears the light blue sash of the Order du Saint-Esprit. The coat, in this print by Bonnard, is all scarlet with strips of silver embroidered lace, gold buttons and button hole lace, but the coat could be blue or other colours; there was no regulation for general's uniforms. Anne S.K. Brown Military Collection, Brown University Library, Providence, RI, USA. Author's photo.

Some Liveries

The King: blue lined with red; some guard and "royal" units wearing blue coats with silver or gold lace for officers. The royal livery lace was red and white or red and blue edged white, usually in small squares from at least the 1660s. According to the January 1678 *Mercure Galant*, the lace's design changed every year on 1 January so that its magnificence increased "more and more" every year. This stopped in about 1687 when a white chain on red or crimson lace was permanently adopted and is still the livery lace of the Bourbon royal family (notably in Spain). The royal lace was worn by drummers, trumpeters and other musicians of the guard and designated "royal" and provincial units, by all the Cent-Suisses de la Garde company and also by servants attached to the king's service, for instance horse grooms, that would also be with the king's suite on campaign. For the king's royal guard and servants, two slips of livery lace had a white lace with red or crimson triangles in between, or silver lace for non – commissioned – officers such as drum-majors. This was the *Grande Livrée* (grand livery lace). The *Petite Livrée* (small livery lace) was usually worn by musicians in the troops of the line that made up the rest of the army insofar as royal or provincial units were concerned.

---

régentes, des princes du sang et des grands officiers de la couronne', *Uniformes* (No. 119, October 1988), pp. 13–17.

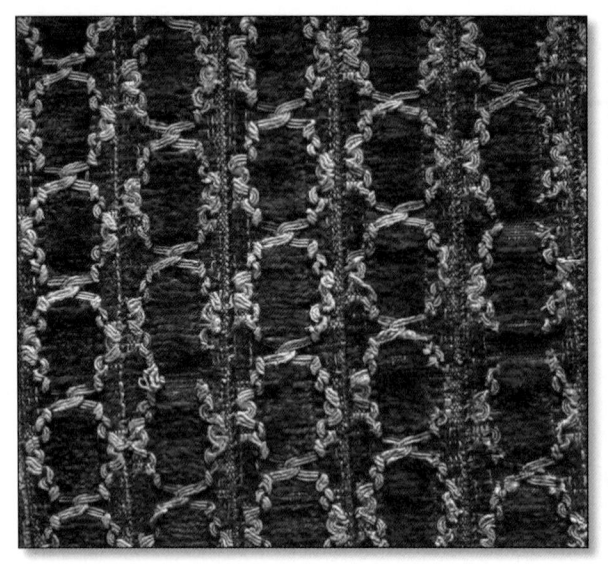

7-5 The King's livery lace, from about 1687. These five rows of the king's livery are of the pattern adopted permanently from the late 1680s instead of changing patterns every year. The lace was red or, often, crimson with a white chain thereon and is still in use today by the Bourbon royalty of Spain. Musée de l'Armée, Paris. Author's photo.

An important aspect is that Louis XIV frowned on anyone else using the same colours for their livery and eventually forbade the practice by royal order on 10 February 1704. In her *Souvenirs*, the Marquise de Créquy noted that in the early 18th century, the blue in the royal livery was still "azure" – she likely meant a medium to royal blue – instead of "the sad innovation" of the "vile obscure blue" that appeared during the reign of Louis XV. The only exception to this rule appears to have been for the Dauphin and for members of the Estaing family who were permitted since the Middle Ages to have the same coat of arms and livery as the king. All the same, blue coats gradually became the insignia of royal government service in many fields apart from the armed forces.

Drummers, trumpeters and other musicians of other units wore their colonel's livery as well as guardsmen of high-ranking nobles, marshals and generals. Below is a sample of liveries of various high-ranking princes and officers:[6]

Duc d'Anjou: green lined with orange.

Duc d'Aumont: red with silver embroidered lace.

Duc de Beaufort: scarlet cassock laced with silver, silver cross, without cipher, and with crowned lilies.

Duc de Berry: Red lined with blue, black cuffs, black lace with a white chain.

Marshal and Duc de Berwick: yellow.

Marshal and Duc de Boufflers: green lined with red, white lace with small red crosses.

Duc de Bouillon: white and black cassocks in 1649; later white coat with black cuffs, black and white lace.

---

6   The data on liveries is taken mainly from: Beneton de Morange de Peyrins, *Traité des marques nationales* (Paris: G. Le Mercier, 1739) which is the main source for French liveries; Bourrassin, 'Les gardes des reines-régentes…', pp. 15–16; Dunoyer de Noirmont and Alfred de Marbot, *Costumes militaires français* (Paris, c.1846), vol. 1; *Journal des guerres civiles de Dubuisson-Aubenay, 1648–1652*, Gustave Saige, ed. (Paris, 1883), Vol. 1, p. 143; *Souvenirs de la Marquise de Créqui* (Paris: Fournier, 1834), Vol. 1, pp. 144–145 and Vol. 3, p. 119. The house of d'Estaing was said to have earned the right to have the royal coat of arms and livery at the battle of Bouvines when a d'Estaing saved King Philippe Auguste as per the *Mercure Galant*, March 1708, p. 269.

THE WORLD OF SENIOR OFFICERS

Duc de Bournonville: yellow cassock and bandoliers lined with green, red, blue and green velvet lace in 1660.

Lieutenant-General and Prince de Carignan: red lined with blue, white and blue lace.

Major-general Comte de Chavagnac: green with wide gold lace at seams in 1667.

Marshal de Choiseul: green, white lace.

Prince de Condé: blue and *isabelle* (according to the 1651 *Gazette*, p. 310; *isabelle* is a buff hue) and changed (probably in the early 1660s) to yellow or buff lined with red, red cuffs, red velvet lace.

Prince de Conti: his guards had scarlet cassocks and housings with silver lace and buttons, silver cross on chest and back with gold lilies at the cross ends, gold embroidery between branches of the cross and gold A and B cipher (for Armand de Bourbon) in 1649; blue cassocks trimmed with silver lace in 1657; later yellow coat with blue velvet cuffs, silver lace on all seams, blue bandoleer laced silver.

Duc d'Elbeuf: green cassocks with white satin double cross (of Lorraine) and silver edging in 1649.

Duc d'Epernon: green or green-brown.

Marshal and Duc d'Estrées: red lined with white.

Duc de Grammont: yellow coat, red horn buttons, red and blue lace on all seams in 1688.

Duc d'Harcourt: Red lined with yellow.

Marshall and Marquis d'Huxelles: scarlet with green velvet cuffs and gold lace.

Marshal and Duc de Luxembourg: buff lined with blue, silver lace.

Duc de Maine: red lined with blue, gold lace.

Marshal Mirepoix: buff, amaranth-red lace with silver thread.

Duc de Montausier: green lined with yellow, green breeches and stockings.

Marshal de Montmorency: see Marshal and Duc de Luxembourg.

Marshal de La Mothe: scarlet cassocks with white satin crosses in 1649.

THE ARMIES AND WARS OF THE SUN KING 1643–1715: VOLUME 1

7-6 (left): Fifer of the Gardes Suisses Regiment, early 18th century. His blue coat lined with red is lavishly decorated with the king's grande livrée (grand livery) wide lace as is the sword belt. This consisted of a white lace with a red central pattern set in between two rows of the basic royal livery lace. Anne S.K. Brown Military Collection, Brown University Library, Providence, RI, USA. Author's photo.

7-7 (right): Guardsman of a personal guard unit, c.1675. While not formally identified as such, this figure from a larger woodcut published at Chalon-sur-Saône is almost certainly a rare view of a trooper of the guard escorting a senior officer. He wears luxurious dress, has a distinctive bandolier with a zig-zag pattern of lace. He appears to be armed with a rifled flintlock carbine. Musée Denon, Chalon-sur-Saône. Author's photo.

Marshal and Duc de Noailles: red.

Duc de Lauzun: brown (almost black according to Saint-Simon), blue and white lace from the 1680s.

Duc d'Orléans: blue with red and white lace probably until the death of Gaston d'Orléans in 1660. *Monsieur*, the Sun King's brother, then became the Duc d'Orléans and since the King wished to have blue exclusively, it was changed to red lined with blue, half white and half blue lace bordered with red and white chequers.

Duc de Penthièvre: red lined with blue, yellow and blue lace.

Duc de Toulouse: red lined with blue, yellow lace between two blue laces.

Marshal Turenne: white lined with black, black and white lace.

Marshal Vauban: red lined with blue, gold lace.

Duc de Vendôme: red lined with blue, yellow lace between two blue lines.

Marshal Villars: maroon brown lined with crimson or red, silver lace in 1703.

Marshal and Duc de Villeroi: green lined with orange, orange and gold lace.

Military Pageantry

The Sun King loved elaborate displays and parades to show off his army. It was not a merely vain practice; he understood the influence that pomp and circumstance had on human minds and, by association, the great prestige that France in general and its army in particular harvested by such festival-like spectacles. Reviews of royal guard units took on an hitherto unseen grandeur and display of power with uniformed soldiers marching in step to military music accompanied by richly dressed ensigns carrying a forest-like assembly of beautiful regimental colours fluttering by the breeze. Many onlookers were not military nor religious, but hundreds if not thousands of courtiers, nobles and even commoners were there to watch such event, which, if it dragged into the evening, might be followed by a fireworks display. Such events became much larger with the King as the prime feature which all eyes sought.

Even originally solemn events presided by the clergy for a select audience of royal and military figures became far more than religious ceremonies. The *Mercure Galant* of January 1683 reported that the colours of the Gardes Françaises Regiment of the royal guard were ceremoniously blessed at Notre-Dame church in Paris. The colours arrived carried by 30 ensigns mounted on horses, each carrying a colour. The first was the colonel's which was white

7-8 Equipage of a marshal of France, 1690s–1700s. Senior officers and especially marshals were not always on horseback during campaigns. Many had more comfortable small carriages such as seen in this print after Edmond Lajoux. The carriage driver would wear the marshal's personal livery, green in this case, which was worn by the servants and the horse guards of Marshal Boufflers and Villeroi. Private collection. Author's photo.

"with five crowns painted on this colour. The 29 others were of blue taffeta silk sprinkled with lilies also in gold, with a white cross bearing the five [actually four] crowns." It was a religious service turned into an extraordinary festival-like event proclaiming the military pageantry and power of the realm that many thousands could admire right in the centre of Paris.

Perhaps a peak in military parades and reviews was reached in 1698 following the end of the War of the League of Augsburg. Although it had been a difficult war at times for France, Louis XIV wished to show that the French army was still a very lethal and imposing force. He wanted to impress on all Europe that it should think twice before going to war against France. To do so, he resolved in March to gather many troops to form a large military camp on the plain next to the town of Compiègne near Paris. He had organised such a gathering there in 1666, but that was nearly nothing compared to the one now being planned. Dangeau's journal of 23 March mentioned that 35 infantry battalions and 130 cavalry squadrons would join the King to parade, train, have mock battles and be reviewed. It was initially scheduled to occur in June, but more preparations went on. By the end of August, over 70,000 men were camped near Compiègne, which were many more troops than initially planned. Marshal Boufflers was in overall command.

Officially, the event was organised by Louis XIV to further the military education of his 16-year-old grandson, the Duc de Bourgogne, so he could see what a large army was really like. The King arrived with a numerous suite on 1 September at the nearby village of Coudon and established his quarters there; as a result, the camp also became known as the *Camp de Coudon* as well as of Compiègne. With the Sun King on the spot, his whole galaxy at the court of Versailles also wished to be there and the area was inundated with

THE WORLD OF SENIOR OFFICERS

7-9 Marshal Boufflers apprehended at Namur, 5 September 1695. Surrounded by a powerful army led by King William III, the French garrison of the fortress city of Namur capitulated. Within was Marshall Boufflers and it was the first time in memory that a marshal of France surrendered. Having obtained the honours of war for his worthy garrison, all came out with drums beating and colours flying. Boufflers, however, chose not to salute or acknowledge William III, an outstandingly improper behaviour, and just rode on with his escort, notably his guard that wore green coats lined with red. As shown in this print, he was soon apprehended by a party of English Life Guards and led back a prisoner in Namur. Private collection. Author's photo.

thousands of courtiers, *courtisanes*, camp followers as well as dukes, their duchesses and every level of the nation's nobility accompanied by an army of servants and lackeys, often dressed in their master's liveries while their carriages created "traffic jams" on the rough country roads.

Naturally, foreign diplomats and observers were also on the spot; one of them, a German named Corfey, wrote a detailed account of what he saw, which obviously impressed him. Other invited observers included the princes of Hesse-Cassel, of Parma, of Lockwitz in Saxony and a great number of ambassadors and lords from other German and Italian states, Austria, Sweden, Great Britain, Denmark and other nations. This was exactly what Louis XIV was hoping for. He had earlier advised his army officers to keep their expenses and gold lace to a minimum. However, once at the camp, senior French officers and high nobles hosted lavish parties often accompanied to music in a display of luxury that would be remembered for generations. Regimental drills, parades, mock battles, lavish dinners – over a hundred tables were constantly filled with fine food and fine wines – and great parties went on until 22 September when the camp ended. All this gilded luxury camp was soon the celebrated setting for a popular novel titled *La Rivale*

Travestie ou les aventures … arrivées au camp de Compiègne (the disguised rival [girl] or adventures … that occurred at the camp at Compiègne) where we learn that, besides romantic events, the princes wore alternately their own diamond-studded coats or the uniform of their regiments while generals were "superbly dressed" without having a particular colour imposed for their coats. They were distinguished by wide silver sashes worn over the shoulder "which is done in France" on a special feast day.[7]

As for the Duc de Bourgogne, the excuse for this lavish festival, his military education does not seem to have been enormously improved judging from his future battlefield command achievements. Nor were the main foreign powers fundamentally impressed. From the 1690s, they knew their armies were just as good as those of the Sun King's so, while admiring the remarkably fine appearance of French regiments parading at Compiègne and taking advantage of fine food and wines, their mostly Protestant and therefore less ostentatious values frowned at the near-sinful luxury displayed there, knowing that all this supposedly military training camp was a far cry from a real combat zone. They further knew their own main challenge was cohesion for strategic objectives and a unified high command should they ever have to again form allied armies to counter the ambitious Sun King.

---

7   Philippe de Courcillon, Marquis de Dangeau, *Journal du Marquis de Dangeau*, M. Feuillet de Conches, ed. (Paris, 1854–1860), Vol. 6, pp. 406–425; *Mémoires du Marquis de Sourches sur le règne de Louis XIV*, Comte de Cosnac, ed., (Paris: Hachette, 1886), Vol. 6, pp. 60–73; A. Pinan Delaforest, *Voyage du roi à Saint-Omer suivi de la relation de ce qui s'est passé au camp de Compiegne en 1698* (Paris: Delaforst, 1828), pp. 409–464; Lambert Friedrich Corfey, 'Reisetagebuch 1698–1700', ed., Helmut Lahrkamp, *Quellen und forschungen zur geschichte der stadt Münster*, neue folge, Vol. 9 (1977), pp. 57–61.

8

Orders of Chivalry

Portraits of the Sun King and many of his officers, from the grandest to, eventually, the much more humble, show the sitters with sashes and medals with coloured ribbons and sometimes richly embroidered badges on coats and capes. These were signs of honour and distinction for those who wore them. All were a sign that the wearer had been received as a knight since all were orders of chivalry. The four orders awarded by the King were: The Order of Saint-Michel, the Order of Saint-Esprit (the Holy Spirit), The Order of Mont-Carmel and Saint-Lazare and the Royal and Military Order of Saint-Louis.

The Order of Saint-Michel and the Order of the Saint-Esprit were largely destined for the high nobility of long standing. They were combined as awards given out somewhat simultaneously in the 16th century and both were known as *Les Ordres du Roi* (the King's Ordres of Chivalry). Also for the high nobility was The Order of Mont-Carmel and Saint-Lazare. However, in 1693, Louis XIV created the Royal and Military Order of Saint-Louis to spread awards amongst many officers in his army. Abolished for a short time during the French Revolution, it was recreated by Napoleon as the *Légion d'Honneur*.

The Order of Saint-Michel

It was created by King Louis XI on 1 August 1469 in the chapel of Saint-Michel d'Ambrose, hence its name. It honoured gentlemen exclusively attached to the personal service of the king and its recipients were to abandon all other orders, the allusion being specifically aimed at the Order of the Golden Fleece that was awarded by Charles the Bold, Duc de Bourgogne, to French nobles. Charles conspired to take over the crown of France. In this way, Louis XI was eliminating from his inner circle those who favoured Charles. The question was settled when Charles was killed in 1477. Thereafter, the Order was much more honorific than political. Initially, 12 knights named by the King were inducted; this rose later to 36 and many more. They were to abide by the rules of chivalry, to assist each other, be Roman Catholics and have filled an important army or government post for at least 10 years. The Order's administrators were a chancellor, a prevost master of ceremonies, a grand treasurer, a herald and a secretary.

THE ARMIES AND WARS OF THE SUN KING 1643–1715: VOLUME 1

8-1 (left, top): The gold collar and medals of the Order of Saint-Michel, 17th century. Mural painting. Château d'Ancy-le-Franc, Burgundy. Author's photo.

8-2 (left, below): A gold and silver collar and its medal of the Order of Saint-Michel, c. 1662. An extremely rare artefact for its age and in perfect condition. Dutch Admiral Michel de Ruyter was awarded the order by Louis XIV following his outstanding 1666 raid up the Thames River. Courtesy Rijksmuseum, Amsterdam. NG-384-A.

8-3 (below): A knight of the Order of Saint-Michel, early 18th century. He is dressed in the order's magnificent ceremonial dress. It is a portrait of Philippe-Joseph Perrottin de Barmond who was received in 1719, but an excellent view of the knight's full dress during the reign of the Sun King. Musée de la Légion d'Honneur, Paris. Author's photo.

During the reign of Louis XIV, the seat of the Order was in the Cordeliers convent in Paris. On 8 May, the anniversary date of the Archangel appearing to Saint-Michel, the knights gathered for a solemn mass attended by the king who then offered a dinner. He also held the yearly review of the activities of the knights; in quite rare instances, they could be demoted for immoral behaviour or treason by votes of fellow knights and the King (who had two votes). By 1661, this knighthood had been somewhat debased as it now had some 1,500 members, some of them "false" knights. As a result, in 1665, the Sun King totally reorganised the Order, limiting its numbers to 100 knights to be henceforth exclusively of French nationality. He also awarded the Order to honour artists and authors such as Le Notre and Mansard.

The insignia of the Order was an oval badge bearing the enamelled figure of Saint-Michel slaying a dragon. This event that occurred in Heaven made the knightly saint very popular during the Middle Ages and he was credited with many apparitions on earth, including one in France when he ordered that a fortified abbey be built on an island off the coast of Normandy whose low tides would allow access: the famous Mont-Saint-Michel. This badge was hung on a golden collar of 23 small shells, symbolic of pilgrimage, with links. Knights of Saint-Michel were to always wear their insignia, especially in battle, which could be fatal. At the 1690 battle of Fleurus, the Knight of Villarseaux was captured by five German soldiers who then fought each other for the medal, strangling the unfortunate knight in the process.

The ceremonial dress in the 17th and 18th centuries consisted of an all silver cloth 16th century-style suit over which a white silk long cassock richly embroidered in gold with the Order's insignia. A scarlet shoulder cape embroidered in gold was worn over the cassock and the Order's gold collar and oval badge was upon it. A black velvet cap with a white plume was the headdress.

The Order of Saint-Esprit

King Henri III created the Order of the Saint-Esprit (of the Holy Spirit) on 31 December 1578. At a time of civil and religious strife, the Order was meant to honour the nobles who were the most devoted and loyal to the king. It initially had 27 knights, a number that increased to 100. Of these, 87 were required to be of noble families for at least three generations, be at least 35 years old and already members of the Order of Saint-Michel so that they were also designated as *Chevaliers des Ordres du Roi* (knights of the Orders of the King) since they were automatically recipients of both orders. They wore its gilt and enamel collar and received a pension varying between 8,000 and 3,000 pounds a year. There were also four grand officers including a grand treasurer and a secretary that were not required to be noble. This allowed the king to reward his ministers into the Order. For instance, Louis XIV named Colbert into the Order as grand treasurer. The Roman Catholic church was represented by nine of its prelates: the grand chaplain of France, four cardinals and four prelates. They only received the Order of Saint-Esprit so had a special cross that just had its insignia on both sides.

8-4 (above): The cross of the Order of the Saint-Esprit, 17th century. Gold with silver dove and silver edged cross. Mural painting. Château d'Ancy-le-Franc, Burgundy. Author's photo.

8-5 (top right): Charles Henri, Comte de Clermont and Duc de Clermont-Tonnerre wearing the luxurious black velvet cloak embroidered with gold of a knight the Order of the Saint-Esprit, mid 17th century. The Clermont-Tonnerre family had successive generations of senior field officers, Charles-Henri shown here passed away in 1640. His son, François (1601–1679), also became a general and was made a knight of this order and thus probably wore this cloak. Château d'Ancy-le-Franc, Burgundy. Author's photo.

There were also a number of members that were admitted into the Order, but not formally received as knights. They were designated *Commandeurs des Ordres du Roi* (Commanders of the Orders of the King). All members were nominated by the king as the chief and sovereign grand master in respect of its motto: *Duce et Auspice* (Under his guidance and auspices).

The Order's insignia was an eight-pointed green and white enamel medal edged with gold with gold lilies at the angles and, at the centre, a silver dove descending symbolising the Holy Spirit. It was hung on a wide sky blue silk ribbon. A large all-silver embroidered version of the medal could be also worn on the left breast of a knight's coat and this is often seen on portraits of senior officers.

The knight's ceremonial dress was an all silver cloth 16th century-style suit over which a black velvet cape with a long trail elaborately embroidered in gold with palms and the Order's insignia. A white short cape embroidered with gold was over the shoulders with the Order's gold and enamel collar. A black velvet cap with a white plume was the headdress.[1]

---

1 François du Chesne and Haudicquer de Blancourt, *Recherches historiques de l'ordre du Saint-Esprit* (Paris, 1710), 2 volumes; Gilles-André de La Roque, *Traité de la noblesse* (Rouen: Boucher & Callioue, 1710), pp. 432–434; Charles Marchal and Sophie Michel, 'Les ordres du roi', *Art & Curiosité*, October-December 1981; Nicholas Carlisle, *A Concise Account of the Several Foreign Orders of Knighthood* (London, 1839).

The Order of Mont-Carmel and Saint-Lazare

This order had roots going back to the crusades as charitable knights that took care of other knights who suffered from leprosy as well as fighting Muslim enemies. It was reorganised in France by King Henri IV in 1607 and 1608 by uniting the Roman Catholic Orders of Saint-Lazare and Mont-Carmel to manage hospitals and particularly to care for lepers. This was confirmed by Pope Paul V. For support, the Order had estates set up as *commanderies* with a grand master and no more than 100 knights whose families had at least four generations of nobility. It was known, by Louis XIV's reign as the *Ordres Royaux, Militaires & Hospitaliers de Notre-Dame de Mont-Carmel et de Saint-Lazare de Jérusalem, Nazareth et Bethlehem* (Royal, Military and Hospital Orders of our Lady of Mont-Carmel and Saint-Lazarus of Jerusalem, Nazareth et Bethlehem) to quote the January 1696 *Mercure Galant*. By 1672, the Order was in financial and administrative peril and the Sun King intervened with an edict that corrected the situation by providing it with better revenues. Its 140 *commanderies* and its knights would mainly be veteran officers. Between 1672 and 1693, the King granted this order the management of hospitals and lazarettos of other orders that were henceforth abolished. Its services now also included pension funds for maimed soldiers and military hospitals. At that time, its grand master was the influential Marquis de Dangeau and the Marquis de Louvois, who was the minister of war, with many high-ranking army officers as knights who solemnly swore fidelity to the Sun King at ceremonies.

The medieval knights' surcoat had a green cross. The 1608 statutes mentioned a cape bearing a brown cross with the image of the Virgin Mary at its centre and a cross-shaped medal with the same image on both sides suspended by a brown silk ribbon. The Order's cross was eight-pointed since the mid 16th century. This rather plain dress was considerably improved insofar as luxury by the Sun King's reign. By early 1696, the received knights wore amaranth-red coats embroidered with gold embroidery, the novice knights with silver lace and buttonholes, and all coats lined with green and gold brocade, a waistcoat-like silver silk cassock upon which was a large amaranth-red and green cross, amaranth-red breeches and stockings, an amaranth-red velvet cap with an heron's plume held by a diamond pin. The grand master also had a long cape with a trail in the same colours and embroidery and his sword's guard was studded with diamonds. Its medal was a gold and enamelled amaranth-red cross of eight points with a gold fleur-de-lys at each angle with the image of the Virgin Mary on one side and Lazarus rising from the grave on the other, the medal being suspended round the neck by a wide green ribbon. For all it "military" designation, it was not really a fighting organisation, but it did gather as its knights some very rich military noblemen that might be seen with a cross of the order as well as other awards.[2]

---

2   R.-D. Stiot, 'L'ordre royal, hospitalier et militaire de Saint-Lazare et de Notre-Dame du Mont-Carmel', *Carnet de la Sabretache*, December 1956: 274–279; André Souyris-Rolland, 'Louvois, vicaire général de l'Ordre de Saint-Lazare', *Histoire, économie et société*, 1996, 15e année, no. 1: 155–158.

The Royal and Military Order of Saint-Louis

Up to 1693, the French royal orders of chivalry were reserved to a privileged small number of generally wealthy and members of the high nobility of long standing. Louis XIV was sensitive to the fact that all other officers in the armed services could not have such prestigious honours. It appears that Marshal de Luxembourg suggested that one way to solve the problem was to create a new order of chivalry under his own supreme authority. The Sun King agreed. On 5 April, a royal edict created *L'Ordre Royal et Militaire de Saint-Louis* (Royal and Military Order of Saint-Louis) and, in his office at Versailles on 13 May, the King knighted members of the royal family, namely the Dauphin, the Dukes of Orléans and of Chartres, the Prince of Conti and Marshal de Bellefond by tapping each with the blade of his sword on the shoulders and saying: *Par Saint-Louis, je vous fais chevalier* (By Saint-Louis, I make you a knight). He then gave them a cross of the order.

This simple ceremony involved only the king, no church members were required and the new order had no monastic rule or religious requirement except that its members be Roman Catholics. It was exclusively reserved for officers of the army or of the navy. Furthermore, the Order, once its recipient was approved by the king, could also be bestowed by a senior royal official such as a governor-general. By its statute, the King was its "Chief Sovereign, Grand Master and founder wishing that its Grand Mastery be united and incorporated … to Our crown…" which meant, amongst other things, that a knight of the Order was only bound by the authority of the king and no other. This meant that a knight of the Order of Saint-Louis could not concurrently be a knight of, for example, the somewhat foreign Order of Malta, but a knight of the *Ordres du Roi* could also be a knight of Saint-Louis.

Possibly the greatest innovation was that a knight did not need to be noble. Every officer, no matter what the circumstances of his birth were, was considered worthy. A Saint-Louis knighthood was not a nobility certificate, but it was certainly a big step up the social scale insofar as esteem and respect for its recipient. Especially as at that time, rich commoners were increasingly buying nobility titles, a despised practice termed by the people: *savonnette à vilains* – the soap (meaning the money) scrubbing that cleaned up common villains until they were noble. There could be no bartering of the Order of Saint-Louis; when people saw an officer wearing its cross on his uniform walking down their street, they knew that he had earned it through long service and had risked his life battling France's enemies.

There were three grades of knights: 1) eight grand cross, 2) 24 commanders and 3) a variable number of knights according to the wishes of the sovereign. It was clear there would be many more than 100 knights as in other orders. Seven eights of the nominations went to army officers and one eight to the navy. To be considered for a knighthood, officers had to have served 10 years (later raised to 24 years) and have distinguished themselves in combat or have performed a truly outstanding battle action in which case the long service requirement could be waived. Pensions came with the knighthood: 6,000 pounds to a grand cross, 3,000 to 4,000 for a commander, 800 to 2,000 for a knight. From the creation of the Order in 1693 to the end of the War of

ORDERS OF CHIVALRY

8-6 (below): The knight's cross of the Royal and Military Order of Saint-Louis, 1693. This plate, which appeared in the May 1693 issue of the Mercure Galant, was probably the earliest publication showing the new honour that Louis XIV bestowed to the officers of France's armed forces. The front had a figure showing the pious king of France Louis IX (1214-1270) who led the Eight Crusade and was canonised to sanctity. The obverse had a sword with a laurel wreath. Author's photo.

8-7 (right): The large gold embroidery cross of the Royal and Military Order of Saint-Louis, early 18th century. This was worn of the breast of the coat of grand cross officers of the order only. Commanders and ordinary knights were not allowed to wear it. Musée de la Légion d'Honneur, Paris. Author's photo.

8-8 (bottom right): The knight's cross of the Royal and Military Order of Saint-Louis, 1698. This medal was awarded to Philippe de Rigaud de Vaudreuil (c.1643–1725), King's Musketeer in 1672, commandant of troops in Canada in 1687, governor of Montreal in 1699 andgovernor general of New France in 1703. De Vaudreuil was promoted commander of the order in 1712 and honourary grand cross in 1721. Gold cross with white enamel edge with gilt tips, blue centre with gilt figure and letters, gold lilies and attachment to a scarlet silk ribbon. Château de Ramezay Museum, Montreal. Author's photo.

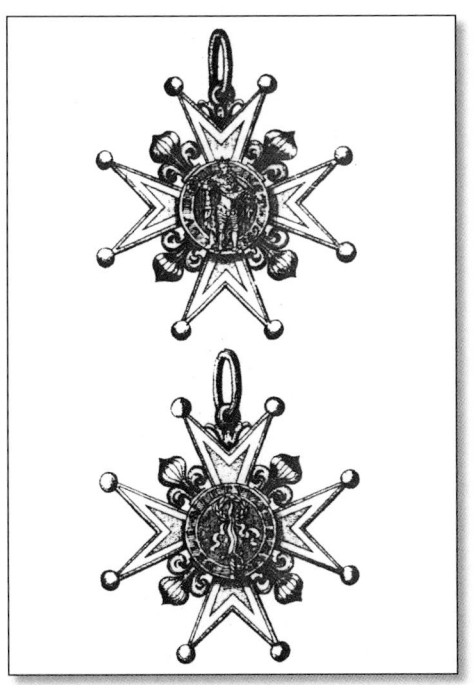

the League of Augsburg in 1697, a total of 591 officers received the honour. From thence until 1714, there are no precise numbers known and estimates suggest that some 1,300 to 1,500 officers were awarded the Order so that about 2,000 officers became knights of Saint-Louis during the reign of the Sun King. Seniority was determined by the admission date to the order without regard to the rank of the knight. A marshal could thus be junior to a lieutenant. In order to reward certain senior officers, honorary grand crosses were created to surpass the eight allowed.

The medal of the Order was an eight-point gold and white enamel cross with gilt lilies at its corners and, at centre, an image of Saint-Louis at its centre one side and a rendering of a sword with laurel leaves on the other. Knights wore their cross suspended on a scarlet silk ribbon attached to a buttonhole on the chest of their coat. Commanders wore the cross suspended from a broad scarlet silk sash over the right shoulder over the waistcoat, but under the coat. Grand cross recipients had a similar sash and were further to add a silver and gold embroidered cross on the left breast of the coat. There was no uniform prescribed for the Order until 1719.[3]

Order of the Golden Fleece

This order was created at Bruges on 10 February 1492 by Philippe le Bon, Duc de Bourgogne when he married Isabel of Portugal. It consisted 24 and later 31 noble knights. In time, the order became common in the Holy Roman Empire due to the descendance of Marie de Bourgogne and, from the 16th century, in Spain by virtue of the Hapsburg royal family. With the nomination to the Spanish throne of Louis XIV's grandson, Philippe Duc d'Anjou, as Felipe V, the order was maintained and certain French high officials, such as Marshal Boufflers in 1703, were made knights of the order by the King of Spain. This explains why it can be seen on some French officer's portraits.

Its badge consisted of an intertwined gold collar whose links formed a slanted "B" for the word *Bourgogne* (Burgundy) with red jewels formed into the shape of flammes with the motto: *Ante ferit quam flamma micet* (It strikes before the flamme appears). Its badge was a golden fleece with the motto: *Pretium non vile laborum* (No mean reward for labour). The knights had a red cloak lined with ermine. On solemn occasions, they wore a silver cloth robe with a violet velvet hood.[4]

---

3 A. Cloarec, 'L'Ordre Royal et Militaire de Saint-Louis & l'Institution du Mérite Militaire', *Art & Curiosité*, November-December 1975; Aegidieus Fauteux, *Les Chevaliers de Saint-Louis en Canada* (Montreal, 1940); Alexandre Mazas, *Histoire de l'Ordre de Saint-Louis* (Paris, 1855), Vol. 1. The 1719 uniform consisted of a black coat with scarlet cuffs and lining, gold buttons and buttonhole lace and a black cloak with scarlet lining for grand cross and commanders; for the knights, simply a black coat with scarlet cuffs and lining with gold buttons only.
4 *Mercure Galant*, September 1703, pp. 18, 25–27.

The Order of the Hospitaliers of St. John of Jerusalem (Knights of Malta)

This order was not awarded by the king, but it was prestigious and played an important role in the diplomatic as well as the military affairs of France. Its French recipients were not only approved by royal authority, but also encouraged to spend time serving with the Knights in the Mediterranean since it was an excellent way acquire military and naval knowledge as well as combat experience. Originating shortly after the capture of Jerusalem by the Crusaders in 1099 AD, the knightly Order of the Hospitaliers of St. John of Jerusalem looked after the safety and health of pilgrims to the Holy Land. After the fall of Acre (now in Israel) in 1291, the order moved to Cyprus, then Rhodes in 1310 until driven out by the Ottoman Turks in 1522. Having been granted the islands of Malta in 1530, the Knights proceeded to transform it into one of the most powerful fortresses in the Mediterranean. The modest, but redoubtable Maltese fleet engaged any Arab or Ottoman Turk ship and its contingents of knights, with their sergeants and soldiers, were often part of military expeditions sponsored by Venice and other Christian European powers. They thus became known as the Knights of Malta.

To sustain their activities in the Mediterranean, the Knights obtained property in several western European countries where they set up *commanderies* that were knight's lodges with the blessings of their respective governments. On the whole, their military activities were lauded by Europe's monarchs from both a religious and a strategic point of view. Malta was the key to the western Mediterranean and if it ever fell to the Ottoman Turks, as it nearly did in 1565, it would have been a disaster for western powers. During the 17th and 18th centuries, there were some 2,000 Knights and at least half of them were French. The Knights were not all in Malta and, indeed, France had nearly 50 *commanderies* in its territory. Each had several resident knights that, much like senior monks, managed hospitals and land estates whose profits would sustain the order in Malta while others served at Valetta, the capital of the islands. French influence in the Order of Malta was substantial since at least half of its revenues and its knights, often from wealthy noble families, came from France. Indeed many young noblemen in France were sent to Malta to learn the arts of war and navigation, be received as Knights and eventually come back home as fully experienced military men; many would then join the French royal army or navy. Knights of Malta were to be celibate and, if French, could not be admitted to orders like that of Saint-Louis. Unless, and it occasionally occurred, a Knight of Malta resigned to marry and thus became eligible to be received, usually, in the Order of Saint-Louis.[5]

Following the 1565 siege of Malta by the Ottoman Turks, which was repulsed, the knights embarked on an ambitious fortification programme that went on until the end of the 18th century. Its aim, shared by western nations, was to

---

[5] La Roque, *Traité de la noblesse*, pp. 457–458; M. de Saint-Allais, *L'Ordre de Malte* (Paris, 1839); Louis XIV. *Lettres*, Vol. 2, pp. 101–102; Delphine Gautier, *Le château de Bellecroix, ancienne commanderie de l'order de Malte/The Castle of Bellecroix, the Ancient Commandery of the Order of Malta* (Chagny: Centre de Castellologie de Bourgogne, 2014).

8-9 (above): Martin de Rédan, Grand Master of the Order of Malta from 1657 to 1660. He has the black robe bearing the white eight-pointed cross worn when knights were not on campaign. Portrait at the Palace of the Grand Master, Valetta, Malta. Author's photo.

8-10 (top right): Hugues de Rabutin, knight of the Order of Malta and, from 1644, "Grand Prieur" of the order in France. He wears the scarlet cassock bearing the white cross, which was the campaign and war dress of the knights. This portrait may be posthumous to his death in 1656. Château de Bussy-Rabutin, Burgundy. Author's photo.

make Malta next to impregnable as a massive first line defence against invasion attempts into the western Mediterranean and its coastlines by the mighty Ottoman Turks. As decades went by, mighty citadels rose around Valetta, the capital, built according to the latest trends in fortifications. These were at first of Italian designs, then increasingly French during the 17th century. Indeed, the government of the Knights shifted gradually away from the Imperial Hapsburg sphere of influence to that of Louis XIV's France. The Sun King's rays shone ever stronger on Malta thanks to France's growing military and naval might as well as its undisputed mastery in military architecture.

At the beginning of his personal reign, Louis XIV had sent expeditions to fight the Ottoman Turks in Hungary and Crete, but thereafter adopted a somewhat more neutral stance. He could do so since, in a way and although not part of the French army, many French knights and soldiers belonging to the Order of Malta did fight the Turks for Christianity, thus contributing an indirect French presence in various local Mediterranean operations. The neutrality between the Ottomans and France basically held unit 1714 when the Ottomans, perhaps thinking that western nations were exhausted by the War of the Spanish Succession, threatened a massive attack on Malta. The French response from Louis XIV was swift: artillery, ammunition, money and a group of military advisers including some of the best engineers of the French army arrived in Malta, reorganised its troops and defences and built yet more state-of-the-art fortifications. The Ottomans changed their plans and shifted their efforts elsewhere.[6]

Initially, the members of the Order of the Hospitaliers of St. John of Jerusalem wore a long black robe bearing a white cross until August 1259

---

6   Stephen C. Spiteri, *The Art of Fortress Building in Hospitalier Malta* (Malta: BDL Publishing, 2008) is the most complete and outstanding study of fortifications.

ORDERS OF CHIVALRY

8-11 (right): Model of the Knights of Malta's Commanderie of Bellecroix, 16th to 18th centuries. Commanderies were not lodged in great castles, but usually in rather small fortified keeps such as this one in Burgundy near Beaune. The chapel was at the top, lodgings at upper right whose small tower was the dungeon and other utilitarian structures with its wall. It was surrounded by a ditch and access was through a fortified gate. The resident knights managed the order's property in the area and had a small hospital within. This Commanderie was expanded in the 19th century and is now a small hotel whose owners have remarkably preserved. Model by Pierre Tison after land survey plans and research at the site by the Centre de Castellogie de Bourgogne. Author's photo.

8-12 (below): Interior of the modest chapel of the Commanderie of Bellecroix as it probably looked in the 17th century. Note the insignias of the Knights of Malta. Château de Bellecroix, Chagny, Burgundy. Author's photo.

8-13 (above): Cross of the Order of Malta in the chapel of the Commanderie of Bellecroix in Burgundy. This white cross on red was the combat insignia of the order and was also used as the order's flag. Château de Bellecroix, Chagny, Burgundy. Author's photo.

when Pope Alexander IV ordered that, to distinguish the Knights from the other friars of the Order, that they wear in peacetime a black cloak with the eight-pointed white cross. For instance, on 8 September 1669, the Chevalier de Bouillon's 70-gun French warship arrived in Valetta and was he received by the Grand Master escorted by over a hundred Knights marching two by two wearing "a black cloak with a white cross and with a small sword at the side". When going to war, they were assigned a red cassock with a large white cross without points on the breast and at the back. This remained the basic dress of the Order of Malta. During the Duc de Beaufort's failed expedition in Algeria in 1664, the Knights of the Maltese contingent were seen fighting wearing "their red cassocks with the white cross" according to the *Gazette* of 28 August. The *Mercure Galant* of September 1684 reported amongst the troops attacking the Ottoman Turks at "Sainte-Maure" was a battalion of a thousand troops from Malta whose "first line … was made up of one hundred knights wearing their red satin cassocks with the white cross." The soldiers and sailors appear to have usually worn red coats. Grand cross recipients wore a white enamelled gold eight-pointed cross suspended by a black collar ribbon. Commanders and their Knights hung the cross as a medal suspended from a black ribbon fastened through a buttonhole.[7]

---

7 La Roque, *Traité de la noblesse*, p. 459; the Chevalier de Bouillon quoted in *Correspondance du maréchal de Vivonne relative à l'expédition de Candie (1669)*, Jean Cordey, ed. (Paris: Renouard, 1890), p. 156; Herbert S. Vaughan, 'Some notes on uniforms in the navy of the Order of St. John', *Mariner's Mirror*, VII (1921): 298–307.

9

The Royal Guard: Units *Au Dedans du Louvre*

It was during Louis XIVs personal rule that the royal guard went from being a rather strong personal guard to an army corps-sized organisation that was meant to be the elite and the example for the rest of the army to follow. The 1659 peace treaty with Spain had brought the usual sharp reductions in the army, but this time, there was a new twist. No doubt on the advice of Minister of War Le Tellier, some of the army's best officers and men were incorporated into the royal guard instead of being sent home and this continued when Louis XIV assumed full power in 1661. Eventually, the guard cavalry mustered at least 3,200 men and the infantry some 6,000 men. The guard was not a collection of parade units. It was a group of fighting units and its privileged members could even be found in combat as far as Algeria and Crete. Guard units were privileged to serve near the Sun King and had precedence over all other armed formations in the nation.

The guard also assumed and defined what elite troops were supposed to be. They were subject to stricter discipline, but had better pay. Ranks in the guard were much higher than in line units, but then, so was the price of officers' commissions. They had superior-quality weapons and also had finer uniforms, the officers being required to have magnificent ones, especially as the guards were always under the eyes of the Sun King and his attention to detail was exacting. Minister of finances Colbert was opposed to such a luxurious expansion that would, in his opinion undermine finances as well as morale in the bulk of the army. Louis XIV ignored his advice and went ahead. The rest of the army might grumble while admiring and respecting guardsmen as warriors of great valour. Overall, the Sun King had sensed correctly the French nation's love of grandeur and also that the sun's rays might well project France's *gloire* all over the world.

There are many anecdotes in memoirs of guardsmen who came under the scrutiny of the King's eye, which obviously terrified them. For the King, it was important to have the grandest, best-appointed, finest-looking guard to awe both the King's subjects and foreign visitors. To make sure of this, proposals for new uniforms had to be submitted to the King's consideration until he was satisfied that they could be adopted. These garments may not have been always practical to wear, but the magnificence the Sun King demanded was much more than a fashion show. His guardsmen had to have the look of the best and most powerful such unit in Europe and impose its appearance and prestige on the guards of all other kingdoms, which it did. On the battlefield, these same gilded troops were expected to have outstanding bravery since they were the very flower of the army, the pride and honour of France and its ruler. Under Louis XIV, the royal guard also assumed a leading role in the education of young gentlemen, notably in the King's Musketeers, that were expanded to become a military academy.

The royal guard was called *La Maison du Roi* (the King's Household) and, from 1671, the Sun King specifically stated that, henceforth, when deployed during hostilities, it would be a distinct army corps. This allowed to King to directly control his guardsmen on campaign. This special body of troops was divided into two entities:

The guard units that served *au dedans du Louvre* (within the royal palace of the Louvre) and later Versailles. These were: the Garde du Corps which included the 24 Gardes de la Manche, the Cent-Suisses and the Gardes de la Porte. All these units wore blue uniforms and were sometimes called *la maison bleue* (the blue household).

The units that served *au dehors du Louvre* (outside the royal palace of the Louvre) were: the Gendarmes de la Garde, the Chevau-légers de la Garde, the Mousquetaires du Roi and the Grenadiers à Cheval de la Garde. These cavalry units were sometimes nicknamed the *maison rouge* (red household) due to the colour of their uniforms although the Grenadiers à Cheval switched to blue in 1692. The guard outside the Louvre also included the two infantry units of the Gardes Françaises, the Gardes Suisses infantry regiments.[1]

Finally there was the company of the Gentilshommes Ordinaires de la Garde (also called *au Bec de Corbin*), a unit of noble gentlemen that only served at certain state ceremonies.

Dressed to Impress

The dress of the royal guard that served near the sovereign was always impressive. The clothing was in the colour of his livery and the arms the guardsmen carried were of fine quality. In the first half of the 17th century, cassocks were commonly worn by soldiers and those of guardsmen were always more luxurious being often trimmed with silver and gold lace and embroidery. They were seen in their finest garbs by the populace at solemn ceremonies or festival-like parades entering cities. From the accounts of chroniclers, these events were aimed to give a spectacle of luxury and power thus impressing the beholders of all classes of society. Young Louis XIV clearly understood this and, once he assumed power, took steps to have the most superb-looking and numerous guard yet seen in France.

---

1 Frédéric Chauviré, 'La maison du roi sous Louis XIV, une troupe d'élite', *Revue historique des armées*, 242/2006 and 255/2009. Online: <http://rha.revues.org/4012> and 6764.

By an ordinance of 16 January 1665, the King "…ordered and orders that all the officers of his troops serving at the guard of his person, and others of his household, will be able to wear blue coats with gold or silver lace, specifically the officers of his Regiment of Gardes Françaises with silver lace; those of his Regiment of Gardes Suisses with gold lace; those of the companies of Gardes du Corps with gold and silver lace; those of the Musketeers without silver [only gold], and other officers of his household gold and silver, or all silver at their choice." This was the guard's version of the much coveted *justeaucorps à brevet* amongst courtiers and surely meant by the King to provide his guard's officers with unquestionable prestige at court.[2]

While each unit had its own uniforms as indicated below, several descriptions of ceremonial dress events also reveal that, in some cases, a special dress would be worn by several guard units, which was not their regular uniform. On such occasions, and notably to greet and impress embassies from important countries outside of western Europe, the royal guard would be dressed in special uniforms so as to suitably project the grandeur and luxury of the Sun King's court on festive days.

For instance, William Perwich's dispatch of 7 December 1669 noted that, for the reception of the Turkish ambassador at Saint-Germain on the previous Thursday, "All troops [of the guards] were in rich new habits, especially the King's Musketeers, who had all black velvet coats with gilded buttons & were on foot next to the palace; the officers had rich embroidered coats, and the King had a coat on so much valued for the great number of diamonds. *Monsieur*, the King's brother, was in black cloth, had diamond buttons, & a belt covered with pearls and diamonds." This sparkling array must have been suitably impressive.

When an embassy arrived from Siam (Thailand) at Versailles during the summer of 1686, the ambassador and his party were greeted by *Monsieur* and Minister of War Louvois in the first courtyard. There were 1,000 men of the Gardes Françaises and Gardes Suisses "who were all dressed with embroidered red coats, and formed in five ranks on each side, all the officers holding their pikes." The obviously impressed embassy was told that this was the ordinary guard outside the chateau. They then went on to meet Louis XIV.[3]

The Gardes du Corps

This unit was in all respects the equivalent to Britain's Life Guards. It marched ahead in precedence of all other guard and line units. Its 1st Company was originally raised from Scots in the mid 1400s – the exact date is not verifiable although given as 1440 by Susane – by King Charles VII who felt he needed a totally trustworthy and non-political personal guard; these were the days of Joan of Arc and the final stages of the Hundred Years War when would-be assassins might be French, but from territories controlled by the rival Duc de

---

2 BMA, Ordonnances, 16 January 1665.
3 *The Despatches of William Perwich … 1669–1677*, Beryl Curran, ed., (London, 1903), p. 47); *Mercure Galant*, September 1686, 2nd part, pp. 177–178.

Bourgogne or the English. The Scots recruits of both officers and men became rarer during the 16th century so the company became increasing French while retaining Scots features. For instance, during roll call according to the 1708 *État de la France* register, the troopers would answer *Hhay hhamier*, a corruption of "I am here" that seems to indicate that its original members spoke more English than Gaelic. The last recorded Scots trooper of the Gardes du Corps was one David Seyton (or Ceton) who vanishes from the muster rolls in 1693. Whatever they spoke, they had a reputation for being valiantly killed on the spot rather than exposing the king. Indeed, they were credited with saving the life of King Louis XI at Montléry in 1465.[4]

This company became the 1st *Compagnie écossaise* (Scottish Company) when more guard companies recruited from Frenchmen were raised in 1474, 1479 and 1515. At that time, they all were denominated Gardes du Corps and eventually given a double numbering system.

The precedence of the companies was not according to its date of organisation, but according to the seniority of its captain. There are contradictions on how this actually worked and, like most modern authors, we follow the numbering of 1st to 4th, which seems to have been the system mainly used from the middle of the 17th century. The 1st Scots Company was the king's and the colonel's company of the unit so it was always senior. The three other French companies could shift in precedence depending on the latest appointment to captain. This changed the colour of the company's distinctive bandolier.

9-1 Trooper of the Gardes du Corps, 1649. At that time, according to the *État et gouvernement de la France*, each of the Gardes du Corps' four companies had 100 troopers that wore scarlet cassocks laced with silver. They were armed with swords, carbine and halberds for service on foot. Print after Alfred de Marbot. Canadian War Museum, Ottawa. Author's photo.

During the reign of the Sun King, the captains were:[5]

1st Gardes du Corps Company and *Compagnie écossaise* (Scottish Company).
　François de Rochechouard, Marquis de Chandenier, October 1642.
　Anne, Comte de Noailles, 10 January 1651.
　Anne-Jules, Duc de Noailles (Marshal in 1693), 5 February 1678.
　Adrien-Maurice, Duc de Noailles (Marshal in 1734), 17 February 1707.

2nd Gardes du Corps Company and 1st *Compagnie française* (French Company).

4　André Corvisier, 'Les gardes du corps de Louis XIV', *Bulletin du XVIIe siècle*, 1959, pp. 265–291 has been our main source for this notice.
5　Louis Susane, *Histoire de la cavalerie française* (Paris: J. Dumaine, 1874), Vol. 2, pp. 211–220.

Louis de Béthune, Comte de Charost, 1 June 1634.
François-René du Plessis, Marquis de Jarzé, 17 August 1648.
Louis de Béthune, Comte de Charost, 9 November 1649.
Armand de Béthune, Duc de Charost, 1663.
Jean-Henri de Durfort, Marquis de Duras (Marshal in 1675), 1 April 1672.
Louis-François, Duc de Boufflers (Marshal in 1695), 10 December 1704.
Armand de Béthune, Duc de Charost, 21 October 1711.

3rd Gardes du Corps Company and 2nd *Compagnie Française* (French Company).
François Potier, Marquis de Gandelus, 10 August 1643.
Léon Potier, Duc de Gesvres, 1646.
Antoine Nompar de Caumont, Duc de Lauzun, 28 July 1669.
François-Henri de Montmorency, Duc de Luxembourg (Marshal in 1675), 11 February 1673.
François de Neufville, Duc de Villeroi (Marshal in 1693), 1 February 1695.

4th Gardes du Corps Company and 3rd *Compagnie française* (French Company).
Antoine, Duc d'Aumont (Marshal in 1651), 23 November 1632.
Louis-Marie-Victor d'Aumont, Marquis de Villequier, 3 June 1651.
Henri-Louis d'Aloigny, Marquis de Rochefort (Marshal in 1675), 10 March 1669.
Guy-Aldonce de Durfort, Comte de Lorges (Marshal in 1675), 12 June 1676.
Henri, Duc d'Harcourt (Marshal in 1703), 26 February 1703.

Up to the 1660s, not only officers but also troopers bought their post in the unit. In the Gardes du Corps, prospective troopers paid captains so they could be admitted; they were nearly always the sons of wealthy businessmen from families that were not nobles and thus escaped paying substantial taxes since members of the unit were exempt. The Sun King felt that money and tax evasion did not mix well with the prospect of having blindly loyal elite troopers of such efficiency and heroism in battle that they would be examples to follow. The royal wish for a real guard unit was acted upon.

The Gardes du Corps was nearly unique in the army in that Louvois managed to suppress the purchase system for its officers, except the captains who remained venal posts. A royal regulation of 30 September 1664 announced that all commissioned ranks below captain would henceforth be appointed directly by the king rather than by the captains. That effectively ended purchase. Many of the previously appointed officers were wealthy noblemen not especially keen on a military career, but purchasing commissions in this unit gave them a permanent presence at court where they could lobby officials for privileges in pleasant surroundings with the prestige of being a guards officer. The incumbent officers were probably encouraged to leave the unit unless they resolved to be real soldiers; new officers were to be noble gentlemen, Roman Catholics and, as much as possible, experienced and battle-tested cavalrymen. The Sun King wanted real fighting men as guards officers that would enforce much stricter discipline on all guardsmen.

9-2 Anne-Jules, Duc de Noailles, captain of the 1st (Scottish) Company of the Gardes du Corps from 1678 to 1707 and marshal of France. He succeeded his father who was captain from 1651 and his son assumed the post of captain from 1707 with Noailles' family descendants assuming command until the French Revolution. Command of the other Gardes du Corps companies was also passed on by generations of "grand" noble families. Print after Hyacinthe Rigaud. Rijksmuseum, Amsterdam. RP-P-1941-278.

In effect he totally militarised the unit to make it a real elite corps. The captain's rank, however, remained accessible to noble persons with money. An outlandish example was the commission of the Duke de Lauzun bought for 750,000 pounds by his immensely wealthy mistress, Mademoiselle de Montpensier, the famed *Grande Mademoiselle*. These venal captains had the honours and their names were published in the registers, but they were not the day-to-day commanders.[6]

Henceforth, the Gardes du Corps was in fact more like a large cavalry brigade than a regiment. At the beginning of the reign, each company had 100 troopers and this grew to 360 in 1667, which was about the size of a line cavalry regiment. This was, according to the King, because of the large number of noble gentlemen "of quality" that constantly asked him for "a place" in the corps. To be accepted as a trooper, one also had to be Roman Catholic, be five feet five inches tall (1.77 m), be about 22 or 23 years old, have a sturdy physique, be handsome and originate from a family with sufficient income for a gentlemanly lifestyle. So the unit's four companies amounted to 1,440 men, reduced to 300 men per company in 1668, but raised to 400 men per company in 1676 and finally stabilised at 360 per company in 1692. From the 1670s, the unit having become much larger, each company served a quarter year at the royal palace. For the 1st Company, this went from 1 January to 31 March, its ordinary quarters being otherwise at Beauvais; the 2nd from 1 April to 30 June with quarters at Coulomniers;

---

6 Louis XIV. *Lettres*, Vol. 2, pp. 247–248. Purchase had been ordered abolished on 19 August 1648, but this was just a few days before the outbreak of the Fronde uprisings and it remained unenforced until 1664. On the cost of Captain Lauzun's commission, a marginal note on a letter from the King to the Duc de Montmorency dated 21 October 1672 at Saint-Germain-en-Laye states that: 'the king has settled the price of the charge of captain of the Gardes du Corps of Monsieur de Lauzun at the price of 400,000 pounds and to pay it and satisfy … 200,000 pounds that His Majesty has given to Madame de Nogent and her children, on the charge of *Maître de la Garde-robe* (Master of the Wardrobe), he gives to Mr. de Luxembourg the said charge of Monsieur de Nogent, from which he will make 550,000 livres; therefore the charge of Monsieur de Lauzun will only cost him 50,000 livres.' From the opacity of this note and the different prices quoted for the commission, one can see there was a great deal of financial manoeuvring at the highest levels.

the 3rd from 1 July to 31 September with quarters at Pontoise; the 4th from 1 October to 31 December with quarters at Dreux.[7]

Until 1664, there was one lieutenant and one ensign per company when this was raised to two lieutenants and two ensigns, both ranks raised to three in 1677. There were 10 exempts in 1664 and a dozen later on; this rank was an NCO in line units, but considered an officer in the guard cavalry. In 1665, there were 10 brigadiers raised to a dozen in 1677 with a dozen sub-brigadiers created; again, NCO ranks that were officers in the guard. For the staff of the four units, the ranks of major with two *aides-majors* were created on 29 November 1666, these last being four from 1674. They were in charge of the details such as lodging, food supply, discipline, transmission of orders and so were very busy officers. From 1693, majors had the rank of *mestre de camp* (colonel in the line) and *aide-majors* posts were filled by senior exempts. Being in the Gardes du Corps was a good path for promotion.

The 24 Gardes de la Manche were the most trusted of guardsmen and were posted nearest to the king. It was said that their name *de la Manche* (of the sleeve) was because proximity to the King sometimes made them slightly brush his coat's sleeve. They belonged to the Scots company and were the best paid soldiers of the guards, not only because of their unique prestige, but also due to having to be almost constantly at court to stand guard. During the numerous ceremonies the King presided over, six of them stood discreetly nearby ready to intervene to counter any perceived threat. During mass, two of them holding their partizans stood at either side of the King. They were also at the doors of the King's quarters or office, crossing their partizans to prevent entry to any unannounced person. Apart from the corps's uniform, the Gardes de la Manche had a luxurious *hoqueton* sleeveless surcoat described below. The Gardes de la Manche nearly always served on foot throughout the reign. However, until the later 1660s, personnel from other companies could also be found on foot service guarding royal palaces.

The service on campaign were many and glorious since the Gardes du Corps were mixed with other troops; each company was put at the head of a brigade of line cavalry. This was still the case during the War of Devolution. From the 1672 invasion of the Netherlands, the Gardes du Corps henceforth went on campaign together as a large cavalry brigade. They were then under the command of the most senior officer serving in the unit (some captains were marshals commanding armies) with the rank of lieutenant-general in the army. Always a prime fighting force, the Gardes du Corps were especially noted for outstanding valour at Leuze (1691) and Malplaquet (1709).

At the royal palace, the escort and surveillance service of the King only required a small number of guardsmen: three lieutenants, three ensigns, one exempt, two brigadiers, two sub-brigadiers, two Gardes de la Manche and 20 guards. They were tasked with various services amongst which the king's daily dinner was possibly the more involved duty. There were *au grand couvert* state banquets. Also *au public* (in public) dinners when the

---

7   Christian-Gérard and Eugène Lelièpvre, *Maison bleue – maison rouge, cavaliers du roi soleil*, (Paris: Centaure, 1945), p. 11.

king dined in front of quite a crowd since anyone decently dressed could watch him eat (with his fingers as he rarely used a fork). This was a popular form of entertainment that even drew people making the trip from Paris to Versailles to witness Louis' legendary great appetite (explained by his autopsy that revealed his stomach to be twice the normal size).

The most frequent type of dinner was *au petit couvert* that suggests a small, simple meal. Not so in the Sun King's court. As with other types of dinners, some Gardes du Corps played a part in what was something of a gastronomic display parade. At least five Gardes du Corps were on hand in the kitchen discreetly seeing that the royal meal was wholesome (without poison); the dishes and wines were first tasted by the equerry of the kitchen. Once this was done and the meal declared fit for the king, the *cortège des viandes de Sa Majesté* (parade of the meats of His Majesty) was drawn up consisting, at its head, of two Gardes du Corps troopers with drawn swords, a usher, a *Maître d'Hôtel* holding his staff, a gentleman-servant of the kitchen's pantry department, the controller-general of the royal household, the dinner itself borne by servants followed by the equerry of the kitchen, an official of the butler's department and three more Gardes du Corps with drawn swords closing the parade.

The kitchen being in a different building, the escorted dinner parade would then march across and through the palace's courtyard at the sound of the repeated shout of *Les viandes du roi!* (the meats of the king!) announcing that the royal dinner was on its way. Once inside the palace, it then crossed several large rooms until it finally got to the king's table. Relating all this, historian W.H. Lewis aptly remarked: "Did Louis in his life ever taste hot food? It seems improbable except when taking pot luck with generals on active service, even allowing for the fact that in the [palace's] room where he ate there were primitive hot-plates, consisting of bowls filled with red embers." Lukewarm or cold, this *au petit couvert* dinner had a substantial crowd of courtiers milling about standing, and joined at times by a few members of the royal family who were allowed small stools except the Queen who had a chair like the king. There was little conversation as Louis ate voraciously with his fingers; he talked between meals.[8]

Companies of the Gardes du Corps further provided detachments for the escort of royal family members. For instance, in 1689, the Dauphin was accompanied by two officers, two NCOs and 20 guardsmen while his wife, the Dauphine, had an officer, an NCO and 12 guardsmen. When the Duc d'Anjou travelled to Madrid in late 1700 to assume his throne as King Felipe V "of Spain and the Indies", he was escorted by two officers leading 120 guardsmen.

The Gardes du Corps also had important ceremonial functions since the unit's major was the King's representative at such events. At religious ceremonies in church, he would indicate the proper place where the noble faithful should be and would also make sure that everyone was properly

---

8   W.H. Lewis, *The Splendid Century, Life in the France of Louis XIV* (London: William Sloane, 1953), pp. 51, 205

dressed for the occasion. The exempt of the Gardes du Corps tasked specifically for *les cérémonies* had duties that were unheard of for other exempts; for most ceremonies, he would regulate the order of precedence, which required a good mixture of tact with authority as he was surely eternally faced with anxious noble courtiers and ambitious *courtisanes* that would try every trick in the book to be seen as close to the Sun King as possible. For many years, this diplomat in uniform was one Louis-François de Gémaris, Sieur des Essarts who retired in favour of his son in 1717.

Some Gardes du Corps were also tasked with potentially delicate duties that required utmost discretion and swift efficiency. Like the King's Musketeers, they might take people of high standing into custody on the King's orders. Courtly young ladies, such as Mademoiselle de Carignan and Mademoiselle de Soissons, could get into serious trouble by their "conduct, for so long utterly indecent and their debauchery so prostituted" as Saint-Simon put it. In March 1698, the Duke of Savoy and the Elector of Bavaria, these young ladies' relatives, asked Louis XIV to intervene. They were part of princely families that could not tolerate such behaviour since it generated much gossip. So, one day, a Gardes du Corps lieutenant with some guardsmen appeared at Mademoiselle de Carignan's residence, and put her in the carriage of the ambassador of Savoy nearby that took her to the Filles de Sainte-Marie convent escorted by a strong guard. Mademoiselle de Soissons was similarly whisked away to a convent in Brussels. There were undoubtedly many more such incidents involving the Gardes du Corps that were, of course, wilfully unrecorded; it is only by the memoirs of individuals, such as Saint-Simon and Dangeau, that some are known.[9]

Early in his personal reign, the Sun King felt that the Gardes du Corps should also be a military academy leading to an officer's commission in the army. From the time of its reorganisation in 1664–1665, some 80 cadets were part of the unit at the rate of 20 per company "so they could learn their trade" as the King put it. Having a few cadets was a long-standing practice in the line regiments, but less so in guard units, where young noblemen from rich families would have preference for commissions. Henceforth, the King wanted that even royal princes should spend time learning to be officers by carrying out the same duties as ordinary troopers. Saint-Simon felt it was a "useless" notion to ask noblemen to serve with common guardsmen. By 1674, there were over 50 cadets in the unit who usually served as such for a year or two, then earned a lieutenant's commission in the line cavalry. The expenses for these cadets were paid for by the royal funds and there were probably more cadets serving at their family's expense. Eventually, the King decided that cadets were no longer necessary in the Gardes du Corps and none were listed in the musters by 1678.

Although some officers – usually independently wealthy – had many luxuries, the Gardes du Corps troopers, while being paid 15 sols daily

---

9   Philippe de Courcillon de Dangeau, *Mémoires et journal* (Paris, 1830), Vol. 4, p. 214–215; Louis de Rouvroy, Duc de Saint-Simon, *Mémoires inédites du Duc de Saint-Simon sur le siècle de Louis XIV* (Paris, 1830), p. 473.

compared to 7 sols for line cavalrymen, also had their share of hardships. In 1710, when the money supply for the army dried up, many troopers in all four companies had not been paid since the beginning of the campaign and "did not know what to do to stay alive" in such circumstances. The situation was of course the same for their servants, many of whom left. Care and forage for the horses was a further problem. One assumes that some relief did reach them because the unit remained on service.[10]

Main Battles, Sieges and Campaigns[11]

1667 Tournai, Douai, Lille
1668 Franche-Comté
1669 Candie
1672 Rhine, Doesburg, Utrecht, Andernach
1673 Courtrai, Deinse, Brussels, Maastricht, Colmar
1674 Besançon, Dôle, Fauconnier, Senef
1676 Condé
1677 Valenciennes, Cambrai, Kokesberg, Fribourg
1678 Gand (Ghent), Schinghem
1683 Besançon
1684 Luxembourg
1688 Huy
1689 Valcourt
1691 Mons, Leuze
1692 Namur, Steenkirk
1693 Neerwinden, Charleroi
1695 Brussels
1706 Ramillies
1708 Oudenarde
1709 Malplaquet
1713 Landau

The Gardes du Corps were praised for their fighting qualities. At the 1674 battle of Senef, William Prince of Orange is said to have cried out: "If I had such troops, I would be invincible!"[12]

Uniforms, Weapons, Standards

Until the late 1650s, the Gardes du Corps wore scarlet cassocks, possibly lined with blue and certainly trimmed with silver and white, the colours of the royal livery, but with the emphasis being given on scarlet rather than

---

10 Corvisier, 'Les gardes du corps de Louis XIV', p. 285.
11 The regiment's main battles during the reign are given in Susane, *Histoire de la cavalerie française*, Vol. 2, p. 211. Officer casualties are often named in Daniel, *Histoire de la milice françoise*, Vol. 2. For a general account of the battles, see Quincy, *Histoire militaire*, Vol. 1. Official dispatches of the battles are usually found in the *Gazette*.
12 Cited in: Nicolas Plaideux, 'Les Gardes du Corps du roi', *Les grandes batailles de l'histoire*, No. 25 (November 1993), p. 86.

9-3 A detachment of the Gardes du Corps wearing its red cassocks on campaign, c.1656. Detail from an unsigned period painting. Musée Condé, Chantilly. Author's photo.

blue. The *Gazette* of 19 July 1645 describes the Gardes du Corps "…dressed in their scarlet cassocks decorated with gold and silver embroidery…". According to the *Estat et gouvernment de la France* for 1649, each of the four companies had a captain, a lieutenant, an ensign, four exempts, who then acted as sergeant and had a baton as their badge of rank, and 100 guards. The Gardes de la Manche of the 1st Company wore their distinctive *hoqueton* surcoats and carried a halberd with a gilded blade and decorated with a gold tassel. All others had scarlet cassocks decorated with silver. What exactly the decorations on the cassocks were is uncertain, but it was almost certainly a white or silver-white cross with gold lilies at the ends and the corners of the cross, which was on the cassock's chest and back, with sliver lace edgings and small silver buttons. The other garments are not described, but could have been in the blue and red hues of the king's livery. They were armed with rifled carbines, swords, pistols and halberds.[13]

At a 1656 cavalcade in Paris, the Comte de Noailles, captain of the 1st Company of the Gardes du Corps was seen "wearing a coat [covered with] gold and silver embroidery with a magnificent bouquet of red and white plumes [on the hat] and mounted on a beautiful Spanish horse with housings also covered with gold and silver embroidery…". The troopers of the Gardes du Corps now wore "their scarlet cassocks enriched with gold embroidery…". It thus seems that the trimming had been changed to gold. On 27 March

---

13 Noirmont and Marbot, *Costumes militaires français*, Vol. 1, p. 64 citing the 1649 *Estat et gouvernment*. A battle painting at the Musée Condé shows the cassock with the lilies as does an engraving noted by Paul Martin in *Le Passepoil*, No. 1, 1930, p. 14.

9-4 Gardes du Corps escorting a royal carriage across the Pont-Neuf in Paris, mid 1660s. Most guardsmen wear buff coats, others blue or red coats who are probably officers or musicians. Unsigned contemporary painting. Musée Carnavalet, Paris. Author's photo.

1657, two visitors in Paris noted that "the Gardes du Corps, who carry the halberd or the *carabine* [rifled carbine]…".[14]

A much bigger change was on hand. On 23 April 1657, "His Majesty … had 200 men of the Gardes du corps drill on the plain of Montmartre who were chosen from the four companies, and to whom were distributed blue cassocks enriched by various ciphers in gold and silver embroidery…". This was when the Gardes du Corps went into a blue livery, which eventually would become its near-legendary blue uniform. Three years later, the trumpeters of the Gardes du Corps were "all wearing blue velvet coats garnished with gold lace…". For the 1660 entry of the King into Paris, the troopers wore blue cassocks laced silver and enhanced at front and back with an embroidered cross formed by 12 lilies and four royal crowns.[15]

In 1661, the Gardes du Corps were seen without cassocks and wearing breastplates. From early times, the guardsmen wore bandoliers to hook on their bows and later their carbines. The bandoliers "were silver, because the white hue was always the colour of France" Father Daniel related. It was probably some time before 1660 that distinctive colours were added for the other companies. According to the 1661 *État de la France*, the 1st Company (Noailles) had white, the 2nd Company (Tresme) had green, the 3rd Company (Aumont) had orange and the 4th Company (Charost) had blue. By 1669, this had changed to: 2nd Company (Charost), blue; 3rd Company (Lauzun), green and 4th Company (Rochefort), yellow. The colours for the bandoliers remained the same until the mid 1690s. By 1698 however, the *État de la France* had 2nd (Duras), blue; 3rd (Lorges), yellow and 4th (Villeroi), green bandoliers; in 1708: 2nd (Villeroi), green; 3rd (Harcourt), yellow and 4th (Boufflers), blue bandoliers, which would have been due to marshals Harcourt and Boufflers having been appointed as captains in 1703 and 1704 respectively. It must have been as totally confusing then as it is now…

---

14 *Gazette*, 1656, pp. 340, 978; *Journal d'un voyage à Paris en 1657 et 1658, tenu par M. de Somme Indick et M. de Villers*, (Paris, 1862), p. 79.

15 *Gazette*, 1657, p. 407; *Nouvelle relation concernant l'entrevue et serment des rois…et cérémonies qui se sont faites au mariage du roi et de l'infante d'Espagne* (Paris, 1660), p. 13; Noirmont and Marbot, *Costumes militaires français*, Vol. 1, p. 63 after a contemporary account.

THE ROYAL GUARD: UNITS AU DEDANS DU LOUVRE

9-5 Guardsmen of the Garde du Corps, 1660s. Standing at left, a guardsman belonging to Captain de Tresme's 2nd (1st French) Company. The mounted guardsman belongs to the 3rd (2nd French) Company. Both wear buff coats decorated with ribbons and bandoleers of their company's colour. Print after Alfred de Marbot. Canadian War Museum, Ottawa. Author's photo.

Until about the late 1680s, each company's distinctive coloured bandoliers had the three wide and two narrow silver laces. Thereafter, the bandoliers assumed an appearance of little squares of the company colour edged with silver lace. At that time and since some years, housings for each company were, for the 1st Company: red; 2nd (Duras), blue; 3rd (Luxembourg), green and 4th (Lorges), yellow bandoliers and housings, the June 1687 *Mercure Galant* adding that "this company [4th] had orange when it was raised, but has since changed to yellow. Only the colonel's [1st Scottish Company] has housings of a different colour than its bandolier and this is because white is not a colour that should be used for housings."

The silver bandoliers had the distinctive colour applied as stripes or lines until about the 1690s when the pattern changed to small squares. These bandoliers were very important to the Sun King who wished that they would impose a certain respect. They were badges of legal authority showing that the wearer had the power to arrest individuals to carry out the King's justice. It was therefore a signal honour and Louis XIV was adamant that the troopers wear it at nearly all times. He further insisted that it be always worn over the coat, never under, and that the uniform itself be irreproachably correct.[16]

In 1667 and probably for years before, the troopers wore buff coats. The 2nd, 3rd and 4th companies were then distinguished by ribbons of their

---

16 M. de Guignard, *L'École de Mars* (Paris, 1725), Vol. 2, p. 416.

9-6 Two members of the royal guard, 1663. At left, holding a musket, is very likely a trooper of the Gardes du Corps. Next to him, a back view of an officer, possibly of the same unit, but it could also be of another guard unit such as the Gardes Suisses. Detail from a print after Charles Lebrun's depiction of the 18 November 1663 renewal of the Swiss treaties with France. Courtesy Anne S.K. Brown Military Collection, Brown University Library, Providence, USA.

company colour on their coats, clothing and hat plumes. The 1st (Scottish) Company however had red ribbons and plumes. They were armed with a sword, pistols and a wheel-lock carbine.

From January 1665, officers were to wear blue coats with gold and silver lace. In 1668, part of the Gardes du Corps troopers had blue coats with red cuffs and lining. However, this uniform was not totally adopted until the invasion of Holland from 1672. The companies continued to be distinguished by ribbons of their respective colour. British philosopher John Locke saw a review of the royal guard on 1 February 1678 that included the Gardes du Corps looking "…all lusty, well horsed and well clad, all in blue, new and alike even to their hats and gloves, armed with pistols, carbines and long back swords with well guarded hilts … some squadrons yellow ribbons and others all sky [blue]." The *Mercure Galant* of May 1679 reported that they wore new clothing consisting of a blue coat with a silver wavy lace, two fingers wide. It was not applied on all the coat seams when the review took place, but had since been added on all the seams the report added. The cuffs were of red velvet "and covered with two wide laces, one less wide than on the coat." There "were five laces on the bandolier, three wide and two narrow. The buff baldrics had lace similar to that of the coat." They also wore white sashes, silver laced hat and were armed with silver hilted swords, buff gloves and belts laced with silver. The officers had coats "all covered with lace or embroidery." When he was appointed captain of the 3rd Company in 1695, Marshal Villeroi wore a coat of blue velvet of "extraordinary magnificence" that was only exceeded by his good humour, related Madame de Sévigny.[17]

With regards to the instrument's banners for trumpeters and kettledrummers, it has been sometimes stated that they were of the company colour, but they were in fact blue; indeed, it is difficult to imagine the Sun King's own life guards not displaying his royal colours and insignia. Officers were required to mount grey horses. The troopers had no obligations

---

17 BMA, Ordonnances, 16 January 1665. This order was specifically repeated for Noailles' 1st Company on 30 January 1665. Peyrins, *Traité des marques* nationales, p. 125; *John Locke's Travels in France 1675-1679*, John Lough ed., (Cambridge: University Press, 1953), p. 186; *Mercure Galant*, May 1679, p. 280–282. Marie de Rabutin-Chantal, Marquise de Sévigné, *Lettres de Madame de Sévigné*, edited by Gault de saint-Germain (Paris: Dalibon, 1823), Vol. 11, p. 131. According to the *Mercure Galant* of March 1693, p. 305, the four captains had blue *manteaux* (cloaks) 'that are presently ornaments à Brevet (brevet ornaments). The other officers also have them but their ornaments are different.' This appears to mean that officer's cloaks were also richly decorated with embroidery and lace in silver and gold for captains and probably in silver only for the other officers.

THE ROYAL GUARD: UNITS AU DEDANS DU LOUVRE

9-7 (above): A guardsman of the Gardes du Corps, c.1675. The guardsman is probably a trooper. He belongs to the 1st (Scottish) Company) whose origins went back to the 15th century. Blue coat with scarlet cuffs, lining and breeches, silver buttons and lace, white sash, silver bandolier. Print after Alfred de Marbot. Canadian War Museum, Ottawa. Author's photo.

9-8 (right): A senior officer of the Gardes du Corps, 1677. Blue coat with scarlet cuffs, lining and breeches, silver buttons and lace, white sash, silver bandolier, white hat plumes. Print after Philippoteaux. Anne S.K. Brown Military Collection, Brown University Library, Providence, RI, USA. Author's photo..

9-9 (left): A trooper of the Gardes du Corps, c.1695. The bandolier is now has little squares showing the company's distinctive colour. This pattern remained for the next century. Print after Guérard. Anne S.K. Brown Military Collection, Brown University Library, Providence, RI, USA. Author's photo.

9-10 (below): Trumpeter of the Gardes du Corps, 1670s and 1680s. Blue coat with scarlet cuffs, lining, waistcoat and breeches, silver buttons and lace that almost covered the coat, white sash, silver edged bandolier. Print after Eugène Lelièpvre. Anne S.K. Brown Military Collection, Brown University Library, Providence, RI, USA. Author's photo.

THE ROYAL GUARD: UNITS AU DEDANS DU LOUVRE

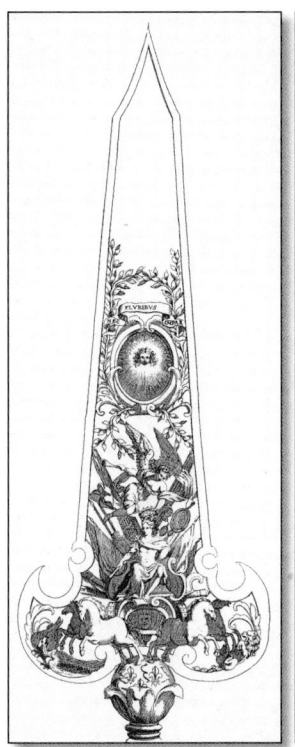

9-11 (far left): A partizan of the Gardes de la Manche detachment of the Gardes du Corps, 1679. This engraving showing the decoration on the partizan's head appeared with an article on the unit in the October 1679 issue of the *Mercure Galant*, one of the most popular periodicals in France at the time. The heads were described as being of steel with all the ornamental drapes, laurels, horse's harness plated with gold, the other decorations being in highly polished steel. This was a new design for the partizans and also for the guardsmen hoqueton by a designer, Mr. Berrin, for the engagement celebrations of the Dauphin. Author's photo.

9-12 (left): Gardes du Corps personnel at the funeral of Henrietta of England, Duchess of Orleans at St. Denis Cathedral on 21 August 1670. Born in 1644, she was the daughter of King Charles I of England and wife of Philippe de France, Duc d'Orléans, younger brother of Louis XIV. The partizans' heads are covered by a black veil and the poles and tassels are scarlet; the bandoliers are covered with silver, which indicate the 1st Company and perhaps members of the Gardes de la Manche. Blue coat with red cuffs, breeches, stockings and ribbons, buttons and lace Detail from a print by Maurice Leloir. Author's photo.

regarding the hue of their horses. Except for stylistic changes due to the evolution of fashion, there were no major variations in the uniform of the Gardes du Corps during the rest of the reign. By the 1670s, the troopers all had flintlock smoothbore carbines until December 1676 when the king ordered some rifled carbines that soon armed 360 troopers. From 14 October 1688, all were henceforth armed with rifled carbines.[18]

By the time of the War of the Spanish Succession, there were repeated orders about the wearing of steel cuirasses and the officers seemingly wore front and back plates while the NCOs and troopers had breastplates only. At least according to Dangeau in 1706, but this was only when in action and even then, it appears to have been grudgingly done by most cavalrymen.[19]

The 24 Gardes de la Manche had, in addition to the blue uniform of the 1st Scottish Company, a luxurious white silk sleeveless *hoqueton* surcoat whose origins as a garment went back to the Middle Ages. Until 1671, this garment was richly embroidered in gold and silver with arms trophies, crowned "LL" and embroidered thereon in silver and gold with Hercules' heraldic mace and King Henri IV's motto *Erit haec quoque cognita monstris* (they will also be recognised for their brilliant deeds) on the chest and the back. In 1671, the Sun King changed Henri IV's badge and motto for his own:

---

18 *Mercure* Galant, June 1687, pp. 33–34; Daniel, *Histoire de la milice françoise*, Vol. 2, pp. 148–149; Peyrins, *Traité des marques* nationales, p. 126; Gérard and Lelièpvre, *Maison bleue – maison rouge*. pp. 12, 14.
19 Robert Hall, Giancarlo Boeri and Yves Roumegoux, *Standards and Uniforms of French Cavalry under Louis XIV 1688–1714* (Farnham, UK: Pike and Shot Society, 2005), p. 4.

9-13 Standard of the Gardes du Corps. This design was most likely adopted during the 1660s and remained unchanged until the French Revolution. The field was in the company's distinctive colour with the central sun badge in gold and its surrounding embroidery and fringes in gold and silver. From an old print in the Journal of the Society for Army Historical Research, Vol. 18 (1938). Author's photo.

the sun badge with his motto: *nec pluribus impar*. They were armed with a sword and a partizan whose head was finely engraved, silvered and gilded, with just below a large silver and gold fringe tassel. The Gardes de la Manche did not wear bandoliers.[20]

Before about 1661, the standards were seemingly blue with gold embroidery, fringes and the embroidered royal coat of arms. Thereafter, the design changed to the Sun King's golden badge of the sun with its long rays surrounded by elaborate laurel embroidery in gold and silver and edged with gold and silver fringes. There were six standards in each company that were of the distinctive colour of its bandoliers (see above). All were square except the 1st Company which had a smaller one slit like a guidon. The white cravat was added from November 1693.[21]

---

20 Peyrins, *Traité des marques nationales*, p. 127; Noirmont and Marbot, *Costumes militaires français*, p. 70; *Mercure Galant*, October 1679, pp. 207–216.
21 Standard in a detail of a pre-1657 painting showing Gardes du Corps troopers with their standard at the Musée Condé, Chantilly; Pierre Charrié, *Drapeaux et étendards du roi* (Paris: Léopard d'or, 1989). p. 115; Robert Hall, Giancarlo Boeri and Yves Roumegoux, *Standards and*

THE ROYAL GUARD: UNITS AU DEDANS DU LOUVRE

The Cent-Suisses de la Garde

This company originated in the last quarter of the 15th century following the 1475 alliance treaty signed by King Louis XI of France with the Swiss cantons. It was a permanent unit from 1496. As it name implies, it had 100 Swiss guardsmen including three drummers and a fifer who were all to be at least six feet (1.94 m) tall. It also included 12 veterans exempted from further service. During Louis XIV's reign, it was led by a captain, two lieutenants and two ensigns. The captain (captain-colonel since he had the rank of colonel) and one lieutenant were French, the others Swiss, but only Roman Catholics were admitted. It was a life guard unit that served in proximity to the King to ensure his personal safety, in conjunction with the Gardes du Corps. There was always a Cent-Suisse at the door of the King's lodging. When the King went out or was on campaign, there was a detachment of the Cent-Suisses nearby. If the King went on foot, the captain of the Cent-Suisses walked in front of him and a captain of the Gardes du Corps was immediately behind. When the captain of the Gardes du Corps went into the King's carriage, the captain of the Cent-Suisses also went in and both captains shared a bench during ceremonies.[22]

For the yearly state dinner offered by the King to the knights of the Saint-Esprit, the Cent-Suisses had the privilege of serving the meat dishes for which service they were allowed to keep for themselves the surplus food and drink of that luxurious meal. Every night, a detachment of the Cent-Suisses was in a guardroom near the royal bedroom. When the King went to holy mass, the guard's squads entered the church with drums beating and fifes playing until His Majesty reached his place. The Cent-Suisses only beat their drums for the King and the Queen. The members of this company were not only seen as ceremonial palace guards, but were also with the Sun King on campaign and, in 1665, he ordered that they had precedence over the Gardes Suisses and would march in front of that regiment. Indeed, he even saw to it that they should have helmets when they accompanied him in trenches during a siege.[23]

Although they were often in battle during the 16th century, they were only deployed in Picardie, Hainaut and La Fère during 1655. The company does not seem to have been in combat in other campaigns during he reign of Louis XIV. In the 18th century, the Cent-Suisses detached on campaign were attached to the grenadiers of the Gardes Suisses.

Uniforms, Weapons, Colour

The dress of this unit had traditional Swiss features that originated in 16th century fashions, notably jackets and ample baggy trousers that were stylishly slashed to show lining of a contrasting colour. This mostly ceremonial dress was worn at court in the colours of the royal livery with black velvet caps garnished with white feathers. The officers wore scarlet and, at the ceremony of the King's majority on 5 September 1654, Swiss Lieutenant Diesbach was seen clothed in

---

Uniforms of French Cavalry under Louis XIV 1688–1714 (Farnham, UK: Pike and Shot Society, 2005), p. 25.
22 Daniel, *Histoire de la milice françoise*, Vol. 2, p. 220.
23 Guyet, *Traité des droits*, Vol. 2, p. 111.

THE ARMIES AND WARS OF THE SUN KING 1643–1715: VOLUME 1

9-14 Detachment of the Cent-Suisses de la Garde, mid 17th century. They are crossing the Pont-Neuf in Paris and wear the peculiar traditional uniform in the colours of the royal livery, blue with red lining and white trim except for the officer in scarlet. They are shown armed with halberds and swords. Detail from an unsigned painting at the Musée Carnavalet, Paris. Author's photo.

THE ROYAL GUARD: UNITS AU DEDANS DU LOUVRE

9-15 (above): Gilded guard of a ceremonial and parade sword of a member of the Cent-Suisses de la Garde, *c.*1700-1725. Musée de l'Armée, Paris. Photo Rama.

9-16 (right): Brass-mounted powder horn of the Cent-Suisses de la Garde, later 17th century. It is marked "CENT SVISSES" on the band of the upper lid (below the spout). Musée de l'Armée, Paris. Author's photo.

that colour garnished with "wide gold and silver embroidery, scarlet stockings and shoes, with silver garters and rosettes" and a diamond stud to hold the plumes on his black velvet cap. On 27 March 1657, French visitors Indick and Villers in Paris saw "…the Cent-Suisses, who are dressed in his [the King's] liveries and are armed with halberds." This is confirmed by paintings and prints of the period that also show that many of these Swiss guardsmen were fond of wearing a full beard. When the King dressed in black for mourning, the company did also.[24]

In 1660 "the Cent-Suisses [were seen] superbly dressed, their coats all garnished with gold lace, with a velvet cap trimmed with beautiful plumes, drums beating, ensign deployed speckled with gold lilies…". The Marquis de Vardes led the escort of Cent-Suisses when the newlywed King and Queen entered Paris on 27 August 1660 and was seen clothed with "green on gold" and looking very good. Thereafter, the King obviously wanted his Swiss guardsmen in the colours of his royal livery. Blue predominated in the jacket and breeches with red as the contrasting colour from about the 1660s, both garments elaborately decorated with royal livery lace. From 1679, the King is said to have restored "their ancient costume" which seems to indicate it had been somewhat changed during the 1670s. An observer of the 1680s noted some Cent-Suisses in Tournai wearing the "black velvet cap, white plumes from which rises a cockade of four brin of the same colour [this seems to mean a standing plume], they wear the *fraise goudronné* [the elaborate 16th century collar], slashed clothing and in these slashes white and blue [silk] *taffetas* … the guard of the sword is quite large and gilded, attached to an antique [style] sword belt edged with fringes." The garters were "blue and red and roses on their shoes were of the same colours; fringed gloves … the cassock [jacket] called Brandebourg is garnished with large red and white buttons in the [colours of the] king's livery. They hold a halberd in one hand and a cane with a silver pommel in the other." The traditional Swiss style remained although the breeches were more red by the later 17th century and the brim of the small hat became much wider with the front turned up *à la Henri IV* (in the style of Henri IV) and thereafter as a tricorn.

During the personal reign of the Sun King, the Cent-Suisses had, besides the above court uniform, another one for ordinary service seemingly

9-17: A soldier of the Cent-Suisses de la Garde, *c.*1680. The guardsmen of this unit wore Swiss "antique" traditional dress arranged in the colours of the blue, red and white French royal livery. The colourist of this plate has omitted the red material both on the uniform and on the livery lace. Many of these Swiss soldiers had beards, which were out of fashion in France by the 1660s. Weapons with this dress consisted of pole arms and swords. Courtesy Anne S.K. Brown Military Collection, Brown University Library, Providence, USA.

---

24   *Journal d'un voyage à Paris en 1657 et 1658, tenu par M. de Somme Indick et M. de Villers*, (Paris, 1862), p. 79.

THE ROYAL GUARD: UNITS AU DEDANS DU LOUVRE

9-18 Colours of the Cent-Suisses de la Garde, late-17th or 18th centuries. This print from Daniel's 1721 Histoire de la Milice françoise shows an ensign carrying a colour that had variations in its elaborate design. For instance, the double coat of arms of Navarre and France are show here, but other sources also show just the arms of France. Private collection. Author's photo.

introduced during the early 1660s. In 1663, it consisted of a blue coat with red cuffs, waistcoat, breeches and stockings edged with narrow gold lace. Laters on, the blue coat had scarlet velvet cuffs, blue waistcoat, breeches and stockings, gold laced hat, white bandolier with red, white and blue silk fringes. On campaign, only 12 guards had halberds, the others being armed with muskets, powder horns and other accoutrements.[25]

The colour of the company was very elaborate. Father Daniel mentions they were blue with a white cross since the late 15th century, but in the Sun King's reign, they had two blue and two red quarters. The blue quarters

---

25 *Nouvelle relation concernant l'entrevue et serment des rois...et cérémonies qui se sont faites au mariage du roi et de l'infante d'Espagne* (Paris, 1660), p. 5; *Souvenirs de Madame de Maintenon*, C. Haussonville and G. Hanotaux, ed., (Paris: Calmann-Levy, 1902), p. 44; Tony Borel, *Une Ambassade Suisse à Paris 1663* (Paris: Fontemoing, 1910), p. 104; Hoverlant de Beauwelaere, *Essai chronologique pour servir à l'histoire de Tournai* (Tournai: author, 1821), Vol. 72, pp. 48–51 quoting a 1680s description.

sprinkled with gold lilies had the King's crowned "L" monogram with the sceptre and the hand of justice in gold tied with a red ribbon. The red quarters were almost filled by a silver stormy sea with a silver rock upon which gold thunderbolts and the four winds blew from angelots heads. The white cross bore the motto: *ea est fiducia gentis* (such is the loyalty of this people) in gold letters. The centre of the cross had the crowned royal arms, with the joint crests of Navarre and France. This appears to have changed to only the crest of France in the early 18th century.[26]

The Gardes de la Porte

This unit was said to be the oldest of the guard, its medieval roots going back to the reign of King Philippe II Auguste (1165–1223). At that time, the king's guard consisted of two bands of men-at-arms, one of which was that of the *portiers* (gatemen) who guarded the royal residence's gates (*portes* in French). It was a relatively small company, but other soldiers could be temporarily attached to it if necessary. In the reign of King Charles VIII (1483–1498), some were detached to participate in campaigns and its captain was killed at the 1495 battle of Fornoue. Its basic duty, however, remained the guard the gates of the palace where the King resided.

During the reigns of Louis XIV and Louis XV, it consisted of a captain, four lieutenants and 50 guards. Only a quarter were on duty for each quarter of the year, 12 serving from January to June and 13 from July to December. They stood guard at the main gate and at the King's apartments door from six in the morning to six in the evening after which time they were relieved by a Gardes du Corps detachment. The keys to the King's lodging were then formally handed over to an NCO of the 1st (or Scottish) Company who would similarly hand them back to the Gardes de la Porte the next morning. When the King, members of the royal family or ambassadors entered or left, the Gardes de la Porte on duty let the guard know so they would form a line in front of the guardhouse and presented arms. They also presented arms to their captain when he came by. At the gates, they would only allow the carriages of persons approved by the King to enter.

Uniforms, Weapons
Up to 1657, the Gardes de la Porte wore a *hoqueton* sleeveless surcoat in the colours of the royal livery with gold embroidery including the crossed keys as their badge on the chest and back and also on the skirts. Thereafter, their clothing would have been of the royal livery colours with a wide buff bandolier garnished with embroidery and bearing the crossed keys badge. Their weapons were a sword and a halberd. From before 1672, the guardsmen's uniform consisted of a blue coat garnished with two wavy silver laces. It most likely then had red cuffs, lining, waistcoat, breeches and stockings, all of

---

26 Daniel, *Histoire de la milice françoise*, Vol. 2, p. 223; Louis Bron, *Le drapeau des Cent-Suisses de la Garde des Rois de France* (Neuchâtel, 1895), pp. 2–6; Charrié, *Drapeaux et étendards du roi*, p. 23.

which it certainly had later. From the early 1680s, the silver lace was replaced by a lace consisting of silver and gold squares, which also edged the hat. The buff shoulder bandolier was embroidered in front and back with the crown and a lily in gold, crossed keys and "L" in silver, and edged with the gold and silver squares lace. They were now armed with a sword and a carbine. Later, perhaps at the end of the 17th century, the bandolier became totally covered with the gold and silver squares lace. Officers had elaborate gold and silver embroidery instead of lace, their hats had scalloped lace and white plumes.[27]

Gardes de la Prévôté de l'Hôtel

The archers du Grand Prévôt belonged to the company of the Gardes de la Prévôté de l'Hôtel, a security unit that dated from at least the middle of the 15th century. That unit was itself descended from the *Oftiaru* bands of men-at-arms that guarded the king in the 8th century, those of the *Portiers* (doormen) at the royal residence, called the *Hôtel*, became this guard unit. It could be deployed on campaign with the royal army and, in the 15th and 16th centuries, was said to be amongst the most valorous combatants. While a military corps, its duties by the 17th century were more those of an armed constabulary unit concerned with the escort and safety of members of the royal family and senior officials in the royal residences. They were also one of the units involved in ceremonial events and were armed and dressed accordingly. For its service during the 17th and 18th centuries, they guarded the main gates of the royal residence and notably made sure that visitors were unarmed, except for those who were allowed arms. The unit was divided into four quarters that corresponded to the four seasons.

The company consisted of 50 guards (or archers) led by a captain and four lieutenants. Officers and archers were selected from men who had served in the army, had excellent credentials, well educated and be at least five feet four inches tall (1.74 m). All archers had the rank of lieutenant in the army, the lieutenants were majors and the captain was a lieutenant-colonel in the line army. It was a very prestigious corps and it was not infrequent that some guardsmen be handed letters raising their personal status to nobility. From 1668, all were granted the title of *écuyer* (esquire). Exceptionally, a few might be detached to escort senior government officials such as intendants who did not have their own guards. Two archers were even posted in Canada between 1665 and 1670 as escorts to the intendant of the fledgling colony.[28]

Uniforms, Weapons
The archers of the Prévôté de l'Hôtel du Roi were dressed in a *hoqueton* surcoat made in the colours of the royal livery: scarlet, white and blue with,

---

27 *États de la France*, 1656, 1661, 1672, 1677, 1678, 1684, 1694
28 Guyet, *Traité des droits, Vol. 2*, p. 112–126. From about 1670, constabulary archers in provinces assumed the intendant's escort except in naval bases and overseas territories in America where such duties were assumed by the Archers de la Marine. Another constabulary unit that was close to the royal court was the Compagnie de la Connetablie. Please see Volume 4 for more details.

embroidered thereon in silver and gold with Hercules' heraldic mace and King Henri IV's motto *Erit haec quoque cognita monstris* (They will also be recognised for their brilliant deeds) on the chest and the back said to have been "the most ancient badge of the guard of the household of the King of France". The whole garment was further decorated with crown "LL" ciphers and gold embroidery. In 1660, they were seen wearing "new hoquetons [surcoats] embroidered in silver" at the King's marriage. This garment remained basically similar during the reign of the Sun King with the badge of King Henri IV. From the 1660s, blue coats lined trimmed with red with gold buttons and lace were worn by the archers. Officers had the same and did not wear the *hoqueton* surcoat. They were armed with a sword and a partizan.[29]

---

29 *État de la France*, 1656, 1661, 1672, 1677, 1678, 1684, 1694; *Nouvelle relation concernant l'entrevue et serment des rois … et cérémonies qui se sont faites au mariage du roi et de l'infante d'Espagne* (Paris, 1660), p. 5; Noirmont and Marbot, *Costumes militaires français*, p. 76. The Gardes de la Porte did not have colours until 1779.

10

The Royal Guard: Units *Au Dehors Du Louvre*

Gendarmerie de la Garde

This unit was created by King Henry IV in 1609 as a company for his son, the Dauphin, who became King Louis XIII so it was sometimes known as the Dauphin's Company. The King was its captain and until June 1675, the company had a captain-lieutenant, a lieutenant, an ensign and 200 troopers. From that year, it was augmented by a lieutenant, an ensign, two guidons, two *maréchaux-des-logis*, a commissary, three trumpeters, a kettledrummer and a quartermaster sergeant. Its establishment was again raised in March 1683 by adding a third ensign and a third guidon. By 1694, the unit now had nine officers, 26 NCOs, 240 troopers, four trumpeters, a kettledrummer, two quartermaster sergeants, a chaplain, a surgeon, a saddler, a shoesmith, a commissary, two treasurers and a controller for a total of 290 officers and men. It was about the size of a line cavalry regiment.

Until 1673, one had to pay the officers to be a trooper in this unit and while many were "honest" men, there were also some gentlemen that were "bad subjects" going as far as having previously committed crimes; joining this select guard unit made them almost immune. This could have a negative effect on the fighting capacity of this unit entrusted with the King's safety. When the Prince of Soubise became captain-lieutenant in 1672, he outlined this problem to the King adding that venality in a guard unit was beneath his dignity. The Sun King agreed and venality to be a gendarme was abolished. The officers were compensated by a substantial raise in pay.

The Gendarmerie de la Garde had their quarters initially in Paris and later at Versailles. They were always with the King when he was on campaign as well being attached to armies in the field when he was not present.[1]

---

1 Daniel, *Histoire de la milice françoise*, Vol. 2, p. 192.

10-1 (top left): Kettle drum banner for the cavalry units of the royal guard. The design of this pattern, which includes the collar and badge of the Order of the Holy Spirit, appears to have been introduced during the reign of the Sun King and was also used during the reign of Louis XV. Blue with gold and silver embroidery, the arms of Navarre being gold on red. Private collection. Author's photo.

10-2 (left): Trumpet banner for the cavalry units of the royal guard. This design appears to have been introduced during the reign of the Sun King and was also used during the reign of Louis XV. Blue with gold and silver embroidery, the arms of Navarre being gold on red. Private collection. Author's photo.

Main Battles, Sieges and Campaigns

1644 Mardik	1677 Valenciennes, Kokesberg
1647 Lens, Vendin	1691 Leuse
1651 Coignac	1692 Namur, Steenkirk
1652 Saint-Denis	1693 Neerwinden
1654 Stenay, Arras	1706 Ramillies
1667 Tournai, Lille	1708 Oudenarde
1672 Rhine, Maastricht	1709 Malplaquet
1674 Besançon, Dôle, Salins, Fauconnier, Senef	

The Gendarmerie de la Garde's valour was often outstanding in combat. Following their conduct at the battle of Ramillies, the King wrote to the Duc de Rohan: "I am convinced that if I had 20 squadrons of Gendarmes and 20 princes of Rohan leading them, the enemy would not be where he is."[2]

Uniforms, Weapons, Standards

The Gendarmes wore red from at least the middle of the 17th century. In 1654, the Duke of York (the future James II of England) saw them wearing red coats. Two years later, one could see "…the Company of the King's Gendarmes of about 200 men … [was] very well mounted and preceded by four trumpeters with their blue velvet cassocks garnished with silver" confirming trumpeters had the king's livery. The company wore scarlet cassocks garnished with lace and trimmed with silver and gold buttons, and white sashes in the 26 August 1660 parade of the Queen's entry in Paris. Its trumpeters had "blue velvet coats garnished with gold lace".[3]

By the early 1670s, the troopers had "a red coat upon which there is a narrow silver lace and black velvet cuffs" according to Richelet's *Dictionnaire françois*. The silver lace was later replaced by gold lace. The *Mercure Galant* of May 1679 describes the uniform of the Gendarmerie de la Garde as consisting of a red coat with black velvet cuffs laced with gold; a white sash; a black hat laced with gold with white plumes and a buff baldric covered with gold lace. The housings were red edged with gold lace accordingly. By the 1690s, the coats were laced at all seams (see illustration of a Guérard print). The black cuffs were changed to scarlet at about that time and are reported as such in 1692, 1698 and 1702. Black velvet cuffs were again worn from 1715. Gold buttonhole pointed lace was added sometime during the early 18th century. Gold laced scarlet waistcoats and scarlet breeches were worn. The officers were to have grey horses. The men's horses could be of any hue. The

---

2   Guyet, *Traité des droits*, p. 169.
3   *The Memoirs of James II His Campaigns as Duke of York 1652–1660*, A. Lytton Sells, editor and translator (Bloomington: Indiana University Press, 1962) pp. 182–183; *Gazette*, 1656, p. 917; *Nouvelle relation concernant l'entrevue et serment des rois … et cérémonies qui se sont faites au mariage du roi et de l'infante d'Espagne* (Paris, 1660), p. 13.

THE ARMIES AND WARS OF THE SUN KING 1643–1715: VOLUME 1

10-3 (above) Troopers of the Gendarmes de la Guard and of the Chevau-Légers de la Garde, 1695. Print after Guérard. Anne S.K. Brown Military Collection, Brown University Library, Providence, RI, USA. Author's photo.

10-4 (left): Standard bearer of the Gendarmes de la Garde, early 18th century. Scarlet coat with scarlet cuffs, lining, waistcoat and breeches, gold buttons and lace. The standards were of white silk embroidered and fringed with gold and silver; the central badge consisted of thunderbolts with the motto *Quo jubet iratus Jupiter* (*To where orders a furious Jupiter*). Print after Eugène Lelièpvre. Anne S.K. Brown Military Collection, Brown University Library, Providence, RI, USA. Author's photo.

10-5 Sub-brigadier and officer of the Gendarmes de la Garde, early 18th century. The sub-brigadier (at left) wears the pre-1715 uniform with scarlet cuffs. The officer (right) has the black velvet cuffs adopted from 1715. Black waistcoats were later seen on officers, but when they were taken into wear is unknown. Print after Alfred de Marbot. Canadian War Museum, Ottawa. Author's photo.

troopers were armed with swords, pistols and carbines. On campaign, rifled carbines were issued to the best shots.[4]

The Gendarmes' four standards were of white silk embroidered and fringed with gold and silver; the central badge consisted of thunderbolts with the motto *Quo jubet iratus Jupiter* (To where orders a furious Jupiter). They were deposited in the King's chambers. On campaign, two were taken with the company.[5]

Chevau-légers de la Garde

This unit is sometimes said to date from 1580, but solid evidence as to its existence appeared in 1589. From the early 17th century, the company had 200 troopers. Until 1670, it was led by a captain, a lieutenant and a cornet. The King then added a sub-lieutenant and another cornet. In March 1684, two other cornets were created. Its service at the royal court was similar to that of the Gendarmerie de la Garde.

A Chevau-léger trooper was selected by the captain-lieutenant in command and would be a *surnuméraire* (over the established strength) for a trial period of three months before being formally admitted. As in other guard cavalry units,

---

4   P. Richelet's *Dictionnaire françois* (Geneva, 1680), p. 368; Daniel, *Histoire de la milice françoise*, Vol. 2, p. 193.
5   G. Daniel, *Histoire de la milice françoise*, Vol. 2, p. 194; Charrié, *Drapeaux et étendards du roi*, pp. 115–116.

the trooper had to pay an advance for his uniform and while noble blood was an asset, gentlemen from families having the means to live "nobly" were admitted and, according to a 1591 decree, would be considered as ennobled after five years of service. Noble or not, experienced troopers of some wealth were obviously welcomed. A 1673 list of 60 accepted troopers revealed that 52 had seen years service in other units. This was also generally the case in the Gendarmes de la Garde and the Gardes du Corps.[6]

Main Battles, Sieges and Campaigns

The Chevau-légers de la Garde always campaigned with the Gendarmerie de la Garde during the reign of the Sun King and thus participated in the same actions. Reputed very brave, they often suffered heavy casualties. A document of 1709 concerning the surviving Chevau-légers de la Garde following the battle of Malplaquet reveals a infrequently seen aspect of battle wounds: the permanent physical consequences. For instance, Chevau-léger Montgardet "had the thumb slit to the bone, received two sabre blows on the arm and a sabre cut on the face"; Chevau-léger d'Origny received "a musket ball that broke his jaw and cut off half of his tongue"; Chevau-léger de Lignevis "lost his arm cut off" by artillery fire; Chevau-léger Vernoix who received "a sabre blow on the head that cut off part of the skull bone" and Chevau-léger Allard who was wounded by a musket ball "that entered at the middle of the arm and had to be extracted in the elbow".[7]

10-6 Captain of the Chevau-Légers de la Garde, c.1660. Portrait by Jean de Reyn. Musée Lambinet, Versailles. Author's photo.

Uniforms, Weapons, Standards

The dress of the Chevau-légers de la Garde was almost the same as that of the Gendarmerie de la Garde. Campaigning with Turenne's army in 1654, the Duke of York (future King Charles II of England) mentioned "seeing one of the Squadrons in red coats, I alter'd my opinion, and believed them to be our horse, taking that particular Squadron to be either the King's Chevau-légers, or his Gendarmes, their coats being of that colour." Later, the Chevau-légers de la Garde wore "…scarlet coats", white hat plumes and sashes in the 26 August 1660 parade of the Queen's entry in Paris. They entered Tournai in 1667 wearing "red cassocks, enriched with six rows of gold and silver lace, with white plumes" on their hats. By the 1670s, the Chevau-légers de la Garde had a uniform consisting of red coats with red velvet cuffs garnished with mixed gold and silver lace; white sash; black hats laced with gold and with white plumes;

---

6 Nicolas Plaideux, 'Les Chevau-légers de la Garde du roi', *Les grandes batailles de l'histoire*, No. 28 (October 1994), pp. 10–11.
7 The 1709 document is taken from Plaideux, 'Les Chevau-légers de la Garde du roi', p. 8.

buff baldric covered with gold lace, red housings edged mixed gold and silver lace according to the May 1679 *Mercure Galant*. This remained the dress of the unit for the rest of the reign. The velvet cuffs were eventually given up, seemingly at the outset of the early 18th century, but worn again from 1714.[8]

Weapons consisted of a sword, a rifled carbine and a pair of pistols. These last were individually procured and thus of no standard model until 1714 when the Duc de Chaulnes had 230 pistols made at his expense and distributed free to the troopers. These were marked with three lilies.[9]

In 1656, the Chevau-légers paraded "with their standards and guidons unfurled, embroidered in silver [and] with the arms of France". The silver embroidery probably changed to gold or to both gold and silver in the mid 1670s. The badge on their four white standards embroidered and fringed with gold and silver consisted of thunderbolts striking down a giant with the motto: *Sensere gigantes* (The giants have felt it). They also deposited them at the king's chambers.[10]

Mousquetaires de la Garde

This unit is today possibly the best-known guard corps in the world thanks to the global best-selling novels of 19th century author Alexandre Dumas that inspired epic swashbuckling cinema productions since the 20th century that have made *The Three Musketeers*, d'Artagnan, the evil Guards of the Cardinal and even the Man in the Iron Mask famously known on all five continents and in just about every culture on earth. The musketeers, d'Artagnan, the Cardinal's guard and the Man in the Iron Mask did indeed exist during the reigns of Louis XIII and Louis XIV. Amazingly, the robust sword-wielding rivalries, dark conspiracies and secret plots really did feature some King's Musketeers involved in the shadows of power.[11]

The King's Musketeers originated in 1622 as a one company guard unit raised by King Louis XIII. It was basically a cavalry unit, but also meant to serve on foot and did in several battles. It was a reputed corps when disbanded on 30 January 1646 by Cardinal Mazarin when he could not appoint his nephew, the Duc de Nevers, as its commander. On 10 January 1657, the King's Musketeers were re-raised with the Duc as their captain-lieutenant and the young Sun King as its captain. From 1660, Cardinal Mazarin's former guard was attached to the King's Musketeers and became known as the *petits mousquetaires* (junior musketeers) as opposed to the original *grands mousquetaires*. Strength often fluctuated being initially 100 men, 300 in 1663 with the 2nd Company formally added on 9 January 1665,

---

8   *The Memoirs of James II*, pp. 182–183; *État de la France*, 1661, p. 677; Quincy, *Histoire militaire*, Vol. 1, p. 280; Daniel, *Histoire de la milice françoise*, Vol. 2, pp. 148.
9   Daniel, *Histoire de la milice françoise*, Vol. 2, pp. 147; Guyet, *Traité des droits*, Vol. 2, p. 177
10 *Gazette*, 1656, p. 917; Daniel, *Histoire de la milice françoise*, Vol. 2, p. 194; Charrié, *Drapeaux et étendards du roi*, p 116–117, 155.
11 The identity of the 'Man in the Iron Mask' remains elusive as ever. See: Danielle and Claude Dufresne, *Le mystère du masque de fer* (Paris: Tallandier, 1998) which, after having studied every known possibility, concludes that he certainly existed but his identity remains a mystery.

10-7 (above): The Mousquetaires du Roi, *c.*1664. They wear the blue lined red cassock with the cross on the back (and (invisible here) the breast, white plumes to their hats and ride grey horses. The figures on foot in the foreground wear the royal livery and likely are pages that accompanied the King on campaign. Detail of a painting by Adam van der Meulen. Musée Lambinet, Versailles. Author's photo.

10-8 (right): An officer of the Mousquetaires du Roi at the siege of Ghent, 1678. He wears a scarlet cloak over his blue cassock. The hat plumes are red and white. Note the multi-branched gilt-hilted sword. Detail from the later 17th century mural painting by Jacques Friquet de Vauroze of the siege of Ghent. Musée de l'Armée, Paris. Author's photo.

THE ROYAL GUARD: UNITS AU DEHORS DU LOUVRE

10-9 (above): Two troopers of the Mousquetaires du Roi at the siege of Ghent, 1678. From their grey horses, they would belong to the 1st Company. Both hold their carbines and are about to go into action. The musketeer at left appears to have folded back his large blue cassock revealing its scarlet lining; the one at right has a scarlet cloak over the cassock. The hat plumes are red and white. Detail of a mural by Jacques Friquet de Vauroze made in 1678 on the wall of the dining hall at Les Invalides in Paris. Authors photo.

10-10 (right) Two drummers and troopers of the Mousquetaires du Roi, 1645. The cassocks appear to have false sleeves with livery lace. A trooper is in front. Print after Stefano della Bella. Rijksmuseum, Amsterdam. RP-P-OB-34.478.

169

250 in each company in 1668 and thereafter hovering at about 280 officers, NCOs and troopers in each company for the rest of the reign. When the king was on campaign, both companies would lodge as close as possible to his quarters. Initially, King Louis XIII meant the unit to serve both mounted and on foot so that it received both colours and standards and also had drummers and fifers as well as trumpeters. During the 1660s, the fifers were replaced by hautbois (flutes). All including drummers were mounted; their drums were smaller than infantry drums and were said to produce a more jolly sound. They drilled both as cavalry and as infantry and the Sun King would often inspect them and have a formal review at least every year.[12]

One day during the 1680s, the King and his suite arrived to review his Musketeers. Meanwhile, the 18-year-old Musketeer Comte de Mirabeau had:

> … found his new shoes so tight that he slit them with a razor; but having thus eased his captive foot, the red stockings made a strong contrast with the shoes. The King was very picky at these reviews. The young musketeer got some ink and, thinking he had blackened his stockings, had in fact only made a dark red spot. The King arrived and the troubled young man put the heel of his right foot on the spot of his left foot. Louis XIV, attentive [to details] and in all of his pomp stopped and said: 'musketeer, you are not properly [standing] under arms.' The proper position had to be assumed and this movement guided [all looks] to the faulty spot; and the whole [of the King's] suite burst out laughing as much as their master's majesty would permit.[13]

All young Musketeers were subject to military training leading to an officer's commission, much like officer-cadets at military academies today. Over and above the established strengths, each company had up to 100 *surnuméraires* who were young noblemen admitted and thus also be trained as officers. They were sponsored by their families and not paid unless serving on campaign. Young Louis XIV was adamant that officers had to have a suitable military education and acquire experience before he would consider them suitable to buy commissions. The King's Musketeers had been providing such training since the reign of Louis XIII and it was now much expanded. Saint-Simon noted that the King required all candidates to spend a year serving in one of his two Musketeer companies and, from thence, "learn to obey in an infantry regiment" before he would give permission to purchase a commission or even buy a regiment if there was enough money. The training was rigorous and strict and was said to produce an outstanding *esprit de corps*.[14]

The King's Musketeers were a good show even when performing silent drills. The *Mercure Galant* of May 1681 reported the visit of an embassy from *Moscovie* [Russia] to the Tuileries Palace in Paris where the 1st Company of the King's Musketeers performed their arms drill every week. The Russian

---

12 Daniel, *Histoire de la milice françoise*, Vol. 2, p. 222; Boullier, *Histoire des divers corps de la maison militaire des rois de France*, pp. 89–92; Frémont, *Les payeurs d'armées*, pp. 49–50, 94–96.
13 *Mémoires de Mirabeau* (Paris, 1834), Vol. 1, p. 55.
14 Boullier, *Histoire des divers corps de la maison militaire des rois de France*, pp. 92, 102–103; Frémont, *Les payeurs d'armées*, pp. 49–50.

THE ROYAL GUARD: UNITS AU DEHORS DU LOUVRE

diplomats were much surprised when they saw that, at a tap on the drum, the troopers would perform a drill movement with "a skill that surpassed [their] imagination" in spite of the many movements of the drill. Captain de Fourbin then treated them to "a quantity of liquors" while the Musketeers' hautbois played. The diplomats were said to be "so satisfied" that hey might try to convince the Tsar to have a such a company that, for this occasion, wore its scarlet uniform decorated with a gold lace on the cuffs and on "several other places" while "marching with its warlike" pride.

The freewheeling street or tavern sword fighting traditions of the King's Musketeers were legendary since the days of Louis XIII. They were less rowdy thereafter, but there were lapses that were definitely disapproved of by the Sun King. In several dispatches in December 1665, he wrote to captain-lieutenants D'Artagnan and Colbert regarding an obviously serious incident between two Musketeers and a Garde du Corps trooper. The king stated his marked displeasure, ordered that the guilty be punished and that all be made aware that he wished that all his guards live in harmony. He further stated to Colbert and to Captain-Lieutenant Romecourt of the Gardes du Corps that he was surprised they had not mentioned the incident to him. The king concluded that the guilty "be punished as an example and to have all my guards live under an exact discipline so that they could not be accused of such irregular behaviour, unworthy of men to whom I entrust the safety of my person." Officers were not exempt. The king added: "I desire to know in detail in which manner the service is performed between them [the King's Musketeers and the Gardes du Corps] and that all officers be assiduous in performing their duties and with zeal in the execution of orders." The message was clear: if you are in my guard, be perfect or get out.[15]

Officers' commissions were purchased. A commission of captain-lieutenant went for 150,000 livres in 1716 and that of a cornet was 100,000 livres in 1672. To enter the unit, one had to be a gentleman, but there was no formal proof of nobility required. Letters of recommendation were essential. Sons of officers, of serving Musketeers or from families "living nobly" were often admitted. Because the unit was also a military academy, entry age was 16 and many troopers were only 17 which was younger than any other guard unit. Many went on to other units or posting, some becoming generals, but some remained as NCOs.[16]

As is well known, certain King's Musketeers made arrests when entrusted by the king with a *lettre de cachet* (secret arrest order) and would secretly

10-11 The Sun King's "James Bond": Charles de Batz de Castelmore d'Artagnan, captain of the Mousquetaires du Roi, *c.*1670. During the 1650s he was sent on secret missions several times in Germany and twice in England where he even negotiated confidential diplomatic arrangements with Cromwell. During disturbances in Bordeaux, he was there disguised as an hermit to spy on the ringleaders. There is no certainty that this likeness is faithful, but it is seemingly the only known portrait purporting to be of the famous musketeer published during the reign of Louis XIV. Frontispiece, 1704 Amsterdam edition of d'Artagan's purported memoirs by Courtiz de Sandras. Author's photo.

---

15 Louis XIV. *Lettres*, Vol. 2, pp. 146–150.
16 Nicolas Plaideux, 'Les mousquetaires du roi', *Les grandes batailles de l'histoire*, No. 27 (July 1994), pp. 10–12.

detain and guard individuals they arrested. A Musketeer officer was the last to see the Sun King for business before he retired for the night and that business might be on secret matters if the officer was discretely handed an arrest order. The difference with arrests by Gardes du Corps officers bearing such orders appears to be that those made by Musketeers were to be absolutely confidential. A few Musketeers were thus permanently involved in intrigues, spying and other activities of what appears to have been a before-the-letter secret service.

Main Battles, Sieges and Campaigns

1659 Dunes	1677 Valenciennes, Cassel
1663 Lorraine	1678 Ypres
1667 Flanders	1688 Philippsburg
1668 Franche-Comté	1691 Mons
1669 Candie	1692 Namur
1672 Rhine	1706 Ramillies
1673 Courtrai, Maastricht	1708 Oudenarde
1674 Besançon	1709 Malplaquet
1676 Condé	

Their outstanding fighting spirit was well known. The April 1691 *Mercure Galant* reported that the "reputation of the Musketeers is so great amongst the enemy that, when they saw the crosses on their *soubrevestes*, they thought themselves lost, and retreated with none daring to resist…"

Uniforms, Weapons, Colours and Standards

The Musketeer's universally known blue cassocks lined red with white crosses were worn from the reign of Louis XIII and continued under Louis XIV. "They all have the blue cassock with the silver cross" when re-raised in January 1657. On 19 January 1657, two visitors:

> …saw the king [Louis XIV]…with his 120 new musketeers … each has a blue cassock with large silver crosses with golden flames [and the ends of the crosses] finishing in fleurs de lis. A silver lace totally edges the cassock. No one is admitted [in this unit] unless he is a gentleman and outlandishly brave…; they have drummers and a fifer; they carry muskets and tie the [slow] match between the two ears of their horses.

On 20 November, they further noted that "…the king has ordered his musketeers to provide themselves with grey horses, wishing that the whole company be mounted [on horses] of that colour, and that their tails be long." When escorting the Queen's entry into Paris on 26 August 1660, they wore their "blue cassocks" with their "brigades" or squads also reported by the Marquise de Villarceaux "with different [hat] plumes. The first brigade had

THE ROYAL GUARD: UNITS AU DEHORS DU LOUVRE

10-12 (top left): A mounted trooper of the Mousquetaires du Roi, *c.*1695. Detail from a print after N. Guérard in his *Les Exercices de Mars* published in Paris. Anne S.K. Brown Military Collection, Brown University Library, Providence, USA. Author's photo.

10-13 (top right): A Mousquetaire du Roi trooper, 1696. Print after Mariette. Courtesy Rijksmuseum, Amsterdam. RP-P-1921-392.

10-14 (left): Side view of a sub-brigadier of the Mousquetaires du Roi, 1st Company, early 18th century. All scarlet coat with gold buttons and lace, blue cassock with silver lace, scarlet housings edged with gold lace, gold-laced hat with white plume border. Watercolour by Rousselot after Delaître. Anne S.K. Brown Military Collection, Brown University Library, Providence, RI, USA. Author's photo.

white ones, the second yellow, black and white, the third blue, white and black, and the fourth green and white."[17]

The early 1660s gradual incorporation of the former Guards of the Cardinal included a change of dress. At a 20 November 1663 review in Vincennes, the *petits mousquetaires* had blue coats embroidered with silver and rode black horses while the *grand mousquetaires* had their blue cassocks with a white velvet cross worn over red coats. At a review in April 1665, Sebastiano Bocatelli, a priest from Bologna on a visit in France, saw the *grands mousquetaires*:

> … [to] the number of 500 [actually 300], well mounted on good-looking horses that were almost all white or pommelled. They all wore blue cloth cassocks edged with silver lace and having on the back and the chest two crosses surrounded by rays that were embroidered in gold and the king's cipher; these crosses were about the size of those of the Knights of Malta. Their cassocks … covered some very handsome blue cloth coats garnished with silver embroidery. The housings of their horses were of the *zinzolin* [violet] colour with four suns embroidered in silver at the four corners … They had very fine plumes on their hats. Their companions, the *petits mousquetaires*, of the same number as the *grands* [*mousquetaires*], were mounted on *moreaux* [black] horses with appointments like those of the *grands mousquetaires*; but they did not have the double silver lace [on their cassocks] and their clothes under [the cassocks] were of ordinary cloth. Their horse's housings were blue with a crowned L. They also had very good-looking [hat] plumes. Their muskets, shinned like those of the *grands mousquetaires* … None can enter the musketeers unless he is a gentleman, and the rivalry that exists between the *grands* and the *petits mousquetaires* is the cause that one always sees amongst them new fashions and clothing of extravagant richness.

From that time, the 1st Company was often known as the *mousquetaires gris* (grey musketeers) and the 2nd as the *mousquetaires noirs* (black musketeers) On 25 June 1667, during the War of Devolution, they entered Tournai wearing their "blue cassocks trimed with silver" over their buff leather coats. It is probably during those years that the distinctive embroidered *flammes* at the angles of the cross for each company were adopted. These were later described as three scarlet points for the 1st Company and five yellow points for the 2nd.[18]

In 1673, the King wished that both companies have a uniform besides the cassock and ordered that its lace be gold for the 1st Company and mixed gold and silver for the 2nd Company. The uniform itself was all scarlet. John Locke saw them on 29 November 1677 wearing "red coats" and on 1 February 1678 "clad all alike in red coats, but their cloaks blue, but with distinction from those

---

17 *État de la France*, 1656, p. 184; *Journal d'un voyage à Paris en 1657 et 1658, tenu par M. de Somme Indick et M. de Villers*, (Paris, 1862), pp. 50, 339; *État de la France*, 1661, p. 677; *Souvenirs de Madame de Maintenon*, C. Haussonville and G. Hanotaux, ed. (Paris: Calmann-Levy, 1902), p. 44.
18 P. de Vallière, *Treue und ehre Geschichte der schweitzer in fremden diensten* (Nuremberg: F. Zahn, 1912), p. 338; Bocatelli quoted in: Eugène d'Auriac, *D'Artagnan, capitaine-lieutenant des mousquetaires* (Paris, 1847, reprint 1993), pp. 275–276 and Odile Bordaz, *D'Artagnan, mousquetaire du roi* (Paris: Balzac-Le Grillot, 1990), pp. 241–242; Quincy, *Histoire militaire*, Vol. 1, p. 280; *L'état de la France*, 1692 p. 85.

of the Gardes du Corps, but half horsed on black horses and half on grey, their coats and belts laced, the grey with gold galloons and the black with gold and silver, their hats and gloves to all the same, even to the ribands on their hats and cravats." The May 1679 *Mercure Galant* reported that the 1st Company had a red coat laced with gold; gold laced hat with a white plume and a blue ribbon; blue ribbons at their cravats; buff baldrics and bandoliers with gold lace; gloves edged with gold lace; white horses; red housings with lace three fingers wide. "Their *pulverin* [powder flask] was a heart [shape] strewn with lilies. There was on the cartouche [pouch] a flaming heart embroidered in gold. They had flames and lilies on their housings. All the officer's coats were red, but with an admirable magnificence and more or less rich according to rank…" The 2nd Company had a red coat with mixed gold and silver lace; gold and silver laced hat with a white plume and a blue ribbon; blue ribbons at their cravats; buff baldrics and red bandoliers with gold and silver lace; gloves edged with gold and silver lace; black horses; red housings with lace three fingers wide. By 1692, the 2nd Company had assumed all silver lace on its uniform.[19] The cassocks had been fairly short up to the early 1660s when they were made somewhat longer and the lower front and back might be slit. In about 1667, before going on campaign during the War of Devolution, they were made much longer reaching down to the knees like cloaks and remained so thereafter. They may have been comfortable but were also cumbersome at times; by the mid 1680s, they were not worn when the musketeers drilled before the Sun King. In 1688, he turned the cassock into a blue *soubreveste*, which was basically a sleeveless coat worn over the uniform coat, slit up the front and back and bearing the distinctive crosses and silver lace trimmings. From about the late 1690s, the trooper's *soubreveste* was edged by two rows of silver laces, a brigadier had three rows and a *maréchal des logis* had four silver laces as well as the King's cipher embroidered in silver at the bottom of the *soubreveste*'s skirt. Up to 1683, the King's Musketeers wore the heavy cavalry boots but that year, the King ordered that they would wear boots when on guard with him on campaigns and lighter "semi strong" boots were henceforth made so they could march more easily. Thereafter, the uniform of the King's Musketeers remained much the same except for changing styles. Officers wore all scarlet uniforms that were embroidered as were their housings and pistol holster covers.[20]

10-15 Mousquetaires du Roi sub-brigadier of the 1st Company, early 18th century. The sub-brigadier's cassock was edged with four narrow silver laces. Watercolour by Rousselot after Delaître. Anne S.K. Brown Military Collection, Brown University Library, Providence, RI, USA. Author's photo.

---

19 *John Locke's Travels in France 1675–1679*, pp. 183, 185; *L'état de la France*, 1692 p. 85
20 Daniel, *Histoire de la milice françoise*, Vol. 2, pp. 212–214; *L'état de la France*, 1692 p. 85; Peyrins, *Traité des marques* nationales, p. 108.

10-16 (top): Standard of the 1st Company of the Mousquetaires du Roi, early 18th century. They were of white silk with gold and silver embroidery and had as a badge a bursting bomb over a town with the motto Quo ruit & lethum (bringing death and ravages). Print after Delaître. Private collection. Author's photo.

10-17 (below): Standard of the 2nd Company of the Mousquetaires du Roi, 18th century. The pattern of the unit's standards remained the same from the later 17th century. The badge of the 2nd Company was a bunch of arrows pointing downwards with the motto Alterius jovis altera tela (other arrows from another Jupiter). Musée de l'Armée, Paris. Author's photo.

Each company had a cavalry standard and an infantry colour. The colours were "much smaller than those of infantry." The standards were the same size as other standards and square. Both colours and standards were white. Those of the 1st Company had as a badge a bursting bomb over a town with the motto *Quo ruit & lethum* (bringing death and ravages). The badge of the 2nd Company was a bunch of arrows pointing downwards with the motto *Alterius jovis altera tela* (other arrows from another Jupiter).[21]

Grenadiers à cheval de la Garde

The company of horse grenadiers was raised in December 1676 by order of the King who was its captain, the actual command being entrusted to N. de Villemeur, Marquis of Liotard. This unit was to have the elite grenadiers of the army. Regimental colonels would periodically receive a royal command to select a grenadier who was tall, strong, brave and wearing a moustache. Before being incorporated, he would be presented to the King who carefully assessed him. If he did not pass the examination, the colonel would receive the King's reprimand with the order to send another grenadier at his expense. It was mounted as cavalry, but served on foot during sieges and had precedence during attacks. The company initially had 100 grenadiers, raised to 120 in 1678, back to 100 at the end of the war that year until 1692 when raised to 150 by the King. This augmentation was caused "by the satisfaction with this corps, of which 50 [grenadiers] beat 800 of the enemy cavalry at the combat of Leuze [on 19 September 1691]." The Marquis de Liotard was killed in that battle and the Sun King, in grateful consideration, appointed his brother François to command the company. It had originally the captain-lieutenant, two lieutenants and two sub-lieutenants as officers, a third lieutenant being added in 1692.

Main Battles, Sieges and Campaigns

The Grenadiers à Cheval were usually brigaded with the Gardes du Corps on campaign. In battle, they had the honour to be posted at right of the 1st (Scottish) Company. Therefore, they were generally present at the same battles often fighting on foot, notably at Valenciennes when, with the King's Musketeers, their "forlorn hope" penetrated into the city. and at Ypres where they captured its counterscarp. Their services, this time mounted, at Leuze were probably the most outstanding of the engagement listed below.[22]

1677 Valenciennes	1691 Leuze
1677 Charleroi	1692 Namur
1678 Ghent	1709 Ramillies
1678 Ypres	

---

21 Charrié, *Drapeaux et étendards du roi*, pp. 117, 155.
22 *Mercure Galant*, March 1692, pp. 279–280; Daniel, *Histoire de la milice françoise*, Vol. 2, pp. 180–181; M. Boullier, *Histoire des divers corps de la maison des rois de France depuis leur création jusqu'à l'année 1818* (Paris: Le Normand, 1818), pp. 123–127.

THE ARMIES AND WARS OF THE SUN KING 1643–1715: VOLUME 1

10-18 (left): Back view of Grenadiers à cheval de la Garde, *c.*1695. Print after Guérard. Anne S.K. Brown Military Collection, Brown University Library, Providence, RI, USA. Author's photo.

10-19 (below): Grenadier à cheval de la Garde, early 18th century. This trooper is show in marching order. The uniform was a blue coat with scarlet cuffs and lining, scarlet waistcoat and breeches, red cap with fur, blue housings, silver buttons and lace. A blue cloak lined red is fastened at the back of the saddle. Print after Eugène Lelièpvre. Anne S.K. Brown Military Collection, Brown University Library, Providence, RI, USA. Author's photo.

THE ROYAL GUARD: UNITS AU DEHORS DU LOUVRE

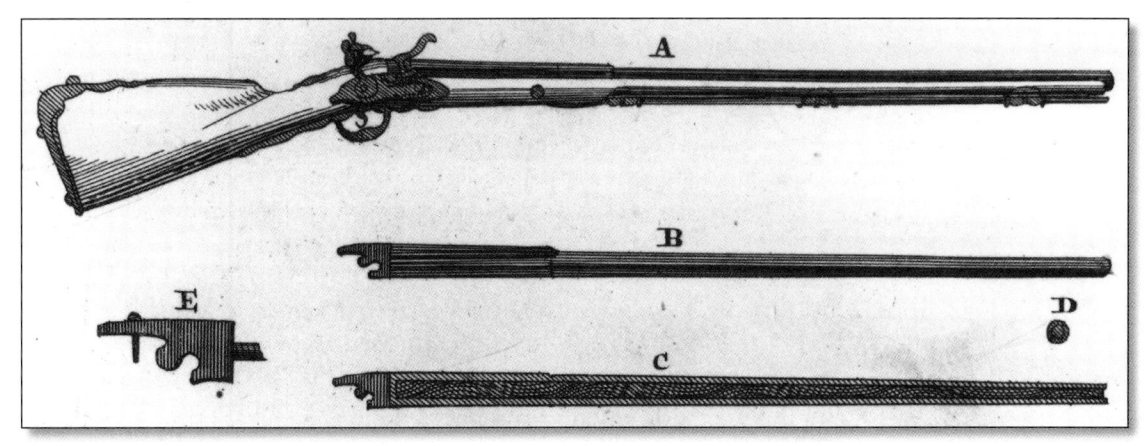

10-20 (top): Rifled carbine used in the royal guard's cavalry, 1690s. Note the rifling of the barrel (C), and the reinforced breech (E). Print after Saint-Rémy. Author's photo.

10-21 (bottom): An assault by the Grenadiers à cheval de la Garde, early 18th century. This illustration from a very small and somewhat blurry print at the head of a book's chapter shows remarkable details, notably what appears to be a flaming grenade insignia on the front of the high fronted cap, the crescent-shaped cap and turned back skirts for ease of movement. These mounted grenadiers could also fight on foot and did in several assaults during the wars of Louis XIV as shown by this illustration in Noeufville's 1734 *État Chronologique et Historique…* Author's photo.

Uniforms, Weapons, Standards

The first uniform colour is given as blue in many works regarding this unit. It was in fact red from when the company was raised. British philosopher John Locke saw the review of the royal guard on 1 February 1678 and was clearly impressed by the Grenadiers à Cheval de la Garde, which he described at length:

…their coats being red, but with loops distinguished from the Musketeers, and so their blue cloaks too…an odd fashion cap…made of red cloth, turned up with fur… standing up with a peak upon top of their heads which turned backwards. These caps both soldiers and commanders all wore [it]… They all wore great whiskers and I think they were all black, whether to make them look more terrible, I know not. Their arms were pistols, carbines and short, broad hanger and pouches, and other things fit for the carriage and management of the granados.

The reporter for the February 1678 *Mercure Galant* was also at the review and further noted that its grenadier troopers were "all well made and can inspire terror to those who see them, because they have often inspired it to our ennemies … They all have crescent sabres [with curved blades], caps with fur and red clothing." The following year, they were seen "dressed in red without lace, with red pointed caps lined with brown plush [fur]."[23]

The red uniform continued to be worn until the spring of 1692. Following the company's brilliant action at Leuze, these troopers were considered really elite and, to quote the *Mercure Galant*, "…since they are grenadiers of the King's Household, it has been found proper to dress them in blue instead of in red as formerly. They appeared with these new coats that were much enriched" with silver lace. This, with the usual changes in styles, henceforth remained the uniform of the Grenadiers à Cheval de la Garde. At Compiègne in 1698, the "Grenadiers à cheval are surprising by their warlike aspect, their moustaches and their clothing. They have blue [coats] lined with red, they have red waistcoats with large *agréments* [lace] and large dragoon [style] caps with fur." Broad silver lace on the coats appears to have been added in the early 18th century according to a 1706 bill. The company rode black horses except for some officers that had grey or piebald mounts.[24]

The company did not have standards until 1692 when Louis XIV granted them a standard as a reward for their capture of five enemy standards at Leuze. The standard was white embroidered and fringed with gold having a central badge consisting of a bursting carcass with the motto: *Undique terror, undique lethum* (everywhere terror, everywhere death).[25]

---

23 *John Locke's Travels in France 1675–1679*, p. 185; *Mercure Galant*, February 1678, p. 230; *Mercure Galant*, May 1679, p. 279. Hall, Boeri and Roumegoux, *Standards and Uniforms of French Cavalry under Louis XIV 1688–1714*, p. 10. According to Noirmont and Marbot, *Costumes militaires français*, p. 93 correctly mentions that the first uniform was *couleur de feu* (colour of fire) and later blue. It seems that nearly every subsequent French author missed that important detail. In 1973, we published a translation into French of Locke's account in the Belgian quarterly *La Figurine*, Vol. XXXV, No. 2 p. 35 which, oddly, was contested by a curator of the Musée de l'Armée. We confirmed the pre-1692 red uniform with the *Mercure Galant*'s description in our *Louis XIVs Army* (London: Osprey MAA, 1988). The full translations are here presented.

24 *Mercure Galant*, March 1692, pp. 279–280; *Mercure Galant*, September 1698, p. 201; ANF, G7, 1778, Bill of 70,000 livres for silver lace for the Gardes du Corps and the Grenadiers à Cheval from Sieur Bounder to Treasurer General Louis Lebalz de Giranchy, 31 July 1706.

25 Daniel, *Histoire de la milice françoise*, Vol. 2, pp. 180–181; Charrié, *Drapeaux et étendards du roi*, pp. 117, 155.

11

The Royal Guard: Infantry

The Gardes Françaises Regiment

This unit originated in 1560 as a single company of guard infantry. Three years later, nine companies were added to form the regiment that became known as the Gardes Françaises. In the following decades, other companies were added and sometimes a few were disbanded. By 1635, the regiment had 20 companies, which was raised that year to 30 companies. This remained the strength until March 1689 when the Sun King created two companies of grenadiers. There were no further changes during the reign. The companies could be grouped into numbered battalions of about six companies. In wartime, there were usually six battalions. The men had to be 5 feet 4 inches (1,74 m) to be admitted in the Gardes Françaises. This was an inch more than in the line infantry in peacetime and two inches more in wartime.

The king was the colonel-in-chief of the regiment so it was the colonel who was the actual unit commander. In the reign of the Sun King, the post was held by Marshal Antoine, Duc de Gramont from 1639 to 3 January 1672, Marshal François d'Aubusson, Duc de la Feuillade to 1 February 1692, Marshal Louis-François, Duc de Boufflers until 26 October 1704 succeeded by Antoine de Gramont, Duc de Guiche until 1725. He was assisted by a lieutenant-colonel, a major and a second major. In 1596, an *aide-major* was created with another added in 1615. They were helped by *sous-aides-majors* and *garçons majors*. The regimental staff also had a *maréchal des logis* and a first sergeant and non-combatants such as surgeons and chaplains. Each company was led by a captain with a lieutenant, a sub-lieutenant and an ensign. From 1701, grenadier companies had two sub-lieutenants and two ensigns. In 1680, the King created four "gentlemen of the colonel's colour" who were ensigns attached to the colonel's company as colour guards. According to Daniel, they did not remain very long on the establishment due to the regimental commander, the Duc de La Feuillade, convincing the Sun King that they were of little use. The number of men in the companies varied, but it was at least 100 or more. In the early 18th century, the fusilier companies had 126 men and the grenadiers 110. Eight *pertuisaniers* (soldiers armed with partizans) were in each company, later reduced to four and finally abolished in 1670. Finally, there were officer-cadets, but the King reduced

11-1 Officer, musketeer and pikeman of the Gardes Françaises Regiment, 1664. The officer (left) wears a scarlet coat with silver buttons and lace. The men are dressed in grey with red ribbons for the musketeer and helmet and cuirass for the pikeman. Print after Alfred de Marbot. Canadian War Museum, Ottawa. Author's photo.

their number to two per company in 1670 and they were eventually abolished. Officer training was gradually concentrated in the King's Musketeers and in the many companies of cadets that were organised in border fortresses during the 1680s (see Vol. 4).[1]

The rank and precedence of guard officers and units was always the source of some contestations from other non-guard officers and regiments when they were deployed together in the field. In early 1691, the Sun King finally made a fairly clear statement on this topic:[2]

> The king henceforth resolved that the captains of his Gardes Françaises would have the rank of colonel … That in any army where there would be companies of the Regiment of Gardes Françaises, he who commands them, although he would not be a brigadier. will command all the other colonels; that only in the trenches, the companies of the Gardes Françaises will never be commanded [by any officer]

---

1 Daniel, *Histoire de la milice françoise*, Vol. 2, pp. 266–275; Louis Susane, *Histoire de l'infanterie française* (Paris, 1876), Vol. 2, pp. 5, 45, 47, 56–63; Noël Lacolle, *Histoire des Gardes-Françaises* (Paris: Lavauzelle, n.d.), p. 387; Verneuil, *L'armée en France*, pp. 177–178..
2 *Mercure Galant*, March 1691.

except the lieutenant-general or the major-general of the day, [and not] by any brigadier unless he belongs to the regiment of the Gardes Françaises.[3]

Main Battles, Sieges and Campaigns

1643 Thionville, Asti, Trino	1678 Ghent, Ypres, Saint-Denis
1644 to 1649 Flanders	1683 Flanders
1650 Burgundy, Picardie	1689 Walcourt
1651 Guyenne, La Rochelle	1690 Fleurus
1652 Paris, Flanders	1691 Mons
1653 Flanders	1692 Namur, Steenkirk
1654 Stenai	1693 Neerwinden
1655 to 1647 Flanders	1694 to 1696 Flanders
1658 Dunes	1697 Ath
1664 Algeria	1701 Flanders
1667 Tournai, Lille	1702 Netherlands
1668 Franche-Comté	1703 Tongres
1669 Candie	1704 Blenheim
1672 Rhine, Netherlands	1705 Huy, Overische
1673 Maastricht	1706 Ramillies
1674 Franche-Comté, Senef	1708 Oudenarde
1675 Colmar, Netherlands, Sarrebruck	1709 Malplaquet
1676 Condé, Bouchain, Maastricht	1712 Denain, Douai, Le Quesnoy
1677 Valenciennes, Cassel, Saint-Omer, Charleroi, Saint-Ghislain	1713 Landau, Fribourg

In battle, the regiment was often noted for outstanding conduct.[4]

Uniforms, Weapons, Colours

Until the late 1650s, the regiment did not have a uniform, but on 6 June 1660 at the mariage of Louis XIV with Marie-Thérèse of Austria at the Island of Pheasants, "… the 600 men detached from the Gardes Françaises were superbly dressed [and garnished] with a confusion of black mixed ribbons, others in the colour of fire [red]". The 1661 *État de la France* mentioned that soldiers in Captain Maupeou's company were dressed in grey with multi-coloured plumes in their hats, Rubentel's wore grey with blue breeches, Castelan's had red clothing and Hautefeuille's red breeches and fur caps. In 1663, Gardes Françaises officers were seen wearing plumed hats, blue coats with three rows of silver lace for captains, two for lieutenants and one for ensigns. "Shortly afterwards, Father Daniel relates, *Louis le Grand* introduced uniforms in the regiments" and "that of the guard of his household [the Gardes Françaises] was of grey-white decorated

---

3 Guyet, *Traité des droits*, Vol. 2, p. 195.
4 The highlights of the regiment's battles during the reign are given in Susane, *Histoire de l'infanterie française*, Vol. 2, pp. 51–81. Casualties were often high and many officers are named in Daniel, *Histoire de la milice françoise*, Vol. 2, pp. 282–287.

11-3 (left) Soldier of the Gardes Françaises, 1684. This guard infantry unit was the first to wear the sword belt around the waist and this is one of the earliest illustrations of this item. A frog was attached at its left to hold the sword's scabbard while the priming horn, bullet bag and slow match (for the matchlock musket) was attached to its right side. This being a guard regiment, the coat and belt have lace embellishments, but the basic aspect was the same for other soldiers. Print after Maneson Mallet's *Les travaux de Mars* 1684 Paris edition. Anne S.K. Brown Military Collection, Brown University Library, Providence, RI, USA. Author's photo.

11-2 (below): Ensign of the Gardes Françaises Regiment, 1668. Print after van der Meulen. Courtesy Anne S.K. Brown Military Collection, Brown University Library, Providence, RI, USA.0

11-4 (above): Musketeer of the Gardes-Françaises Regiment presenting arms, c.1696. Note that no buttons or buttonhole lace are shown on the cuffs in all the prints showing enlisted men in this series. Yet, other details are shown with precision. Print from *L'Art militaire Français pour l'infanterie* drill book (Paris, 1696). David Harding Collection, London. Author's photo.

THE ROYAL GUARD: INFANTRY

11-5 (left): Officer and private soldier of the Gardes Françaises Regiment, c.1670. The officer is dressed in a scarlet coat with dark cuffs, silver buttons and narrow lace, white sash, cuirass and white plumed hat. The private has a light grey coat with red ribbons, breeches and stockings. Print after Philippoteaux. Courtesy New York Public Library, New York Cit

11-6 (above): A lieutenant of the royal guard, c.1679. The unit is not identified, but might be the Gardes Françaises. On 1 January 1679, its officers paraded "magnificently dressed" with their coats so covered with embroidery that the ground colour could hardly be seen according to the *Mercure Galant*. Print after H. Bonnart's *Recueil des modes de la cour de France*. Courtesy Los Angeles County Museum of Art. M.2002.57.37.

11-7 (left): Ensign of the Gardes Françaises Regiment, c.1690. The colour is not shown accurately but simply as an evocation. Blue coat with scarlet cuffs, breeches and stockings, silver buttons and lace, white sash. Print after JOB copied from small images. Private collection. Author's photo.

11-8 (top left): Musketeer of the Gardes Françaises Regiment, c.1696. He is armed with a matchlock musket and is shown at the apretez-vous (prepare to fire) position. Print from *L'Art militaire Français pour l'infanterie* drill book (Paris, 1696). David Harding Collection, London. Author's photo.

11-9 (above): Musketeer of the Gardes Françaises Regiment, c.1696. He is armed with a matchlock musket and is shown at the *tirez* (fire) position. Print from *L'Art militaire Français pour l'infanterie* drill book (Paris, 1696). David Harding Collection, London. Author's photo.

11-10 (left): Musketeer of the Gardes Françaises Regiment c.1696. He is at the *retirez vos armes* (recover your arms) position after firing before loading again. Print from *L'Art militaire Français pour l'infanterie drill book* (Paris, 1696). David Harding Collection, London. Author's photo.

THE ROYAL GUARD: INFANTRY

11-11 (top left): Musketeer of the Gardes Françaises Regiment, c.1690. Blue coat with scarlet cuffs, breeches and stockings, white buttons and lace. Print after JOB copied from contemporary small images. Private collection. Author's photo.

11-12 (above): Officer of the Gardes Françaises Regiment, c.1690. Blue coat with scarlet cuffs, breeches and stockings, silver buttons and lace, silver laced hat with white plumes, white sash. Print after JOB copied from small images. Private collection. Author's photo.

11-13 (left): A fusilier private of the Gardes Françaises Regiment, early 18th century. He wears the uniform in style at the end of the Sun King's reign and the Regency years. He is at the *prenez le poulverin* (take your primer [small powder flask]) position of the regulation drill of 2 November 1703. Print after Delaître. Private collection. Author's photo.

with false silver lace on all the seams of the coats and the officers were dressed in scarlet embroidered with silver." It seems this uniform was being worn by 1664. Other authors, notably Susane, have added that the lace also edged the cuffs and pocket flaps and that they had scarlet breeches and stockings, wide-brimmed plumed hat and white cravat, which is plausible from paintings of the 1660s that also show white sashes and gilt gorgets for the officers. Drummers and sergeants wore the king's livery of blue lined with red with the white and red livery lace as well as silver lace. The *pertuisaniers* also wore "a coat of the king's livery" according to Daniel. During the 1670s, this remained the case for drummers, but by the end of the decade, officers were seen in blue coats and sergeants with red coats laced with gold.[5]

At a blessing of the colours on 1 January 1679:

> All the officers were magnificently dressed and had coat so covered with embroidery that the cloth's colour was hardly visible. All the drummers were dressed in blue. Their coats were covered with a lace of the king's livery for the 1st of the year, because … it changes every year and while the [coat] is always blue, the lace is never quite the same. Between these laces, there is one of silver and these coats are garnished with buttons with shanks. Their drums were painted and gilded and one could see the coat of arms of their captains. The sergeants had cuirasses with gold filets and scarlet coats laced with silver. Their velvet cuffs were of several colours according to the company to which they belonged. [Their hats] all had white plumes.[6]

Four days later, John Locke was at a review of the royal guard. He saw:

> …officers of the French [Guards wearing] gold or for the most part silver embroidery or lace in blue [coats]…French [Guards] common soldiers all in new clothes, the coats and breeches cloth almost white, red vests laced with counterfeit silver, lace under or at least as much of it as was seen before was red cloth, though if one looked farther, one should have found it grafted to linen. Shoulder belt and bandoliers of buff leather laced as their vests, red stockings and new shoes. A new hat laced, adorned with a great white, woollen feather, though some were red. A new pair of white gloves with woollen fringe, and a new sword, copper gilt hilt.

He also later saw soldiers going home to Paris who had "most of them oiled hat cases … and coarse, linen [and] buckskin [leggings] after the fashion of the country to save their red stockings." A reporter also there saw:

---

5   *Nouvelle relation concernant l'entrevue et serment des rois…et cérémonies qui se sont faites au mariage du roi et de l'infante d'Espagne* (Paris, 1660); Borel, *Une Ambassade Suisse à Paris 1663*, pp. 202–203; Daniel, *Histoire de la milice françoise*, Vol. 2, p. 201; Peyrins, *Traité des marques nationales*, pp. 149–150; Normont and Marbot, *Costumes militaires français*, p. 69; Susane, *Histoire de l'infanterie française*, Vol. 2, p. 63. mentions the adoption of the grey uniform for the whole regiment at about 1670 and this has been repeated by countless authors, but Daniel does say *Peu de temps après* (shortly afterwards) Normont and Marbot give their source as Daniel and paintings (notably Lebrun's siege of Tournai) and prints of the period; we feel this agrees best with the King's early desire to put his guard in uniform clothing.

6   *Mercure Galant*, January 1679, pp. 237–239.

THE ROYAL GUARD: INFANTRY

…six battalion [of the Gardes Françaises] in one line, 50 grenadiers armed with axes, flintlock muskets and grenades. The fire-coloured ribbons on their hats were arranged in such a manner as they seemed to be plumes. The sergeants had scarlet coats with a silver lace and the cloth edging their cuirasses was edged with a gold lace. The soldiers were dressed in grey cloth with scarlet waistcoats on which there was a silver lace. The same [silver] lace edged their hats that were garnished with white plumes. They had buff bandoliers also edged with a silver lace. Their stockings were red, and their *gibecières* [ammunition pouches] were ornamented with [the badge] of the sun with silver rays.[7]

The accoutrements described show that the bandoliers with wooden powder flasks had been replaced by the ammunition pouches that were later adopted in the line infantry. This was likely an experiment first tried out in the Gardes Françaises from about the later 1670s.

At a review on the plain at Nanterre reported by the May 1680 *Mercure Galant*, the regiment was seen "divided into five battalions of 500 men each" and noted it would be difficult to find "better looking" troops. The soldiers all wore plumes edging their hat brims, most of which were green and white. In September of that year, the enlisted men wore buff leather jackets with sleeves or cuffs laced with gold and silver at a review in Nanterre. This appears have been an experiment to provide a protective garment, but it was not continued.[8]

During 1680, the King created four "gentlemen of the colonel's colour" to escort it and defend it at all times. Their dress and weapons were:

Grey-white, covered in front, on the pockets, at the side and back slits with silver buttons and 'Brandebourg' [lace] two fingers wide, with a silver lace on the seams. Their sword is silver [hilted], and their baldric [shoulder belt] is buff and edged with two quite large silver laces, as are their gloves, with a silver laced hat that is covered by a white plume tied with a blue ribbon, like their cravat and their baldric, to match with their coat's lining, which is blue, as are their breeches and stockings. They carry a gilt-speared partizan.[9]

Drummers continued to wear blue coats. At a January 1683 review:

[The] Drum-Major, dressed in a blue coat laced with silver, with a grey bandolier embroidered with silver … was followed by 60 drummers, dressed in blue coats laced with the red, silver and blue lace of the King's livery. They had buff drum

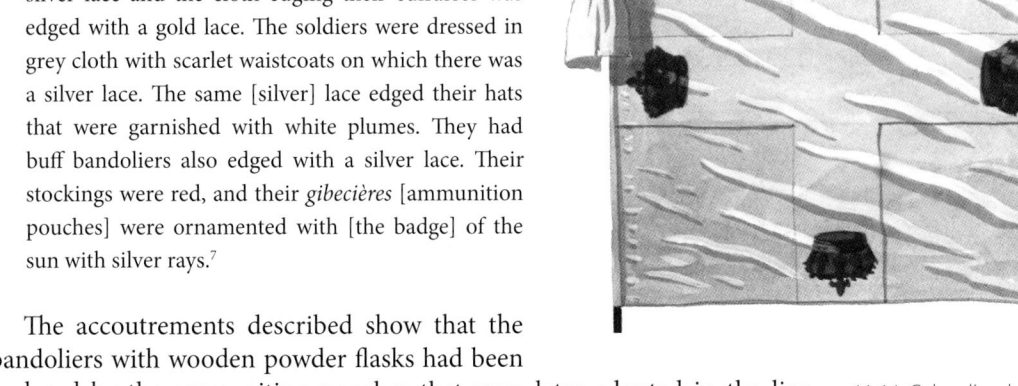

11-14 Colonel's colour of the Gardes Françaises Regiment, early 18th century. White cross and quarters, gold and red crowns. Anne S.K. Brown Military Collection, Brown University Library, Providence, RI, USA. Author's photo.

---

7   *John Locke's Travels in France 1675–1679*, p. 254; *Mercure Galant*, January 1679, p. 254.
8   Noël Lacolle, *Histoire des Gardes-Françaises* (Paris: Lavauzelle, n.d.), p. 379.
9   *Mercure Galant*, November 1680, p. 300.

belts with the same lace ... laced hats, silk sashes, and ribbons on the hats and at the cravats. The King's coat of arms were [painted] on the drums cases.

Some 60 Sergeants who "came after them, carrying their halberds. They were dressed in a blue coat laced with silver and had a buff bandolier laced with silver, red breeches and stockings, a grey hat with fire-coloured ribbons at the sword [guard] and cravat."[10]

From the above cited descriptions, it seems that the enlisted men's grey-white coat was lined and cuffed with the same colour although blue is also possible, but only mentioned in 1680 for the four gentlemen that guarded the colonel's colour. In any event, on 30 September 1684 the Sun King decided that the whole regiment would wear his blue and red livery. On the following day, the Marquis Dangeau wrote that "...it was resolved that night that the Regiment of Gardes Françaises would be dressed in blue and the [Gardes-]Suisses in red." On 24 March 1685, "...The king reviewed the Regiment of Gardes Françaises. The soldiers were all dressed in blue for the first time since they were previously dressed in grey ... The officers ... were all clothed in blue with silver embroidery, and the king told us he had never seen the regiment ... [looking] so good."[11]

It is uncertain if enlisted men and NCOs had the white buttonhole lace from 1685, but they certainly did in the early 1690s since engravings show these. They were initially set even spaced until set in threes, probably from the mid 1690s.

The King was renowned for his attention to details in the uniforms of his guards. Within the 27 March 1691 regulation for the Gardes Françaises, he specified that: "When I [the King] order the regiment to be dressed, the colonel will request pattern models from the major and will dress a soldier or two with a sergeant [in the pattern uniform], and will present them to me." He further ordered that: "... The sergeants' coats ... [would only have] one silver lace on the cuffs and edging the pocket flaps."[12]

The uniform, which remained essentially unchanged except for stylistic evolution until the 1760s, was a dark blue coat with scarlet cuffs, lining, scarlet waistcoat, breeches and stockings, white metal buttons and white buttonhole lace and hat lace. Musicians wore the same colours, which was the king's livery, with in addition the king's grand livery lace. Officers had the same colours as the men, but in finer materials and heavily laced and embroidered in silver.[13]

There was a white colonel's colour for the senior company and a blue *ordonnance* colour for each company. However, when on campaign, the number of colours was reduced to three, one white and two *ordonnance*, like the line infantry regiments. A contract of 17 October 1661 for colours described them

---

10 *Mercure Galant*, January 1683, p. 191.
11 *Journal du Marquis de Dangeau*, M. Feuillet de Conches, ed. (Paris, 1854–1860) 18 volumes, Vol. 1, pp. 57, 140.
12 Zurlauben, *Histoire militaire des Suisses au service de la France*, Vol. 2, p. 412.
13 In 1698, Corfey saw the Gardes Françaises at Compiègne wearing a blue coat with red cuffs, red waistcoat, red stockings. Lace is not mentioned, but is seen in prints. Corfey, 'Reisetagebuch 1698–1700', p. 57.

as "made of good taffetas [silk] blue and white, the four quarters sprinkled with fleurs-de-lys on both sites with four crowns on each side of the cross … mounted and equipped, for 50 pounds per colour, well made … with its pole, gilt tip, cord and lead." The white colour with eight crowns (four on each side) without lilies was 46 pounds. In 1679, "The French [Guards] Colours were in a field azure sprinkled with flower de lys or a cross argent [silver] charged at every end with a crown or [gold]. They were all the same but one, which was azur [blue] 4 crowns or [gold]." Prints of the 17th century occasionally show the gold lilies in the quarters laid horizontally rather than upright.[14]

Gardes Suisses

The Gardes Suisses Regiment was raised at Tours in early 1616 and mounted the guard at King Louis XIII's residence there from 12 March. The nominal honorary command was assigned to the colonel general of the Swiss troops. The actual command was assumed by the regiment's colonel. Its first colonel in 1616 was Gaspard Galatty. When Louis XIV became king in 1643, Colonel Gaspard Freuler had been commanding officer since 1635. He was succeeded by Jean-Melchior Hessy on 6 November 1651, Laurent d'Estavayé de Montet de Molondin on 13 December 1655, Pierre Stuppa on 1 October 1685, Maurice Wagner on 13 January 1701, François de Reynold on 25 June 1702 who held command until December 1722. The colonel was assisted by a lieutenant-colonel. All officers and men in the regiment were to be Swiss. In early 1691, the King decreed that the same regulation regarding precedence for the Gardes Françaises was also "in favour of the Swiss Guards."[15]

The strength of the regiment varied greatly. When raised, it had eight companies of 160 men each. By 1639, this had risen to 19 companies, 23 in 1648, 19 in 1650, 16 in 1656, 29 in 1657, 20 in 1661, 21 in 1667, 10 from 1668 and 12 from 1690. Thereafter the number of companies did not vary so the regiment was really like an infantry brigade of 2,400 men. A battalion was formed by three companies. During the reign of Louis XIII and the early reign of Louis XIV, each company had three officers: a captain, a lieutenant and an ensign. The Sun King, once in power, added a lieutenant and a sub-lieutenant since he felt five officers were needed for a company that could have as many

11-15 Captain Louis de Marval (1624–1654), Gardes Suisses Regiment, 1654. He is shown wearing a black cuirass with a white sash over the right shoulder. His coat or jerkin has its sleeves slashed showing the white shirt sleeve. Sketch by Francis Back from a portrait painted in 1654. Private collection. Author's photo.

---

14 'Une fourniture de drapeaux pour l'armée française sous Louis XIV', *Bulletin de la société d'histoire de Paris et de l'Isle-de-France*, 1890; *John Locke's Travels in France 1675–1679*, pp. 254–255; Charrié, *Drapeaux et étendards du roi*, pp. 21, 83.
15 Susane, *Histoire de l'infanterie française*, Vol. 2, pp. 123, 133–134; *Mercure Galant*, March 1691, p. 342.

as 200 private soldiers. Each company also had eight sergeants, four *trabans* (a peculiar and ancient Swiss rank which originated as guards of the captain), five drummers, a fifer, six corporals and six *anspessades* (lance-corporals). Thus, there were as many as 235 officers, NCOs and men in a company. There were in addition several officer-cadets from some of the best families in the cantons that served as such until they obtained a commission. They wore the soldier's uniform with the additional distinction of a white feather on the hat and a silver hilted sword. The senior company was the *Compagnie générale* and had in addition a grand judge, a quartermaster sergeant, a *grand fourrier* (master sergeant), a *truchement*, surgeon-major and a chaplain. The regimental staff was very large at 88 officers, officials, NCOs and men. Besides the colonel and, from 1689, the lieutenant-colonel, it included two majors, three commissioners, a chaplain, a physician, a surgeon-major, an auditor, three treasurers, a grand judge, a grand *prevost*, 12 juges, 20 archers of the grand judge, one executor, several NCOs and 22 halberdiers for the escort of the colonel general of the Swiss troops.[16]

It should be noted that the regiment's senior company, the *Compagnie générale*, was initially solely for the colonel general of Swiss troops and was sometimes termed as the "ancient company" as it dated from the late 16th century. It served as a guard company, but was not included in the early musters of the Gardes Suisses Regiment. As decades passed, it was gradually merged into the regiment as its de facto senior company. From 1661, it was at last included in the regiment's musters, possibly due to the Sun King's wishes for a more orderly administration.[17]

The Swiss regiments were granted the *Prévôté* that meant they administered their own justice system according to their laws. The judges, *prevosts*, archers and the executor in the *Compagnie générale* were the personnel specifically concerned with the application and respect of justice within the Gardes Suisses Regiment.

Before 1763, the regiment did not have a grenadier company. However, from the later 1660s it did have grenadiers because 16 soldiers in each company were selected amongst the best and the bravest to assume that role as a squad. It was led by a captain-lieutenant and two sergeants. They were grouped into temporary companies from 1696.

Each company was identified with a Swiss canton, which was where its officers went to recruit its men. From 1690, the division was as follows:[18]

> 1st Company: all cantons since this was the *Compagnie générale*.
> 2nd Company: Lucerne
> 3rd Company: Grisons
> 4th Company: half for Zug, half for Zurich

---

16 Daniel, *Histoire de la milice françoise*, Vol. 2, p. 227; Susane, *Histoire de l'infanterie française*, Vol. 2, pp. 133–134. We have followed Daniel regarding the establishment, but Zurlauben, followed by Noirmont and Marbot, *Costumes militaires français*, pp. 71, 92–93, mentions 23, 19 and a half, 20 and a half, 28 and 29 and a half between 1647 and 1661, 15 between 1661 and 1667.
17 Guyet, *Traité des droits*, Vol. 2, pp. 203–205.
18 Susane, *Histoire de l'infanterie française*, Vol. 2, pp. 123, 134–135.

THE ROYAL GUARD: INFANTRY

5th Company: half for Claris, half for Schaffhausen
6th Company: half for Schweitz, half for Fribourg
7th Company: Berne
8th Company: half for Soleure, half for Grisons
9th Company: half for Soleure, half for Berne
10th Company: Soleure
11th Company: half for Soleure, half for Grisons
12th Company: Grisons

According to the agreements made with the cantons, the King could not order the regiment to serve east of the Rhine River in Germany, beyond the Alps in Italy and beyond the Pyrenees in Spain. This might be loosely interpreted at times, but was a standing practice.

As in all Swiss regiments in French service, its officers and men were free to practice the religion to which they belonged. The regimental chaplains were Roman Catholic and Protestant. They were paid for by officers of their respective faiths and both chaplains were to be provided with a suitable place to hold their religious services. Officers were not to tolerate any lack of respect between Catholics and Protestants and were to prevent any disturbances that might be made during religious services by one group of soldiers on the other.

The companies were quartered at inhabitants' homes in the Paris suburbs and nearby villages. They were to quickly assemble and be ready to march off at first call. In general, the Swiss soldiers kept to themselves and were appreciated for their orderly conduct. Their sutlers had the right to set up shop near where the men were posted; local officials could not oppose this.

The Swiss were reputed as excellent, very orderly and outstandingly brave soldiers. Such qualities did not come cheap. Garde-Suisses officers, NCOs and soldiers received double the pay of the Gardes Françaises.[19]

Uniforms, Weapons, Colours

On 4 May 1654, Captain Louis de Marval wrote that "Our company was very costly to equip. Besides having armed it with very fine arms that cost us over 1,600 pounds, we had 70 red coats made that cost us 22 to 23 pound each … We also needed a quantity of breeches, stockings, shoes, bandoliers, hats and shirts…" Thus, during the early years of Louis XIV's reign, red seems to have been the usual colour of the coats, but not exclusively. On 20 November 1663, the regiment paraded in Vincennes wearing grey-blue coats lined with buff with all seams laced with gold. Officers had blue coats with one silver lace for ensigns,

11-16 Musketeer of the Gardes Suisses Regiment, c.1696–1700. He is shown at the 'hold the ramrod' drill position. Red coat with blue cuffs, breeches and stockings, white buttons and lace. Print after JOB copied from contemporary small images. Author's photo.

---

19 Boullier, *Histoire des divers corps de la maison militaire des rois de France*, pp. 185–186, 188.

THE ARMIES AND WARS OF THE SUN KING 1643–1715: VOLUME 1

11-17 (left): Gardes Suisses Regiment, field officer, early 18th century. Senior officers carried canes. Scarlet coat with scarlet cuffs, blue lining, waistcoat, breeches and stockings, silver buttons and lace, white hat plumes. Courtesy Anne S.K. Brown Military Collection, Brown University Library, Providence, RI, USA.

11-18 (above): Gardes-Suisses Regiment, fusilier, early 18th century. A rare back view. Red coat with scarlet cuffs, blue lining, waistcoat, breeches and stockings, white buttons and lace, buff belts. Courtesy Anne S.K. Brown Military Collection, Brown University Library, Providence, RI, USA.

11-19 (left): Gardes-Suisses Regiment, company officer, early 18th century. Company officers were armed with spontoons. Scarlet coat with scarlet cuffs, blue lining, waistcoat, breeches and stockings, silver buttons and lace, white hat plumes. Courtesy Anne S.K. Brown Military Collection, Brown University Library, Providence, RI, USA.

two laces for lieutenants and three laces for captains, all having plumed hats.[20]

From 1664, the musketeers were dressed in red coats again and the pikemen were seen sometimes in red or sometimes in blue coats. The red coats had blue lining, cuffs and ribbons. The breeches and stockings were red with blue ribbons. The breeches and stockings appear to have changed to blue during the 1670s. In January 1679, John Locke saw that "The Swiss soldiers were habited in red coats and blue breeches cut after their fashion, with their points at the knee, and had no feathers [on their hats]. The pikemen … had back and breast [plates] … also head pieces [steel helmets]." The sergeants had new coats of "scarlet or red … with true gold galoon…" and officers had "all gold on red and much the richer." At a review of three battalions at the Nanterre Plain in January 1679, the Gardes Suisses' musketeers "were dressed in red and the pikemen in blue. Their coats were garnished with gold buttons with cuffs covered with lace." Pikemen definitely had red coats from March 1685 following the King's confirmation that the regiment would henceforth always have red coats. The Gardes Suisses pikemen wore the full equipment consisting of the steel helmet, gorget, front and back cuirass with tassets and the half-brassards to protect the shoulders and upper arms right up to 1703 when pikes were abolished.[21]

From 1685, the uniform of the regiment was henceforth a red coat with blue lining, cuffs, breeches and stockings. For enlisted men, the buttons were of white metal and the hat lace was white. White buttonholes were seemingly added then or shortly thereafter. They were set equally and, from the 1690s or early 1700s, set by three. Officers wore scarlet coats with blue lining, breeches and stockings, silver buttons, lace and embroidery; their coat cuffs were scarlet and it appears this was the case throughout the Sun King's reign. Drummers, fifers and *trabans* continued to wear the king's livery with the grand livery lace. Waistcoats became regular wear during the 1690s and, in 1698, Corfey noted them as being orange [more likely red] at Compiègne, but they soon changed to blue.[22]

The colours of the Gardes Suisses Regiment were in the hues of the livery of the colonel general of Swiss troops. The regimental colours were seen in 1679 by John Locke as having "a cross argent [white], the four cantons, filled with stripes of yellow, azure [blue] and red, wavy, all pointing to the centre of the cross." This remained unchanged until about 1715 when a black wavy stripe was added. The colonel's colour was white.[23]

---

20 Letter of Captain Louis de Marval, Gardes-Suisses Regiment, 9 May 1654, in: *Soldats Suisses au service étranger*, A. Jullien ed. (Geneva: Jullien, 1915), Vol. 6, p. 57; Vallière, *Treue und ehre*, p. 292; Noirmont and Marbot, *Costumes militaires français*, pp. 71–72; Borel, *Une Ambassade Suisse à Paris 1663*, pp. 202–203.
21 *John Locke's Travels in France 1675–1679*, pp. 254–255; *Mercure Galant*, January, 1679, p. 255; *Journal du Marquis de Dangeau*, Vol. 1, pp. 57, 140.
22 'In the [Swiss] Guards Regiment, the [*trabans* wear] the king's livery, in the other [Swiss regiments] they have the livery of the colonels like the drummers and fifers.' Daniel, *Histoire de la milice françoise*, Vol. 2, p. 226; Corfey, 'Reisetagebuch 1698–1700', pp. 57–61.
23 Daniel, *Histoire de la milice françoise*, Vol. 2, p. 226; *John Locke's Travels in France 1675–1679*, pp. 254–255; Charrié, *Drapeaux et étendards du roi*, pp. 21–22, 83.

Main Battles, Sieges and Campaigns[24]

1643 Rocroi, Thionville, Sierck
1644 Gravelines
1645 Mardyck, Saint-Venant, Bethune, Perpignan, Roses, Agramont, San Feliu
1646 Piombino, Elba, Longwy, Flanders, Dunkerke
1647 Flanders
1648 Ypres, Lens, Cremone
1649 Cambrai, Condé
1650 Burgundy, Bellegarde
1651 Guyenne, Béneau, Étampes, Paris, Coucy
1653 Mouzon, Sainte-Ménehoud
1654 Stenai, La Roquette, Bormida, Arras
1655 to 1657 Flanders
1658 Dunes, Dunkerke, Ypres
1663 Marsal
1667 Tournai, Douai, Lille
1668 Franche-Comté
1672 Rhine, Netherlands
1673 Maastricht
1674 Franche-Comté, Senef
1675 Colmar, Netherlands, Sarrebruck
1676 Condé, Aire, Lenck, Maastricht
1677 Valenciennes
1678 Ghent, Ypres, Saint-Denis
1683 Flanders
1684 Luxembourg
1689 Walcourt
1690 Fleurus
1691 Mons
1692 Namur, Steenkirk
1693 Neerwinden
1694 to 1696 Flanders
1697 Ath
1701 Flanders
1703 Eckeren
1704 Blenheim
1705 Nodoue, Groendael
1706 Ramillies
1708 Oudenarde
1709 Malplaquet
1711 Bouchain
1712 Denain, Douai, Le Quesnoy
1713 Landau

---

24   Susane, *Histoire de l'infanterie française*, Vol. 2, pp. 139–152.

12

Other Guard Units

Gentilhommes Ordinaires de la Garde (also called *au Bec de Corbin*)

Originating in the 15th century, this unit could be compared in status to Britain's Gentlemen at Arms of the Guard. It was created by order of King Louis XI on 4 September 1474 consisting of a company of 100 gentlemen, augmented to two companies totalling 200 men in 1498, that, by a regulation of 1585, had a quarter of its numbers available for service. They were armed with a sort of short partizan with an hammer head and this brought them the nickname *Bec de Corbin* (falcon's beak). Louis XIII disbanded the unit in 1629, but it was re-established in 1649. From then on, it was a parade unit rather than a real bodyguard. The *Grande Mademoiselle* saw both companies on 7 June 1660 at Saint-Jean-de-Luz for the King's marriage. One was commanded by the Marquis d'Huxelles and the other by young Comte de Péguilin of the Lauzun family. She added in her memoirs that it "only served at ceremonies" but had been "in its day very much in fashion and enjoyed great consideration." These gentlemen were also seen by a reporter who mentioned they had "their blue batons" that were surely the handles of their *Bec de Corbin*. The two companies were reduced to one in 1688. It was then commanded by a captain, a lieutenant and an ensign with 200 gentlemen divided into two *bandes* (bands or groups). During ceremonies, they marched two by two before the King wearing their swords at their sides and holding the *Bec de Corbin*.[1]

Gardes Écossais Regiment

In 1642, a regiment of Scots was raised by the Earl of Irvine and some 2,000 of its men arrived in Boulogne, France, during January 1643 and was incorporated into the French army's foreign establishment on 19 January. Its

---

1 *Nouvelle relation concernant l'entrevue et serment des rois … et cérémonies qui se sont faites au mariage du roi et de l'infante d'Espagne* (Paris, 1660), p. 14; *État de la France*, 1712, pp. 547–548; Boullier, *Histoire des divers corps de la maison militaire des rois de France*, pp. 16, 32.

12-1 Colours of the Royal Écossais, c.1643. Blue field with white St. Andrew's cross, the crowned coat of arms of France and Navarre with laurel wreath at the centre. Print after Cecil C.P. Lawson. Private collection. Author's photo.

establishment initially was 30 companies of 150 men each although it appears to have had 15 to 20 companies in later times. The French authorities promised high pay, incorporation in the royal guard with precedence after the Gardes Suisses and that a company would guard the King. None of the promises were kept. According to Father Daniel, the regiment was nevertheless named *Gardes Écossais* (Scots Guards) and was said to have been present at the Battle of Rocroi in May 1643, the capture of Thionville in August and the siege of Trin when the *Gardes Écossoises* took an enemy redoubt with outstanding valour on 18 September. However, the unkept promises may have had a negative effect on morale and the regiment was badly mauled at Tuttlingen in November. Sir Robert Moray, its lieutenant-colonel, was captured there, eventually ransomed and went to Scotland to enlist recruits, but only got about 400 men. Nevertheless, the depleted corps fought alongside the Gardes Françaises Regiment in the battle of Lens in 1648. By then, its *Gardes* denomination was surely a courtesy title since the regiment was not listed with the guard units belonging to the *Maison du Roi*. It nevertheless served under that name until 1662 when it was incorporated into Douglas's Scots Regiment.

No livery or uniform clothing is known for this unit, which existed when uniforms had not yet been generally adopted in the army at large or even by the guards. Drummers and sergeants might have worn the king's livery, but this is purely speculative. According to Lawson, its regimental colours were the flag of Scotland, a blue field with the white St. Andrews cross, bearing the royal crown, the arms of France and Navarre with gold laurels and palms and a white scroll with *Memo me immune l'accessit* (no one attacks me with impunity) in black letters. The colonel's colour had a white field with the white St. Andrews cross, the arms of France and of Navarre at the centre.[2]

Guards of the Royal Family and Prime Ministers

These few units were not formally part of the royal guard yet enjoyed a prestige that was nearly equal to it.

---

2 Ledieu, *Esquisses militaires de la Guerre de Trente* Ans, pp. 59–60; Francisque-Michel, *Les Écossais en France, les Française en Écosse* (Paris: A. Frank, 1862), Vol. 2, pp. 287–288; Daniel, *Histoire de la milice françoise*, Vol. 2, pp. 232–233; *Gazette*, 1643, pp. 861, 864; Stephen Wood, *The Auld Alliance, Scotand and France: the Military Connection* (Edinburgh: Mainstream, 1989), pp. 56–58; Cecil C.P. Lawson, *History of the Uniforms of the British Army* (London, 1942), Vol. 2, p. 82. It should be noted that Morlay was paid in advance by the French army for 800 recruits and was thus charged with fraud as per Stephen Wood.

OTHER GUARD UNITS

Gendarmes de la Reine. Raised in about 1638 for Anne of Austria, retitled Gendarmes de la Reine-mère (Queen Mother) when Louis XIV married Marie-Thérèse of Austria in 1660. The Comte d'Interville was its first captain-lieutenant until 4 April 1642 succeeded by Jean-Antoine, Marquis de Franquetot and followed in July 1649 by Edme-Claude de Simiane, Comte de Monchat. It consisted of 120 troopers dressed in red coats. Existed until the death of Queen Mother Anne of Austria in 1666. Crimson standard with silver embroidery and fringes, cipher "MA" and "1646" with crown on left side, motto: *À coeur vaillant rien d'impossible* (nothing is impossible for valiant hearts).[3]

Chevau-légers de la Reine (Chevau-légers of the Queen). Raised on 18 June 1643, retitled Chevau-légers de la Reine-mère (Queen Mother) in 1660. Seen in 1653 as having over 100 troopers "led by the Chevalier de Saint-Mégrin, lieutenant of [the company] dressed in a coat covered with gold and silver embroidery, mounted on a very fine white horse … whose mane was garnished by a great number of ribbons, having in front of him four trumpeters dressed in black velvet, decorated with silver." Existed until the death of Queen Mother Anne of Austria in 1666.[4]

Gendarmes d'Orléans. Raised for Gaston d'Orléans, younger brother of King Louis XIII who was addressed as *Monsieur* in the French court's protocol. The date of its creation has been given as 1643 by Susane, but correspondence between Louis XIII and Gaston indicates that it may have been in 1635. In October 1634, an agreement was made to raise a company of Gendarmes and a company of Chevau-légers of 100 men each, of which 50 would serve as his bodyguards. This seems to have replaced the previous Gardes de Monsieur who were seen in 1626 numbering 80 troopers wearing velvet cassocks and bandoliers of his livery colours, "the cassocks decorated at front and back with his embroidered ciphers highlighted in gold." On 25 February 1635, Gaston asked that his Gendarmes company have 200 men to provide "a better service in the armies of His Majesty" and Louis XIII agreed. This implies that the Gendarmes d'Orléans were deployed on campaign. The Marquis de Mauny was captain in the early 1640s followed by the Marquis de Genlis on 10 April 1645 succeeded by his son in September 1658. The unit existed until Gaston's death in 1660. His livery was blue. After his death it was changed to red for Louis XIV's young brother who also assumed the title of *Monsieur*.[5]

---

3 Susane, *Histoire de la cavalerie française*, Vol. 1, p. 255.
4 Madame de Motteville, *Mémoires pour servir à l'histoire d'Anne d'Autriche épouse de Louis XIII roi de France* (Amsterdam: F. Changuion, 1731), n.p.
5 Susane, *Histoire de la cavalerie française*, Vol. 1, p. 270. The 1634–1635 correspondance is at: <http://rohanturenne.blogspot.ca/2009/10/gendarmes-de-monsieur-dorleans>; on the 1626 Gardes de Monsieur: <http://rohanturenne.blogspot.ca/search/label/Uniforms>; A. Jal, *La France maritime* (Paris, 1837), n.p. The Chevau-légers were not raised.

12-2 Guards of the Cardinal, second third of the 17th century. Cardinals Richelieu and Mazarin, who were prime ministers, each had a company of life guards – famously known for their rivalry with the King's Musketeers – wearing red cassocks with white crosses. Detail of a print after Maurice Leloir. Private collection. Author's photo.

Garde du Cardinal. The first was the guard of Cardinal Richelieu that served until his death in 1642. Its men wore red cassocks with white crosses, which were made famous in "Three Musketeer" novels and movies as the dress of the "bad guys" fighting the King's Musketeers. The next Garde du Cardinal was raised in 1650 for Cardinal Mazarin. In 1656, the *Gazette* mentions his guard wearing "new scarlet cassocks" which probably indicates that they were generally similar to those of Cardinal Richelieu's guards. In 1660 Mazarin gave his guard company to the King who made it a fully mounted unit in 1663 and, on 9 January 1665, as the 2nd Company of their former arch rivals, the King's Musketeers.[6]

Pages of the Royal Household. Serving with the royal guard near the King were the pages of the royal household. They were organised in two groups: pages *de la Chambre* (of the Chamber) and pages *de la grande et de la petite Écurie* (of the small and large stable). They performed various duties at court and some travelled with the King, those of the stable being near or on the back of his

---

6   Daniel, *Histoire de la milice françoise*, Vol. 2, p. 218; Boullier, *Histoire des divers corps de la maison militaire des rois de France*, p. 90; Normont and Marbot, *Costumes militaires français*, p. 53.

12-3   A royal page or servant of the king's household, *c.*1680. He wears a blue livery coats with scarlet cuffs and lining. The coat was nearly covered with royal livery lace, which changed design every year until about 1687, had little red squares edged with white. Print after Chavignard. Private collection. Author's photo.

carriage drawn by eight horses. They were dressed in the blue and red royal livery and are often seen in the vicinity of the King in battle paintings. Before 1661, these colours could result in scarlet cassocks surely lined with blue trimmed with lace and bearing royal insignias. In 1660 for instance, pages were seen in "fire-coloured velvet cassocks all covered with gold" lace. Thereafter, the King changed the ground colour to blue and the pages were thereafter seen in blue coats lined red with silver or red and white lace. Those that accompanied the King on campaign were thus often exposed to enemy fire. They were, in theory, not armed and not officially fighting troops, but there were obviously times they did engage in combat. According to the May 1677 issue of the *Mercure Galant*, the King recognised that pages had distinguished themselves "in the most perilous occasions" and to "begin to testify of his satisfaction" commissioned their dean as an ensign in the guard. This opened future prospects to a military career for deserving pages. Ten years later, pages even had a campaign dress that appears to have been less decorated with lace. They also had laced hats with white plumes and red housings edged with silver lace for their horses.[7]

---

7   *Souvenirs de Madame de Maintenon*, p. 44; *Mercure Galant*, December 1687, p. 320.

Appendix I

Royal Guard Cavalry Uniforms in Army Lists*

Etat General des Troupes, 1692

Gardes du Corps: blue coat, red cuffs and lining.
    Compagnie de Noailles: white bandoliers.
    Compagnie de Duras: blue bandoliers.
    Compagnie de Luxembourg: green bandoliers.
    Compagnie de Lorges: yellow bandoliers.

Gendarmes de la Garde du roi: red coat, red cuffs and lining, gold lace.
Chevau-Légers de la Garde du roi: red coat, red cuffs and lining, gold and silver lace.
Mousquetaires gris: red coat, red cuffs and lining.
Mousquetaires noirs: red coat, red cuffs and lining.
Grenadiers à cheval: red coat, red cuffs and lining.

Etat General des Troupes, 1702

Gardes du Corps: blue coat, red cuffs and lining.
    Compagnie de Noailles: white bandoliers.
    Compagnie de Duras: blue bandoliers.
    Compagnie de Lorges: yellow bandoliers.
    Compagnie de Villeroi: green bandoliers.

Gendarmes de la Garde du roi: red coat, red cuffs and lining, gold lace.
Chevau-Légers de la Garde du roi: red coat, red cuffs and lining, gold and silver lace.

Mousquetaires gris: red coat, red cuffs and lining.
Mousquetaires noirs: red coat, red cuffs and lining.
Grenadiers à cheval: blue coat, red cuffs and lining.

* MBA, Ms A1b, 1626, 'Les Tiroirs de Louis XIV' for the 1692 and 1702 lists and Corfey, 'Reisetagebuch 1698–1700', pp. 57–61.

Appendix II

Order of Battle at the Compiègne Review, September 1698 (by Corfey)

Gardes du Corps: blue coat, red cuffs and lining, silver lace.

Gendarmes de la Garde du roi: red coat, red cuffs and lining, gold lace, white hat plumes.

Chevau-Légers de la Garde du roi: red coat, red cuffs and lining, gold lace, white hat plumes.

Mousquetaires du roi: red coat, red cuffs and lining, blue soubreveste, gold lace, white hat plumes.

Grenadiers à cheval: blue coat, red cuffs and lining, gold [actually silver] lace.

Appendix III

Opposing Armies: the Spanish Army of the 17th Century

Spain was France's and its Sun King's main opponent during the period covered in this volume. Its land and sea forces had been very redoutable in the 16th century. However, its sea power had been humbled by the loss of the 1588 Great Armada against Britain and later by the Dutch navy. The reputedly nearly invincible Spanish infantry *tercios* of the 16th century faded in the next century and were crushed by the French army at Rocroi in 1643. A Spanish *tercio* at the time had about 1,200 men divided into 12 companies, a third of which were pikemen and the rest musketeers. By then, the Spanish kingdom was in serious decline and its armies could not gain the initiative against the Portuguese who won their independence by force of arms while the French realised that their nation could be the dominant European power.

The Spanish military *esprit de corps* degraded during the 17th century. The army was badly supplied, the men were indifferently paid and often wearing rags, officers were largely uninspired in their service and discipline was somewhat lax at times. The Spanish soldier was nevertheless known to be very brave in battle, but good recruits were lacking and vagabonds were enlisted in ranks that were plagued by frequent desertions. Apart from several veteran *tercios*, the most dependable units were made up of foreign mercenaries. During the 1650s, the strength of the Spanish army in Europe came to about 77,000 men. The largest contingent was the 19,000 men in Spanish Flanders under the command of Don Juan of Austria and Prince de Condé, 16,000 were in Italy's Lombardy, Naples, and Sicily and the rest were in Spain itself. In 1657, a listing of militiamen that could be embodied in Spain came to only 21,500 men, including 3,000 retired veteran soldiers. It was a largely insufficient army, still hampered by rather antiquated command systems and organisation arrangements. In war, the regular army would have to be deployed in at least four fronts distant from each other: the borders with Portugal and France, northern Italy, and Flanders. All in all, the Conde de Clonard, the great Spanish army historian, concluded correctly after presenting these figures that "it is easy to understand that with

OPPOSING ARMIES: THE SPANISH ARMY OF THE 17TH CENTURY

Ap. 3-1 (left, top): Spanish infantry ensign and musicians, 1650s–1660s. The musicians shown have brown cassocks, but might also wear their colonel's livery. Print after Giminez. Private collection. Author's photo.

App. 3-2 (left, bottom): Spanish cavalry unit, c.1670s. From about 1669, the Spanish army adopted clothing approximating the French styles with the typical justeaucorps coat. Print after César de Floribus. Anne S.K. Brown Military Collection, Brown University Library, Providence, RI, USA. Author's photo..

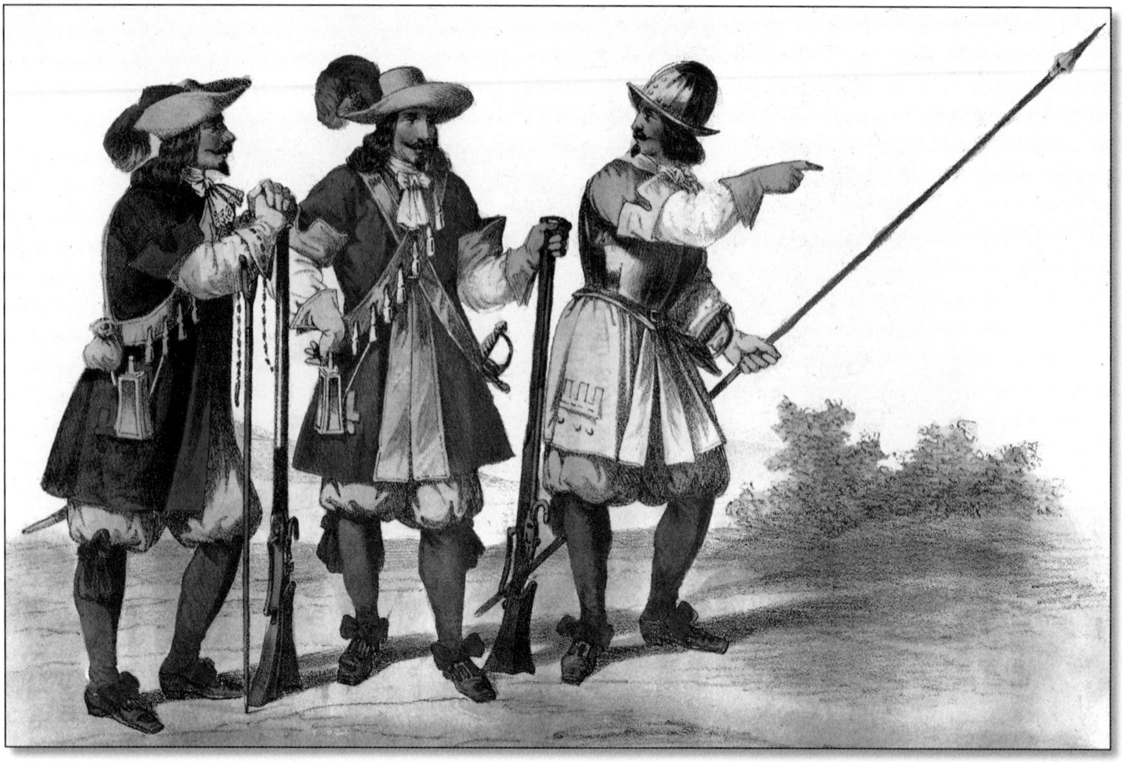

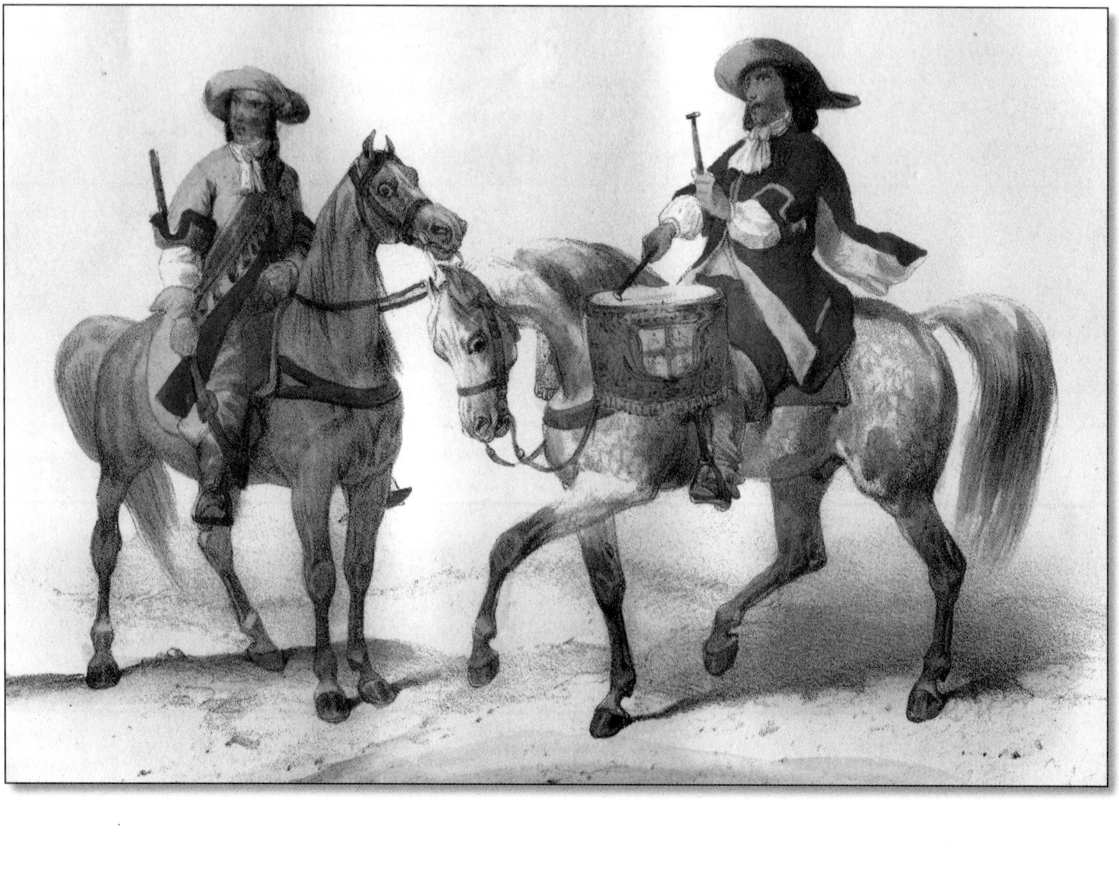

Previous page::

App. 3-3 (right, top): Spanish infantrymen, 1670s and 1680s. At left, a musketeer from the tercio of Morados viejos in a violet coat; at centre, an arquebusier of the Colorados viejos wearing a red coat; at right, a yellow-coated pikeman of the Amarillos viejos infantry tercio. Print after Giminez. Private collection. Author's photo.

App. 3-4 (right, bottom): Spanish cavalry, c.1690. At left, a dragoon trooper in yellow lined red; at right, a kettledrummer of heavy cavalry wearing red trimmed with yellow. There were nine cavalry tercios from 1677: three were in Spain, three in the Milan area of Italy and three were in the Low Countries. Print after Adam. Private collection. Author's photo.

such forces, Spain could not uphold its independence and its honour".[1]

There were attempts to improve the army. In 1652, soldiers in Spain were to receive brown cloth jackets, trousers and stockings, shoes, linen shirts, hats, cravats, swords, matchlock muskets, arquebuses, or pikes on a regular basis. The lighter arquebuses were used to the end of the 17th century; their lighter calibre may have been handier, but also compromised heavier firepower. Pistols replaced lances in the cavalry, the artillery was effective if somewhat antiquated. Wages were still often promised, but less often paid so that such efforts did not greatly improve the troops. In 1685, grenadiers were added. The French-style coat was adopted from the late 1660s each unit having its coats of a distinct colour. Some units became known by the colour of their coats. For instance, the *tercio* of Sevilla was also called *Morados viejos* (the old violet), Madrid was *Colorados viejos* (old red), Burgos was *Amarillos viejos* (old yellow) and Toledo was *Azules viejos* (old blue). In 1678, the French reported that men of the yellow and blue *tercios* surrendered at Puycerda in Catalonia and, in 1689, they noted *Los Amarillos* as the best Spanish infantry at Camprevon. However, when some 4,558 men and 285 officers surrendered at Mons in 1691, The French victors described the Spanish and Walloons soldiers as "very badly dressed and badly armed". From this, it can be assumed that the Spanish army was still neglected and partly explains its demise in the second half of the 17th century. It must further be noted that no outstanding general emerged during the 17th century, which is not surprising; brilliant commanders can only shine when they can depend on a strong and effective force to carry out their strategic and tactical concepts. From the 1667–1668 *blitzkreig* to the end of the War of the League of Augsburg, the Spanish army suffered repeated defeats culminating in the 1697 capture of Barcelona by the French. From France's main opponent in the 1640s, the Spanish army had fallen to a secondary military role. Amazingly, within a few years, it was resurrected largely thanks to Louis XIV as will be seen in volume 4 of this series.[2]

---

1   Conde de Clonard, *Historia organica de la infanteria y caballeria española* (Madrid, 1853), Vol. 4, pp. 416–418; Gabino Enciso, *El Arte Militar* (Barcelona: A.J. Bastinos, c.1880), pp. 43–49.
2   Clonard, *Historia organica*, Vol. 4, pp. 458–459, Vol. 5, pp. 7–8, 12, 33; *Mercure Galant*, June 1678, p. 293, September 1689, p. 285 and April 1691, p. 335; Giancarlo Boeri, 'L'esercito spagnolo di G.C.', *La guerra della Lega di Augusta fino alla Battaglia di Orbassano* (Torino: Academia di S. Marciano, 1993), pp. 247–255.

Colour Plate Commentaries

Plate 1 (L–R)

Gardes du Corps guardsman, c.1645–1656
Before 1657, the king's Gardes du Corps (Life Guards) were distinguished by scarlet cassocks laced and embroidered in silver and gold. Artwork of the period shows small buttons edging the sides of the cassock. On the chest and on the back was a white cross edged with silver with golden lilies. These guardsmen served mounted or on foot, often for formal events as escorts to royal family members. They were then, as shown in this future, armed with polearms and swords. The colour of the cassocks changed to blue in 1657.

Guard of the Duc de Beaufort 1660s
Like all high ranking officers in the French forces, François de Vendôme, Duc de Beaufort – who was a cousin of Louis XIV – had his own personal company of guards to attend him. He had campaigned on land as a youth before becoming a senior admiral always keen for action. His guards wore a scarlet cassock laced with silver, the ends of the embroidered silver cross having silver lilies and gold crowns. They were likely armed with rifled carbines and swords when many of them must have perished with Beaufort, fighting to the end against Ottoman Turk soldiers at Candia (Crete) on 25 June 1669.

Gardes du Corps guardsman, 1st (Scottish) Company, c.1667–1668
From the early or mid 1660s, the Gardes du Corps wore buff leather coats that were elaborately decorated, notably their sleeves, with gold and silver lace. The four companies had bandoliers of their distinctive company colours. While it appears to have been gradual, decorative ribbon bunches of their company's colour (which could change, see text) were adopted at about that time except for the 1st Company that had them in red rather than in white. This was the dress worn during the campaigns of the War of Devolution.

Plate 2 (L–R)

Officer, Gardes Suisses, c.1665–1670
Although the Swiss Guards are traditionally associated with red uniforms, there were important exceptions to this practice. For instance, on 16 January 1665 the Sun King signed a royal ordinance stipulating that the officers of the

Gardes Suisses henceforth wear blue coats garnished with gold lace. Scarlet was the lining colour of the blue royal livery and was likely the colour used for the lining, cuffs and ribbons. Of course, the Swiss officers likely wanted to assume red coats like most of their men and, in the long run, succeeded in convincing the king of that during the 1670s. How long the blue coat was worn by the officers of the Gardes Suisses is open to conjecture, but up to the late 1660s or early 1670s would seen reasonable.

Pertuisanier, Gardes Françaises, *c.*1660–1670
Pertuisaniers were literally soldiers armed with the pole weapon called a partizan. In 1659, the Gardes Françaises had eight such soldiers in each company, which, at 30 companies, came to 240 for the regiment. They were considered elite soldiers, and when marching were formed in two ranks at the head of each company. Their status is somewhat unclear, but seems to have been somewhere between sergeant and corporal and had some constabulary duties. They were certainly honour guards as well as professional and experienced fighting men and, like sergeants and drummers, wore the livery of their colonel, which, in the case of the Gardes Françaises, was the king's livery. This consisted of a blue coat with red lining richly decorated with royal lace. During the 1660s this lace had little red, white and blue squares. The partizan had a flat wide blade with lower small crescents or points. In 1670 the king forbade the use of the partizan in the army, feeling the pertuisaniers would be more useful with muskets. By then, their establishment had been reduced to four per company and they soon vanished from the royal army. However, some were found long afterwards as part of local troops in cities.

Pikeman, Gardes Suisses, mid 1660s to mid 1670s
From about 1664, the pikemen of the Gardes Suisses were mostly dressed in red. Their coats had blue lining that could be seen when the lower sleeves were turned up. The ribbons are shown as blue at the 1667 siege of Tournai, yet also seen as red in a painting of the Quai Malaquet in Paris. Blue coats are known to have been worn by Gardes Suisses pikemen in the later 1670s. While most pikemen of the time wore steel breast- and backplates and wore hats, the Gardes Suisses pikemen had more elaborate armour with tassets, pouldrons and rerebraces attached to the cuirass for added protection and they also wore steel helmets. The armour's quality was superior, being imported from Milan, long renowned for its fine craftsmen.

Plate 3 (L–R)

Gardes Françaises, private, *c.*1679
From the 1660s up to 1685, the corporals and private soldiers of the Gardes Françaises Regiment wore a pale grey coat. Other details given in the very few extant descriptions are rather vague. In January 1679 however, two accounts confirm that the coat was grey or "almost white" as were the breeches, that the waistcoat, stockings and ribbons were red, the buttons were silver as was the lace edging the hat and the waistcoat and the fringes of the buff gloves.

The colour of the coat's lining and cuffs are not mentioned and thus may well have been grey-white. The men were armed with matchlock muskets and swords. The equipment, as shown, was starting to change. Instead of bandoliers with charges, the Gardes Françaises were experimenting with *gibecière* ammunition pouches (that were eventually adopted in the rest of the army) whose flaps featured the sun with silver rays.

Gardes Françaises, sergeant, 1679
Sergeants had an important status in 17th century armies and often might be seen wearing coats in the colours of their colonel's livery. Blue lined with red was the royal livery, but before 1685 the regiment and its sergeants would, in principle, wear that colour. During the late 1670s however, the king, while dressing the Gardes Françaises officers in blue and the regiment's men in grey, opted for sergeants to wear scarlet coats with velvet cuffs of their officer's liveries according to descriptions of a 1679 review. We have thus shown scarlet cuffs, which was a popular livery colour, but they could also have been buff, green, etc. The Sun King further allowed them to have steel "cuirasses with gold filets" and white plumes on their hats. A white sash was commonly worn at that time to identify the soldier's French nationality. Sergeants were armed with halberds and swords.

Grenadier à Cheval de la Garde, trooper, 1677–1678
Amongst the innovations introduced in the Sun King's army was this troop of mounted grenadiers as part of the royal guard from December 1676. Its uniform was initially all red until changed to a blue coat with red cuffs and lining in 1692. There are no images yet know of these troopers until the mid 1690s so this reconstruction is based on early descriptions given in the text. They had what appears to be small laced buttonholes until 1679; buttons and lace were probably silver, which they always were later on. The red cap came up to a point that then curved backwards and it had a brown plush fur turnup. This remained distinctive to the corps later on also. They were armed with a sabre with a brass single branch guard and curved blade as well as muskets, pistols and of course, grenades.

Plate 4 (L–R)

Gardes Françaises, sergeant, c.1695
Following the king's decision in September 1684 that his regiment of Gardes Françaises would henceforth be dressed in blue, the unit accordingly paraded on 24 March 1685 wearing the new uniform. It consisted of a dark blue coat with scarlet cuffs, lining, scarlet waistcoat, breeches and stockings, white metal buttons and white hat lace. It is uncertain when and if the white buttonhole lace was worn, but it certainly was by the 1690s. This regulation ensured that sergeants would also consistently wear the same colour coat as the men in the future. An uncertain feature is wether their buttonholes were laced like the men's. On 27 March 1691, a royal regulation for the Gardes Françaises proclaimed that: "…The sergeants' coats…[would only have] one silver lace on

COLOUR PLATE COMMENTARIES

the cuffs and edging the pocket flaps." Two prints published in 1696 show coats that don't have buttonhole lace, but instead narrow edging lace, presumably of silver. Our figure is based on these figures. The one addition that we have added is silver lace edging the cuffs and pocket flaps. Indeed, one print shows a narrow pocket flap edging that was probably about an inch wide. Sergeants were armed with swords and halberds and we have based ours on original specimens rather than the rather crudely rendered ones in the prints. All the same, *L'Artmilitaire François* by Pierre Giffard, the illustrated drill book in which the prints can be found, remains an invaluable source.

Guard of the Prince de Conti, *c.*1690
François-Louis de Bourbon-Conti (1664–1709) was free-spirited and libertine scion of the highest nobility who was disliked by the Sun King. No wonder, since witty Conti had qualified him as "King of theatre". He was nevertheless a good officer who took part in sieges in 1683 and 1684 including leading grenadiers in an assault on Luxembourg. His uncle, the Prince de Condé, perceived his many military talents and mediated with the King. Conti was awarded the Order of Saint-Esprit in 1686, but not his own command as royal suspicion remained, although Conti campaigned as an outstanding battlefield general with his close friend Marshal de Luxembourg during the 1690s. Louis XIV at last recognised his military leadership qualities in early 1709, naming him commander of the army in Italy, but too late: Conti had died of sickness in February. As a prince as well as lieutenant-general, he had his own personal bodyguard dressed in the yellow and blue livery of the princes of Conti laced with silver and equipped with blue bandoliers edged with silver lace. Guarding Conti in battle was quite a challenge. At Steenkirk, taking a French colour from a wounded ensign, he rallied troops and led a successful charge. At Neerwinden, he led six charges until "covered in blood", he narrowly missed being struck down by a sabre blow and instead brought down his foe, no doubt with his guards, in a frenzied victorious fight.

1st Company of the Mousquetaires du Roi (King's Musketeers), trooper, late 17th century
By the 1670s, the King's Musketeers' famous blue cassocks bearing silver crosses had become large and cumbersome; they were more like cloaks. The Sun King called for corrections on this matter and, in 1688, approved a totally new style of surcoat called a *soubreveste*. This blue garment bore the King's Musketeer silver cross badge on the chest and on the back, was edged with lace, had a much better fit, had no sleeves and its skirts went just above the bottom of the skirts of the scarlet coat that was worn underneath. It had open sides and slits in front and back for maximum ease of movement. It was fastened snug at the waist by the sword belt. This was an immediate stylistic success and the *soubreveste* soon replaced cassocks in guard units of other allied or rival armies all over Europe.

Plate 5 (L–R)

Cent-Suisses de la Garde, guardsman fifer, *c.*1700
This company originating in the late 15th century consisted, as its name announced, of a hundred Swiss guards that were amongst the most trusted

of the king's guardsmen. Their dress at the time of the Sun King's reign was basically in the style of the previous century, which was traditional for such guard units (and still seen today by the Pope's Swiss Guards). The dress of the Swiss guardsman shown is based on surviving garments of the Cent-Suisses de la Garde in Paris and Zurich; it was in the blue and red royal livery richly decorated with the livery lace pattern adopted during the later 17th century that also cover the belts. Bellow the knee garters are the pointes peculiar to Swiss costume. They were armed with halberds and swords, drummers and fifers having their instruments.

Gendarmerie de la Garde, trooper c.1704–1714

This elite company was the senior guard unit *au dehors du Louvre* (oustide of the Louvre) palace corps and appears to have always worn scarlet. There were variations and we show the dress worn by an ordinary trooper at the time of the War of Spanish Succession when, even in defeat, the corps was outstanding in combat. Its uniform was also outstanding being all scarlet made with fine cloth with the gilt buttoned coat and waistcoat elaborately laced with gold. Troopers also wore a tricorn hat laced with gold and its brim edged with white feathers. They were armed with the straight-bladed heavy cavalry swords (also called sabre), pistols and carbines. The buff belts were edged with gold lace.

Marshal Villars' Bodyguard c.1704–1714

As a marshal commanding an army, Villars was entitled to a personal bodyguard of 50 officers troopers dressed in his livery. These men were sure to be in the midst of action as Villars was very much a fighting battlefield general; his clothes were often riddled with shot, he was badly wounded at Malplaquet and he led the charge at Denain, his greatest triumph. Some of of his guardsmen must not have survived the honour of serving with him. The Villars livery dress was brown lined with crimson or red laced with silver. The figure shows a trooper wearing a coat of a rich brown hue with red cuffs, brown waistcoat, silver buttons and lace on the coat, waistcoat and edging the brown belts. They were armed with swords, carbines and pistols.

Bibliography

A full and annotated bibliography covering published sources for this whole multi-volume series will appear as the final contribution in the fourth and last volume. This is only logical because many works, such as Quincy's military history or Voltaire's *Le Siècle de Louis XIV*, are used in all volumes. Readers will note that published sources in all volumes are given in full in the first footnote that cites them, with the usual shorter form beginning with the author's name thereafter.

For this volume, we present the notes below regarding some of the data found in manuscripts texts, original and printed artwork. The letters in brackets identifying the institution are cited in our footnotes.

Primary Source Documentary Archives

Archives Nationales de France (ANF), rue des Francs-Bourgeois, Paris. This is where we researched in the 1970s and 1980s, but this institution has since expanded and other centres have opened at the outskirts of Paris and as far as Aix-en-Provence. The G7 and K series in particular have useful data. Some collections have been digitised.

Bibliothèque Nationale de France (BNF), rue de Richelieu, Paris. The manuscript collections are mainly at this location. This is a huge institution, by far the largest of its kind in the Francophone world. Its newer and enormous library on the left bank of the Seine River in Paris is mainly for newer and currently printed books. It has been digitising books and manuscripts for decades and these are accessible mainly through the Gallica and Persée web sites.

Bibliothèque du Ministère de la Guerre later renamed **des Armées (BMA)**, Boulevard Saint-Germain, Paris. The author often researched in this library until the 1980s when it was closed following the passing of its very erudite and helpful chief librarian, the regretted Mademoiselle Madeleine Leloir. Its extraordinary collection was then transferred mainly to the Musée de l'Armée in Paris and to the Service Historique de la Défense at the chateau of Vincennes. We thus use BMA in citations since we cannot be certain where some documents were sent after its closure. In general, our research concentrated in the large Ordonnances collection that consisted of army orders (both printed and manuscript) simply identified by date.

Brown University Library, Anne S.K. Brown Military Collection (ASKB), Providence, Rhode Island, USA. Certainly the most important collection in the Americas of books, prints, manuscripts and original renderings related to military themes. It has a substantial number of digitised works accessible on the web, but there is a great deal more at the university's John Hay Library where the collection resides.

Library and Archives Canada, Ottawa (LAC). This institution is the result of the fusion of the national archives (previously long known as the Public Archives of Canada) with the National Library. The archives have transcripts and microfilms of ANF and BNF documents and the library has original prints, notably by van der Meulen.

Service Historique de la Défense (SHD) at the chateau of Vincennes. This institution, which also had several recent name changes, is the home of the French forces historical section that is also responsible for the very large archives kept in this castle just east of Paris. For the period of Louis XIV to the French Revolution, the vast Archives de la Guerre (AG), series A1, is the main source.

Digital Art Sources

An increasing number of institutions holding vast collections of paintings and prints are at last making them available to the world via websites that offer them in high resolution files. They are to be lauded for fulfilling the primary mandate of any library, museum or archive: the free dissemination of knowledge to all. We note here in particular the **Rijksmuseum** (Amsterdam, The Netherlands), **Library of Congress** (Washington, D.C., USA), the **Brown University Library** (Providence, RI, USA), the **Yale University Library** (New London, CT, USA) and the **New York Public Library** (New York City, NY, USA), as well as many others that permit visitors to take photos.